NO MONEY
But What A Life

STEVIE FARR

The Book Guild Ltd

First published in Great Britain in 2023 by
The Book Guild Ltd
Unit E2 Airfield Business Park,
Harrison Road, Market Harborough,
Leicestershire. LE16 7UL
Tel: 0116 2792299
www.bookguild.co.uk
Email: info@bookguild.co.uk
Twitter: @bookguild

Typeset in 11pt Adobe Garamond Pro

Printed and bound by CPI Group (UK) Ltd, Croydon, CR0 4YY

ISBN 978 1915352 354

British Library Cataloguing in Publication Data.
A catalogue record for this book is available from the British Library.

MIX
Paper | Supporting
responsible forestry
FSC® C013604

To my family, Dad, Mum, Janny, Mike, Merry and Sue.

My daughters Jo and Zoe and all of my friends and others that have made my life what it is.

Thank you, Stevie.

Contents

Acknowledgements

My grateful thanks to those who helped me in the production of this book

Sue Sales
Janet Fulwell
Merry Farr
Melissa Kemp
Barry "Baz" Watts ***
Cliff Birtchnell ***
Joanna and Simon Rose
Zoe and Dean Cattaneo
Tony Hughes
Pete Robbins ***
Bruce and Reece Thomas ***
Stu Blandamer
Bill and Ruth Scott
Ian Gabriel ***
Dave South
John Cannell
Jim Davidson
Bauke Algera
Mickey Pearl
Jeff Stow
Ken Holway

*** Special Photo contribution Thanks
Original Chrysalis Photograper Martyn Goddard

Introduction

STEVIE FARR – NO MONEY BUT WHAT A LIFE!

I am sitting at a table having lunch with Paul McCartney, Ringo Starr, George Martin and some of my best friends in the world. Paul is talking about his relationship with Michael Jackson, and the sale of the Beatles' back catalogue of songs and he speaks fondly of John Lennon and the songs they wrote together… How did this lad from Watford arrive at this moment in time? How had my not so ordinary life become so extraordinary? I will speak more about this encounter, along with the many special and famous people that became my friends, later. Anyhow, back to me.

One

THIS IS STEVIE FARR AND HE'S GOING TO SING A HIT SONG

I suppose a child's life doesn't really begin until their first thoughts are remembered. I certainly can't recall me feeding from my mother, or my first footsteps, or crying as I fell down. But as a toddler I can remember that night in 1952 as clear as if it happened last week. It was the night my father died. The storm had been raging since teatime and he had gone to bed early, feeling unwell, after a few hard hours in the garden. In the middle of the night a large clap of thunder had woken me and as always, I was keen to leave the room I shared with my brother to find the comfort of my parents' bed.

My life started then.

Being shaken, my mother pulled me out from beside my dad, lying still but making strange gurgling, quacking noises as the life drained out of him. My mother was desperately shaking him, calling his name over and over again, and as if by magic Mr Gradley, our next-door neighbour, was there pushing Mum and me aside so he could resuscitate him. My older sister, Janet, burst into the room fully dressed, which I thought was strange. She had been sent out to call the ambulance some time before I woke, only to find that the storm had taken out the local telephone box at the end of the road and she had run out into the night looking for one that worked. Janny was fourteen. I was taken back to the boys' room and

Mike, my older brother by eight years, tried to explain to me that today, Dad had gone away from us and wouldn't be back.

Why was he dressed as well? It was the middle of the night. The first service to get to us was the Fire Brigade. I can still see these men walking into the hallway from my vantage point at the top of the stairs. Great giants in black heavy uniforms wearing helmets as they walked through to the kitchen; their conversation muted to a low hum, they all stood there while Janny made them tea. As I sat at the top of the stairs, I noticed that the last man had not shut the front door, and I remember to this day, my thoughts remain quite clear, that Dad had left for death through that dark front door into the raging storm. In the morning, the ambulance still hadn't arrived, but the doctor had been, and my father's body was still upstairs in his bed. My mother had Sellotaped the handle of the door so I couldn't go in, something years later she told me that I had tried to do quite often.

Within a few days, my other sister, Merry, and I were sent over the road to Mr and Mrs Senegal, our elderly neighbours, and we watched from the window as my dad's coffin was brought out and placed into the hearse. I couldn't understand as I saw all my aunties and uncles looking very sad and coming out looking very sombre and getting into the large black cars. Hardly anybody was speaking. It was so strange as whenever I had seen them everyone was always laughing and singing. I wanted to be over there with them. After all, Mike and Janny were, but it wasn't the place to be for Merry and me. Not me, a four-year-old. On his death certificate, Henry (Harry) James Farr, my dad, had died from syncope due to congestion and oedema of the lungs, the result of chronic parenchymatous nephritis. His kidneys had stopped functioning and he had drowned when his lungs filled up with water in his body.

He was thirty-nine, and as lives go, he hadn't had much of one. He worked for Saxones, a well-known shoe shop chain, and had grown up happily in a family with six brothers and sisters in Enfield, North London. He met my mum, Edith Patricia Brierly, at a local dance and as the war with Hitler loomed ever more possible, they were married. Janny was born in 1937 and Mike followed in 1939. By now the Blitz of London had started and Dad became an Auxiliary Fire Fighter at night after work. His fire engine was a taxicab in its day job. On one occasion two taxi fire engines arrived together to tackle a fire that was raging at the London docks. Dad and his team were ordered to go and help put fires out in the street next door. As the second taxicab entered the docks a warehouse collapsed, engulfing them. There were no survivors.

One night, after a very busy shift, the Tottenham (Dad's) brigade were stood down and my father and a friend, absolutely exhausted, could not face the trip home but sought somewhere quiet to get a few hours' sleep before battling the fires again. They found a darkened building where many others seemed to have the same idea and there were rows of sleeping figures. They woke in the morning to find that they had stumbled on a makeshift mortuary and the other sleeping figures were in fact dead bodies. They fled in terror and didn't stop running until they reached their homes several miles away.

On another occasion a large departmental store in London had been bombed and the firemen were digging to reach the shelter in the store's basement. A bomb appeared to have gone straight down the lift-shaft and exploded at the bottom. Eventually my father's team reached the shelter door and prised it open. Inside everything appeared normal and they expected the people inside to welcome their arrival and rescue. Instead, one after another, the people sagged and collapsed to the floor. It transpired that they had been killed instantly by the blast, but the shelter had been vacuum-sealed, preserving the scene exactly at the moment of the explosion until the firemen broke the seal and let the air in many hours later.

Later he and his brothers joined up together and an association with the Royal Navy was well and truly formed. Over the next six years, my mum would receive several yellowy-brown envelopes, the dreaded War Office telegram… "Your husband sunk, missing, believed dead." Not the best news to receive once, let alone three times. Miraculously he and all his brothers survived the war, and they all went home to their mum only to be told that their dad, my Grandpa Farr, had been knocked off his bike and had been crushed by a London bus on his way home from work. The boys had been dive-bombed, torpedoed, shelled and rescued after hours in shark-infested waters, capsized and tortured by the Japanese and come through it. Grandpa had been covered in tyre marks and killed by the No. 7 Enfield to Southgate special. What a strange world.

My mum was evacuated out of London when the Blitz was bad and for some reason, she ended up in a small village in North Wales called Meliden, just outside Prestatyn. With the war at an end, and Hitler and Grandad dead, Dad eventually found Meliden and soon after that, my younger sister, Meriel, was born. A fine Welsh name, that is if you're living in Wales, but Dad took his family immediately back to London and from that day Meriel became Merry, and it stayed like that forever. The family then settled in Haringey, North London, and on a miserable rainy day in November 1947, I was born, the youngest of the Farr family, Stephen Francis.

With the country rebuilding after the war, all new towns were springing up in the counties around London and young families were encouraged to move out into the fresh air and perhaps a fresh life. Dad, having got his job back in shoes, was doing well and climbing up the wages ladder, when a job opening came up in Watford. Mr and Mrs Farr and their four young children moved excitedly into Hertfordshire. We were to live on a council estate in South Oxhey, three or four miles from Watford. Great for Dad's work, although we didn't have a car the new local bus service was very good, and in the spring of 1948, we arrived at Number 10 Caldwell Road. The house was brand new. The downstairs walls were prefab concrete, the upstairs metal, and the roof was asbestos sheeting. There was a garden back and front. None of that mattered. Mum and Dad had great plans to stay there for five years and then move into a small house of their dreams that they could buy. Oh, how that night in 1952 changed things.

School-wise, Watford had their grammar schools. A girls' grammar school for Janny, and Mike soon started to do very well at the boys' grammar school down the road. The Hertfordshire Education Authority in 1952 awarded three bursaries to England's premier public schools, Harrow, Eton and Winchester. Each of these famous educational institutions was to receive a boy from the real world and set a stiff entrance examination for those clever enough to put their name to the paper. Imagine the delight and fear when my mum and dad received a letter to invite Mike to be a pupil at Eton College. Oh, how that night changed things in 1952.

Wait, there was help. The school fees were being paid by the Hertfordshire County Council and they generously awarded Mike extra help for books, travelling expenses and uniform, so Mike, having lost his dad only a few weeks before, very nervously entered his boarding house at Eton. Years later he told me it felt so strange making friends with the other boys in his class whose parents had mansions, land, horses, ships and even servants. His best friend was a boy called Cadbury, and his dad had a chocolate factory.

Merry and I went to the local infant and junior school, Oxhey Wood. Not quite the same thing, but at least our school was brand spanking new. Mum now had to work and luckily there was an offer of a job at the same shoe shop that Dad had worked at in Watford. It was full-time for her, so Merry and I were on our own when most of the other kids were home from school. There was no-one to look after us and we weren't allowed into the house, so in the warm summer months we walked home together, and there would be jam sandwiches in a paper bag in the garden shed where we would have to wait for Janny to get home from her grammar school around 5.30pm.

Mum would get back around 6.30pm and we would have more jam sandwiches and a cup of tea. We had no television yet, so it was bed for Merry and me. Janny would help Mum in the house with the housework and the washing up, and then she was allowed to play a few of her records in the house before she was sent up to finish her homework. Mum followed suit and the house would be so quiet some nights we could hear Mum crying through those thin walls; probably wondering what she had done so wrong to end up, left stranded on a getting rougher council estate with four children.

Most evenings a daily paper came home with Mum. Merry would read me the children's page and make up stories to the pictures on the other pages. One day she noticed a picture of a puppy being offered as a prize in a competition. Janny explained what a competition was, and Merry and I excitedly made up a letter to be our entry. We had to write to the paper, the Daily Mirror, and say why the puppy would be happy to live at our house. Merry, a great storyteller, wrote of how Daddy had just died, and Mummy was sad, and we needed a puppy to love. Apparently, my input was that I was keen to let the Daily Mirror know that we didn't have many flowers in our garden which was good for when the puppy wanted a poo; it wouldn't spoil too much. Janny promised to post our entry and some weeks later, it was late when there was a knock at the door. Merry and I were asleep in bed when Mum let the man from the Daily Mirror in. He explained that our letter had won the puppy and the paper would like us to go to their offices in London, and after a slap-up tea, be presented with the dog with photographs for the next children's page. Mum explained that basically what Merry and I had written was the truth, and she had to work full-time, and the poor dog would have to be left alone most of the day, so it was agreed that we were not suitable for the prize. Days later, there was a picture in the Daily Mirror's children's page of a little girl with a beaming smile holding her new puppy. My mum told me that story when I was twenty-two years old, and I didn't speak to her for the rest of the week.

School holidays were a problem. So were Saturdays. Janny, a keen sports girl, wanted to play hockey for her school and the school wanted Janny badly. She was one of their star players. So Merry and I had to go to Watford Grammar School for Girls each Saturday morning to watch hockey. We soon tired of this, and come to think of it, soon tired of each other, and it wasn't long before Merry and I couldn't stand the sight of one another. And that meant open war.

During the holidays, all the children in Caldwell Road and the adjoining streets would play on the green opposite our house. Merry made a best friend of a girl of her own age, Stephanie Gray, who lived next door. Now I had two adversaries, as they giggled and whispered and plotted to bring me down. Soon after the sun came up, it wasn't long before all the kids were getting together to play games, ride their bikes or hammer down the hill sitting on a book balanced on a roller skate. This one very hot day, some builders had left some wood and pallets by the side of the green, so it wasn't long before the leaders had organised a small stage, inviting those who wanted to entertain in Caldwell Road's first summer show. My favourite song at the time was "Cherry Pink and Apple Blossom White", a huge hit by Eddie Calvert, a trumpet player. There were lyrics that I had learned perfectly from the radio. It was a perfect time for me to impress all the other kids older than me, and perhaps I would find a best friend like Stephanie. So, dressed only in a pair of swimming trunks, I lined up to do my act. It was my turn next, and as I was about to climb up onto the wobbly platform I was hurriedly joined by Merry and Stephanie. "Stephanie will introduce you, and I will make sure you're standing in the middle of the stage," Merry said.

"What's introduce me?" I asked.

"She says your name and the song you're going to sing, and her voice is louder than yours so everyone will hear."

"OK," I said. I was on. I jumped on the platform with Merry and moved to the middle of the stage, with my sister behind me. Stephanie Gray shouted, "This is Stevie Farr from Number 10, and he's gonna sing a hit record." I looked out to see a small sea of faces all sitting neatly cross-legged in a tidy fashion across the grass before me. I waited for the name of the song to be shouted, but it never came. Merry was still behind me but her hands were in the waistband of my trunks and in an instant, she had pulled my trunks to the floor. Nothing happened for a second, and then through sheets of laughter, I started to cry. I was not sure if it was from not being able to get on with the song, or from the embarrassment of standing there naked with my little winkle resembling an acorn, a very small acorn indeed. I pulled up my trunks and ran sobbing back to the house, which was close by, thank God. Before I made it, I ran straight into the arms of the postman, a kindly old man who had witnessed the whole thing. He cursed out Merry and I can't remember what punishment she got from Mum when he grassed her up. Anything would have been great. Stephanie didn't talk to me for months either. Perfect!

Two

I'M GOING TO PRISON FOR NICKING A FEW APPLES

Mum was an attractive widow in her early thirties and it wasn't long before men were hovering around. One such individual was Len Blott, a balding, thick-moustached man who worked with Mum at Saxones. He boasted that he had a new car and that he would call round to the house for tea one Sunday. Mum told Janny that although she thought it was an idle threat, we were not to answer the door if he came. Sure enough, on a warm Sunday there was a knock at the door. Mum peered through the curtains. "Oh no," she hissed. "Blott!" She immediately gave Merry, Jan and me commando-type silent hand instructions to hit the floor, just like the soldiers in the films, and we crawled and shuffled on the floor from room to room, until he gave up knocking and left. Janny and Mum had the giggles about it, and they were very pleased that Merry and I hadn't blurted out and given the game away. Time for tea and a slice of cake as a victory feast, but just as we were sitting down at the table, Blott was back. No frantic arm waving from Mum this time as Merry and I knew the drill and we made base camp under the table, still with cake in hand.

Another fifteen minutes of total silence, he was gone again. The third visit an hour later came as a complete surprise and we were all in the hall and very close to the front door and Mr Blott's knocks made us all jump. Thank God the glass in the front door was opaque. Again Mum, through sign language, ushered us to the stairs, where we all sat down staring at the front door and the shape of Mr Blott through the glass. It seemed that we were in silence for ages and just as we thought the shape would move away from the door and go back to his car, the shape bent down and flipped the letter box and he put his finger through to open it, only to see us all sitting on the stairs. It stayed like that for a moment, then the letter box flap was dropped and Blott was gone.

Years later Mum told us that she had been so embarrassed at being discovered, she confessed to hiding during his earlier visits and some weeks later he turned up and had some tea. It was clear that there was no way that Mum had any intention of becoming Mrs Blott, although we teased her about it for years afterwards.

In 1953, Princess Elizabeth was crowned as our new Queen of England. The excitement that spread through the British Isles that year was like bushfire. Schools were decorated in every class and every corridor and in every street, parties, games and entertainment planned for the great day. There weren't too many televisions on the estate, so those who had, invited those who hadn't, especially the elderly, to watch the ceremony. Tea and biscuits were passed round, and there was no walking space left as children sat neatly on the floor. Ladies had their seats and men stood at the back, watching an 11 by 7-inch flickering television in black and white. Early days.

We now know just how long it takes to crown a queen so it was a lot of looking at nothing much inside a cathedral other than a choir singing, so it wasn't long before the adults were talking and even singing. However, all us children were only interested in the party and the games that were happening in the afternoon, and what a party. Roads were closed and long trestle tables were laid with white tablecloths and with Union Jack flags and bunting displayed across the road going from bedroom to bedroom, families passing the flags from one house to another. The week before, they had hardly even spoken to each other. It was decided that Mum, Merry and I would stay home for the party. Janny and Mike had asked Mum if they could go to London the night before the coronation to find a good spot for the procession. They would actually sleep on the pavement all night to be ready to cheer Her Majesty as she passed right in front of them. I wasn't at all jealous as sleeping on the roadside didn't appeal to me at all. Imagine rolling over in your sleep and getting the same treatment as Grandpa Farr. No, not for me!

Merry and I were entering the street's fancy dress competition. Merry was to go as a pixie and I was going as a Royal Navy sailor. I didn't know where it had come from, but I had a tiny uniform, an exact replica of a Naval Rating No. 1 best uniform, pressed bell bottoms, T-shirt and naval collar and it fitted perfectly. I won the competition hands down and was presented with a large toy lorry made of tin. It became a prized possession which I kept for years afterwards. God knows whatever happened to that sailor suit.

During those early years, the summers always seemed to be hot. Mum always took us away on holiday, God knows how she did it. It was either the village in Wales, Meliden, where she still had friends from the war years, and we always stayed in the same cottage Merry was born in, or one year we went to Prestatyn holiday camp a few miles away down by the beach. This was Hi-de-Hi! at its best. I remember Mike putting me into the camp's Mr Universe competition. Imagine the surprise when contestant Number 6, me, flexed my non-existent muscles. Everybody laughed and I got an ice-cream out of it. I remember one of these holidays I got too close to the sea and a wave knocked me over and I was completely soaked. Mum this time was furious and said I could have drowned and gave me a whack round the ear. Happy times!

At home in Caldwell Road, I was making friends, being involved in football games on the green in front of the house; most of the boys were slightly older than me and none of them went to my school. Brian Crockett was by far the best footballer, Peter Gooden was next, Jimmy Faulkner was OK, and the Reedy boys, Bernand and Robert. Their third brother, David, didn't play at all. The Reedys and Faulkner were a rough lot, and my mum didn't approve, but she didn't stop me playing with them. I would be off with them, whilst she was at work. At school, I was popular, and around this time started taking an interest in girls. Pauline Borman was the girl for me. Her dad worked in insurance and had been very helpful to my mum when my dad died, so the two families knew each other quite well. One morning every week, our entire class were put on a coach and we were taken to Watford Public Swimming Baths to learn how to swim. The rewards were certificates for being able to reach 25 and 100 yards, and I was proud when I reached these goals, especially in front of Pauline Borman, as the end of term certificates were handed out on stage during the last assembly.

Another new pastime with the Caldwell Road gang was train numbering. The main Euston to Northern England line was only a few streets away and all the engines were still steam trains. We would sit on the high bank above the tracks on the grass in a camp we had made and write the numbers of the smoking giants as they thundered through London towards Watford and the North, and the other way too. The carriages at that time were red and yellow, later to change to maroon, and they carried boards above their windows stating where the train was going to and where it had come from. Between trains, we would check the numbers against the complete rolling stock book iSpy, and mark those off as spotted; many of the engines had name plates, the Royal Family, famous people, regiments and places and I can still remember one of the most sought-after spots was an engine called the Black Watch. You were somebody if you saw that train pass through. The camps were built and had milk crates for seats, and we always made a fire to cook potatoes and a sort of bread made from flour and water wrapped round a stick during the warm afternoons. When the railway schedule was at a low, we would get bored and that's when the smoking started. For a penny you could buy a cigarette from the newsagent, no questions asked about your age; then if we all clubbed together, we could buy a packet of ten cigarettes for a shilling, which is 5p.

There were cigarettes at my house that weren't being smoked. Mike, my brother, had done well at Eton, and was now at Dartmouth Naval College, training to be a naval officer, and was given his tobacco ration. This was several packets of RN cigarettes a month. He didn't smoke, so he brought them home to give to Mum so she could give them out to guests and relatives when they came to visit. When there were enough packets in the cupboard for one not to be missed, I would take the RN cigarettes, twenty in a packet, to the boys at the train camp. They were strong cigarettes for strong seamen and try as we might we smoked them between coughing our hearts up.

Scrumping in the autumn months became another quest for the boys. We would walk along the tops of the train cuttings where many back gardens backed onto. We could see where the tastiest apples, pears and plums were, and it wasn't long before we got over a fence or under a hedge to steal the fruit. Jumpers were tucked into trouser waistbands and made a perfect bag to load the fruit into, leaving both hands free. The house owners would come out their back doors, shouting and waving, perhaps with a broom and that was time for us to exit. We were never chased, except once.

The fruit in this one garden was exceptional. It was our second visit and things were going well and we didn't hear the door open or shut and we didn't see him racing down the garden. He must have been about eighteen or nineteen and he was moving fast. We were out of his garden and back onto the railway embankment in a flash and he was heading towards our camp. Someone suggested that we split up when we stopped for a breather, but not for long though as he was still coming. It seemed that every time one of us looked back he was still there, still coming. We reached the railway bridge and went deep into the brickwork, a camp we had made earlier when the weather was bad. We had candles and matches to make a fire, but for now it was dark and a great place to hide. We whispered and giggled, eating our bounty, and everybody was chatting. One of the Reedy boys would go up to see if the coast was clear. Each time he came back, he said that the man was walking up and down asking different people if they had seen a group of lads on the run. Time was getting on. We had been there a few hours now and it was starting to get dark. Our mums would be getting angry, mine would at least. I had strict orders to be home for teatime and was getting nervous, so decided to make a break for it. Brian came up with me. He was much taller than me and he could see the young bloke was close by. At first, we thought he'd given up, but then we saw him at the other end of the bridge. If I ran now, Brian said, I would have 200 yards on him, down the side alley of the school and into Caldwell Road. I would be safe before he got close. I went as fast as I could, down the side alley looking around, nothing, into Caldwell Road, nothing, into my backyard, a quick look to see if he was there, nothing, I had made it. I was still late for tea and got it from my mum.

I couldn't tell her the story, she might turn me in, so I took a whack around the ear and said nothing. A few days later I met the train gang again. They'd waited until they'd seen him disappear for good. They'd all arrived home late, and all got punished in some way; so we agreed that the fun had gone out of it and we wouldn't be scrumping again.

So, we turned our activities onto pastime number two, that was birds-egging. All along the railway bank were trees and bushes of all sizes and a haven for different birds. Birds-egging was a national pastime then, and there were iSpy books, the same iSpy books we used for the train number spotting. We had pictures of every species of egg. Once the egg was taken from the nest, we would put a pricked hole in each end and blow out the yolk. Then the delicate egg would be placed in a tray of sand to keep it safe. Rare eggs were worth money, but we didn't care about that. One warm sunny morning we gathered and Brian, our leader, said that we were going to see if we could get a coot's egg. I'd never heard of a coot. He said that they made their nests on the water and we were going to a lake that he knew not far away, on the estate of a private school. So that afternoon, we gathered for the walk across South Oxhey Golf Course, to the Merchant Taylors' School, a very posh place by the sound of things. We figured that if we were on school holidays, they must be too, and it was late in the afternoon when we got into the school grounds under the fence and to the lakeside. Brian recognised the small birds swimming around the island on the small lake and told us where the nest would be. Bernard Reedy, Peter Gooden and I were the only swimmers, and we soon had our swimming trunks on and were ready to explore. What we hadn't taken into consideration was that the water was bloody freezing! All of us jumped in, and then jumped out again just as quickly. Brian and the non-swimmers were pleading for us to try again, but I'm pleased to say that the swimmers stuck together and there was no way we were getting back in. A wasted afternoon, but we bought some chips at the chip shop on the way home and hoped we could come up with another plan.

A couple of weeks passed and I hadn't seen the train gang for a few days, and I was at home with Mum, Merry and Jan. There was a knock at the door, and there was a large policeman standing there asking to come in. My heart was pounding. Had the man from the scrumping tracked me down? The policeman removed his helmet and said to Mum that he would like to speak to me. Mum and I went into the front room with the police constable. God this is it, I was going to prison for nicking a few apples. Mum looked nervous as she placed her hands on my shoulders. Where was I on such and such a date: was I at Merchant Taylors' School, by any chance?

"Yes, I was there," I told him. "We went off to find coots' eggs."

"Is that all you did?" What did he mean?

"Yes, why? Did we break a fence?"

"No, only the school was broken into that day and several classrooms were vandalised. Was that you and your mates?"

"No," I protested, as the tears rolled out of my eyes, "we didn't do that. All we did was try to get the coots' eggs but the water was too cold." The policeman seemed to accept my story. He told Mum that he'd interviewed the rest of the gang and we'd all said the same thing. Before he left, he gave me a stern telling-off and a warning never to go into private property again looking for eggs. I didn't mind that; I was terrified of what was going to happen after he left. Mum saw him out, and then turned to me in the room. I was expecting the punishment of a lifetime but instead she burst into tears. This frightened me more, so then I burst into tears too. She hugged me tight, and I apologised and told her that I had thought he had come for me for scrumping. I told her the story and we sat quietly and wiped away our tears. Mum told me later that her worst fears were beginning to come true. She was trapped on this council estate, and it was getting rougher and there was nothing she could do about it. She hated the train gang and asked me to keep my distance from them as they would get me into trouble again if I didn't. She said she also knew about the cigarettes, and I promised to pack that in too.

On the family front, things were changing. Mum went on the occasional date and Janny had left school to get an accounting job at a London firm called Deloittes. She had met a nice lad there called John Fulwell. He was an instant hit with me. With no dad, and Mum working full-time and Mike away in Dartmouth in Devon, he filled the gap perfectly. I was playing in the school football team regularly now and had complained to Mum that I had no-one to watch me. John immediately volunteered and roared encouragement, making me feel really good. He'd been a keen boy Scout, and now I had passed up from the Cubs, which had been good clean fun. We'd had a lovely elderly woman as our Akela, although if she saw a naughty Cub, she would pick him up with one hand and spank his bottom. I loved her and she loved me, no sore arses for me! The only one thing I didn't like were the thick fogs we would get, and on the walk to the bus stop she would insist that we walked in a chain, holding hands so we wouldn't get lost in the smog. Sometimes you couldn't see your hand in front of your face. The bus would crawl along and when it came to my stop the conductor would shout Caldwell Road, and then it was thirty seconds to my front door. Mum was always relieved when I got in and made cocoa.

In August 1957 there was the World's Scout Jamboree to be held in Sutton Coldfield in the Midlands. John asked Mum if he could take me. I was bursting with pride when he showed up to take me. I was dressed in my Scout uniform and so was he. The train took us to Sutton Coldfield from Watford Junction, and it seemed to stop a few times and already there were hundreds of Scouts with their parents and Scout leaders all getting excited to be at this massive event. Scouts had come from all over the world, and we spent all day walking amongst the African Scouts, European Scouts, American Scouts exhibiting their camps and singsongs. The Canadians were my favourites as they had red jackets and Scout jackets and were always friendly when you walked into their section. I had a great day and will always be thankful to John.

A couple of years later, he was married to Janny and for me I couldn't have been happier. The wedding was to be held on 1st March 1958 at the new church, All Saints, that had been built at the same time as the estate. Mike, who had two years to go before he finished at Dartmouth Naval

College, was going to be giving Janny away. Merry was to be a bridesmaid and Mum had a new outfit. I was looking forward to being suited and booted. I was very disappointed when I found that my suit had short trousers. I was ten, for Pete's sake! My brother missed his connecting train that took him from Exeter to Paddington; he then had to cross London to get to Euston on the Tube and then the overground to take him to Carpenders Park, our local station. Had things gone to plan, he was to arrive at the house at teatime on Friday, the day before the big event. As he stood trying to think of a plan B in his uniform on the platform at Exeter, the station master explained that the next train would be in the morning, the morning of the wedding. The ceremony was at 1pm, but even that didn't give Mike enough time to get there. After a while, the station master said, "Wait a minute, I can get the milk train to stop, or at least slow down to walking pace. Would you be prepared to travel like that, sir? It won't be any picnic though, you might need to travel in the guards' van, but at least you would be in London for about 5am." Mike jumped at the offer, so the station master made a call, and the driver of the milk train got the message and agreed to stop at Exeter station.

Mike found out later that the actual message the driver got was that a very famous naval officer was going to miss his own wedding if he didn't get the milk train, so plan B plus one worked well and Mike arrived at the house three hours before the wedding, looking dirty, his uniform creased and drab. Mum was worried his shirt wouldn't dry in time, and his uniform definitely needed brushing and pressing, but as quick as a flash, Mike had his clothes off, and Mum ran all the way to the local dry cleaners and explained the problem. They cleaned the shirt and uniform while Mum waited so everything was back on track. At least at the reception at the local golf club Mum, Janny, John and Mike could now all relax, and the day ended with a great party, which I suspect John's parents had paid for.

John's dad was a station master at Ealing Broadway in London and said later that he felt very proud that his fellow rail worker in Devon was such a great guy and did a good thing for Mike so he could get there in time for the wedding. Just before the end of that school year, in June, a letter was given to each child in my class when I came back to Oxhey Junior School.

Next year was my final year as a junior and we were all very excited about the contents of the letter. The letter said next May there was to be a class trip lasting just over a week to Wengen in Switzerland. It was the first time that a junior class would make that type of European visit, certainly from our school and even from our county or country. Each child was to pay £20 which would include hotel, travel and food. Pocket money could not be more than £1 and would also have to be added to the fee. As the forms were returned to Mr Johnson, our form master, and the summer holidays were over, it seemed that everybody in the class would be going.

Mum had read the letter and had said that it was impossible for me to go. She just could not afford it. John and Janny had just paid out for the wedding, Mike was still at naval college, and I cried and pleaded for Mum to change her mind but with no luck, but then I came up with a plan. "Can I go if I get a paper round and pay for it myself?" Mum agreed and said that she would take my wages off me every week and give me a shilling for sweets. She worked it out and if I worked until the trip, I would have enough. Getting a paper round was easy. My round was on the estate, and it was every evening that I was to deliver the late papers, the Evening News, the Standard and the Evening Star. I didn't have a bike, so I would have to run. On the first day the man from the paper shop who marked up the papers said that my round was all together except for one house that was on the other side of the rail track. Getting to that one house and back would take me about twenty minutes. I came in exhausted when I finished and explained my lateness to Mum. "We can't have that, now," Mum said, and she came up with a plan.

Merry was almost thirteen and by now was falling in love with rock and roll. Most of the time at the house, she and Stephanie, her lifetime buddy, were practising jive dancing, this new craze that was overtaking the nation. Merry wanted money for records, so she would do the one delivery over the other side of the estate, leaving me to get on with the main paper round. There was another drawback. Once I had been walking with my sister where I had to pick the papers up Mum insisted that we share the wages. I protested bitterly, but Mum insisted. Paying for the trip made me get on with it. Our eleven-plus exams would be taken just before the school trip and now the teachers were pushing revision hard. In our house, Jan and Mike had sailed through and Merry, on the other hand, had failed.

A couple of months previously we had had a visit from a boy who had been at the school two years ago. I didn't know him. He was introduced as Jimmy Purdy from Woodhall Lane, the next street along from mine. He was dressed in a smart sailor suit, just like the one I wore for the Coronation, with a proper naval hat. He gave a short talk about his school, and although it was a long way away on the east coast of England it sounded great. I went home and told Mum about Jimmy Purdy's visit. Unbeknown to me, Mum found out where Jimmy Purdy lived and one evening after I went to bed, she went round to Jimmy Purdy's house to speak to his mum about the school and how she might apply for me. Since those days with the train gang, Mum had been desperate to get me off the estate, as it was becoming rougher, and crimes were becoming more frequent. When the brochure and the forms to apply arrived, Mum sat me down to show me more school photos. It was called the Royal Hospital School, built in 1933 at Holbrook, by the River Stour in Suffolk, not far from Ipswich. It had been there since 1933 when it was moved from its old site in Greenwich by the River Thames. The school took boys if their fathers had been, or still were in the Royal Navy, hence Jimmy's uniform. He had been wearing No. 1 uniform, as they all did on Sundays, and when they went out of the school, otherwise it was navy socks, trousers, shirts and jumpers when they all went to classes. The brochure said that most afternoons were sports, with football, rugby, athletics, rowing, sailing, cross-country, boxing, tennis, the list went on and on. In the evenings after tea there was an hour back in the classrooms for homework. Table tennis, snooker and a hot drink before bed back in the houses. I didn't need to ask twice, I was hooked, and I never thought about being away from home for days on end and not seeing Mum for a couple of months at a time.

All went quiet for a week, then Mr Emling, the Headmaster came into the class and asked me to follow him. Oh Christ, I thought, now what? Because of the paper round I hadn't seen the train gang for weeks. What else could it be? I entered his study. He was a tall dark man who had a voice like thunder when he was addressing the school. He smoked like a chimney even in school those days and his fingers were brown with nicotine stains. He spoke softly to me and sat me down at the small table. He explained that Mum had written to him telling him about the application to the Royal Hospital School, and he said that he knew the school because of Jimmy Purdy and he liked the sound of it very much, and asked what I thought of it. I agreed. "OK then," he said, "you must do another exam, just like the eleven-plus, but right here and now." He gave me the paper and pencil and wished me luck and left the room and now it was up to me.

The preparation for the Switzerland trip was getting quite exciting. All the class were going, and small gangs were forming as Mr Johnson said that we would be sleeping at least six to a room at the hotel. Just before leaving, three things happened that changed my life. The first was that the letter came to say that I had failed the eleven-plus. Mum was upset and I cried, saying that I had tried my best. When I went into school that day, I was relieved that I wasn't the only one by a long chalk. Next another letter came to say I had passed the entrance exam to the Royal Hospital School, and I had to go there for a medical and formal interview. The third came, which was the biggest bombshell of all. We were moving. "At last," my mum said, "we are going to get away from this dreadful estate." To Merry and me, it seemed like the end of the world. We were moving to Boxmoor, Hemel Hempstead.

Three

BYE GIRLS, I'M OFF TO BE A NEW JACK!

Mum had been successful and arranged a council house exchange. She had seen a house and came back and told everyone that the garden needed doing and we would have to get stuck in and decorate the whole house.

The handy bit for me was that the move was going to happen whilst I was away in Switzerland and then when we got back there were a couple of weeks left of the term where Merry and I would have to travel from Boxmoor to the Oxhey estate every morning on two trains.

My class at school was 4J because we were in the fourth-year juniors and soon to go onto secondary education. And the J was for Mr Johnson, our form teacher, who took us for all subjects from swimming to maths. He was a good teacher, making lessons fun to learn. I loved him and I loved my class. There wasn't one arsehole, and I couldn't wait to get there every morning. The girls were great too, and bloody clever. During the last few months of 4J a few girls asked if they could put on a story-play every Friday during the afternoon. Marlene Smithson was the instigator and wrote parts for the rest of the girls in the class. It was as though Marlene was writing one of the very first soaps. They rehearsed hard and the storyline was good. Even we boys looked forward to watching each episode. The cast certainly impressed me – perhaps I was a little jealous as I would have liked a part too.

When the morning came that 4J would depart for Wengen in Switzerland, parents were fussing around their kids, mine included. Mum was checking I had gloves and a hankie and to my great surprise slipped me a ten-shilling note. "I'm proud of the way you've worked for that trip," she said. "This is for you to get something to eat." She kissed me and left me to go to work in Watford.

The class walked to Carpenders Park station, each of us holding a small suitcase and a blanket. Sandwiches were going to be provided on the journey to Dover, and at the port we caught the ferry across to Calais, France. We were fed in the ship's canteen, many of us too excited to eat. From there onto the train to Switzerland, where we would spend the night, that's what the blankets were for. Somewhere across Europe we would change trains in the very early hours, but most of us were too tired to ask where we were. During the next morning we arrived in Interlaken and then took a funicular train up the mountain to Wengen and our alpine village, which had roads but no cars. Transport for the locals was walking, horse and cart or a bicycle. I thought it was the most beautiful place I'd seen, and the locals were very curious and friendly. The week went by very quickly as we went out in the sunshine every day to learn about Swiss farming, with the cows with the huge bells around their necks and how they made cheeses, and the lovely wooden Swiss houses and the many fantastic flowers that grew by the roadside and in the woods. Just before we left, we were put on the funicular railway again, this time to go further up the mountain to the Jungfrau glacier. Snow and ice in the summertime? It was fantastic. The whole trip was fantastic and by all accounts a great success for all those in the council education department as the people who had thought up the idea. Mr Johnson was a very keen photographer and he had even taken cine films of us all. He announced that we would have lemonade and crisps after school when the film was developed.

We arrived back at school one afternoon just after home time. Merry was waiting for me. It was her job to show me the way home to Boxmoor and our new house. Mum knew that we'd be hardly likely to travel together, so I'd have to learn how to do it myself very quickly. From Carpenders Park it was two stops to Watford Junction, the mainline station. From there, there was another train coming from London and going towards Birmingham, a steam train. I had to be sure that whatever train I got on would stop at Boxmoor, Hemel Hempstead. From there it was a walk across a small park, across a canal bridge and then a walk across another park and then I was home. Our new house was in a small cul-de-sac, called Bishops Mead. There were only six houses in three semi-detached blocks, formed to make a horseshoe. The houses that faced right down the drive were the four-bedroom houses, and the rest were three-bedroomed. Mum had exchanged our house in Caldwell Road for a four-bedroomed house and Janny had just had her first baby, a son called Andrew, and they were going to live with us until Janny and John could buy a place of their own.

The second day I did the journey alone with no problems until I was crossing the second park, which was called the moor, that's why the place was called Boxmoor. A boy on a bike came up to me and asked why I was walking across the path.

"To get home," I said, "I live just over there."

"No, you don't," said the kid. "I know everyone who lives around here."

"Well, you don't know me yet," I said.

"Do you want a fight?" he said as he got off his bike.

"OK," I said, and I immediately punched him and he fell over. With that he jumped up and was off on his bike. It wasn't much of a victory though. I later found out he was a bit puny and was terrified of the boys who I later made life-long friends with. That happened a few weeks later during the school summer holidays.

Some months before we moved, John had asked Mum if we could have a dog, and to my surprise she agreed. The only other animal we'd had before was a blue budgerigar called Peter. So, John turned up with this adorable wirehaired puppy and we called him Sasha. Of course, he'd come to live in Boxmoor with us and the park being so close was great for him and for me. Every day, I would slip the lead on Sasha and he would pull me to the park. Most of the time whilst Sasha was doing his thing off the lead, I would be looking at the local girls. There was a group of lads my age playing football, when a wild shot at the goal that was made up of jumpers for goalposts, suddenly found itself at my feet. I quickly teed it up and lobbed it accurately back to them.

"Hey mate, do you want to play? We're short on numbers."

"Yes," I answered, "only I've got to take the dog back, I only live over there." A good opportunity for me to get some friends, not so good for Sasha, who didn't know why he was going home early and ran off. We all had a turn at trying to catch Sasha, and at last he was captured and taken home.

After a great afternoon's football, I was taken to the pub, The Anchor. The pub was a little further up the road from the park and right opposite was the house of Pete and Paul Robbins. Jimmy Gannon's house was a few houses down and Tony's house a few streets away. They were my first mates in Boxmoor, and now we were going to the pub, where we could sit on the wall in the garden drinking Vimto and eating large arrowroot biscuits costing a penny each. I told them about me, and the school I was about to go to and they told me about the area and the other boys who would frequent the pub. Later that day I met Bruce Thomas, Pip Hay and John Hollick. They lived further up the road, past the pub. We sat there until Pete and Paul were called in for tea and I left to go home and tell Mum all about it. Through the holidays, I met the boys' parents and they all seemed to like me, and my mum liked them, she said they seemed polite.

As the school holidays came to a close, all the boys prepared to go back to school. They all went to the same school in Hemel Hempstead, and I was getting ready to show myself at the Royal Hospital School. The day came when Mum and Mike took me to London to Liverpool Street station. I was dressed in my wedding suit and had a large brown paper parcel label hanging from my lapel. On it was my name and where I was bound for, and on the other side was the telephone number for the house in Boxmoor. I had no luggage. In my pocket were some pens, a toothbrush, toothpaste and £2. I thought I was going to look stupid standing like a package on the platform but to my relief there were a hundred other packages on legs joining me. There were a few naval officers getting us settled on the train and it wasn't long before a few boys, called from now on 'New Jacks', were talking.

23

None of us knew too much about arriving at Ipswich station, and buses took us the ten miles or so to the school. I couldn't believe my eyes: the place was enormous, two great Napoleonic cannons at the main entrance and a flagpole stood just behind them flying the naval flag. We were the only boys in the school at the moment. We were told we would have a medical, an interview and a written test the next day. If we passed, we were in, and we would be joined by the other 600 boys ranging from eleven to eighteen. Before tea in the great mess hall, we were given a short tour of the school. First the classrooms, then the science labs, the school hall, the indoor swimming pool, gymnasium; everything was so big, even the school chapel, which seemed more like a cathedral to me, although I'd never been in one. Then there were the houses where we would live. There were eleven in total, almost identical, only one was different. Each house took sixty-six boys and inter-house competition was fierce. Each house was named after a sea admiral, looking over acres of playing fields and soccer and rugby pitches. Beyond that was marshland, the sea wall and the River Stour, which was around two miles wide at this point. This is where the sailing and boating was done, explained the naval chap who was showing us around. Sitting in the mess hall, us New Jacks boys were making a racket eating and talking at the same time. One of the guides had to shout to get our attention.

"Listen up, you bloody noisy shower!" he boomed. "There are only a hundred of you now, imagine what it's like to have 660 of you like that! We have a system; so watch me now." He had our attention. "See these," he pointed to a series of red bulbs, twenty feet apart, ten feet from the floor, going all the way around the great room. He walked to a small, raised stage at the end of the room. "The Duty Master, the Head Boy and a few others sit here, while you lot eat down there. The lights are controlled from a switch under this table and when the red lights are on, you must not utter one word." He flicked the lights on. "Do I make myself clear? Not one word!"

Some of the group started to say, "Yes, sir," but he was down on them immediately. "Not even that, not one word!" The light was left on for a few moments, and then he turned it off. "When the light is off, you can talk," he said. "When the light flashes from on to off, it means other things, you'll learn this from your house mates." After tea, we were given a pair of pyjamas each and shown what houses we were to sleep in.

If we passed the medical and tests, our houses would be sorted out later. We would be living in these houses for the next six or seven years. It didn't seem like a prison sentence; I was so excited. We were getting ready for bed and looking out of the window in our pyjamas when one boy said, "Look, I can see France from here." No one said he was talking rubbish.

"I've just come back from France," I said, trying to impress.

Another kid said, "I've just come back from Hong Kong as my mum and dad are stationed there." I thought he'd have a long journey back if he didn't get in tomorrow and thought, Good luck, mate.

After a good breakfast, we were taken to the school infirmary for the medical. I say infirmary; it was more like a hospital, and I'd only ever been in one of those when Mum had all her teeth out when I was seven. This place, we were told, had its own operating theatre, and mortuary; I'd never been in any of them. Then we were stripped off to see the doctor. He looked at my teeth, in my ears, squeezed my bollocks and told me to cough! He listened to my heart. "You're a bit small, but you've got a strong heart, you're going to be a good runner. Let's see your weight/height." I was four feet and four inches tall and weighed four stones and four pounds. Next was the interview. Mum and I had rehearsed this bit. I had learned all about Dad's ships during the war and how long he'd been with each. He'd ended up in the Australian Navy and of course he had his firefighting records during the London Blitz. It went down like a dream. I even got in that Mike was about to pass out at Dartmouth as an officer. They seemed impressed that I knew all this, especially the naval terms in the conversation. If I did well here at school, I could follow in Mike's footsteps and go to Dartmouth. I told them about the eleven-plus failure; they said they already knew, but that didn't matter. I could get to the grammar school standard if I worked hard. I said I would. Mum and Mike would have been proud of me.

Onto the written test, which was more general knowledge than English and Maths. Later that afternoon, all the New Jacks were assembled, well, not all; I'd noticed that some of the boys I had spoken to, including the kid who could see France from Suffolk, weren't there. These kids didn't get in and were on their way home. Hong Kong boy was here with us. "Well done, boys," said the master. "You're all welcome to the RHS," which stood for Royal Hospital School. "When your name is called out, go to your house matron." Eleven women, each representing their houses, were standing patiently. My name was called out quite early, as my surname started with an F.

My house matron was a woman in her late forties/early fifties and she had a broad Suffolk accent from living in Thetford for most of her life. There were nine of us New Jacks going to the house called Cornwallis. Andrews, D; Burton, N; Cross, C; Farr, S; Flemwell, V; Loveday, B; Loveday, J (they were twins) Quaid, A; and last of all Showell, D. Like a mother hen, she gathered up her chicks and we toddled off to the clothing store. Vests, pants, dark blue short trousers, and a dark blue crew-necked jumper made of wool. The socks were heavy dark blue wool, just like football socks, and we were given second-hand black lace-up shoes; the plimsolls were new, though. Then to the raincoat section, then we walked to Cornwallis and were given a number. It was the number of our locker and our bed. No shoes could be worn in the house outside of the boot room. In a week or so, we would be measured for new black shoes, and new leather sandals, which was to be the footwear for inside Cornwallis. A naval tailor would come to measure us up for our new No. 1 uniforms, the same as Jimmy Purdey's uniform.

It was hard to take it all in, I said to the matron, and she answered, "That's just the tip of the iceberg." For the next few weeks, I found out that she certainly wasn't wrong. We changed into our dark blue daywear and the plimsolls we had been given.

"You should all have your toothbrushes and toothpaste," she said. We all held them up. Tiny tin mugs were passed around and the three items were put in a bedside locker together with the clean pyjamas that we had been given the day before. The pocket money was logged in a book and taken away from us.

The next job was to parcel up all our civvy clothes and address them back to our mums. That was it, I was in now, no going back or changing my mind. At 4pm that day, the rest of the school would be showing up and it would be a noisy afternoon, so we were told to sit quietly and watch and learn. We waited in the day room, where there was a snooker table, a table tennis table and some long tables and chairs. All around the walls there were lockers at waist height, again with our numbers on. It was buses that first gave the signal that term was about to begin for 660 boys. We looked out of the windows as bus after bus entered the school and followed the road around the massive parade ground. We were told never to call it a playground, how was I supposed to know! I could see as each of the double-decker buses stopped outside the appropriate houses, hundreds of boys, each dressed exactly the same in dark blue raincoat, bell-bottomed trousers and black shoes and white naval caps, exactly what a naval rating in the Royal Navy would be wearing except that he would have had a black band around his cap which would have had the name of his ship embroidered in gold. Around theirs, they had Royal Hospital School and I thought it looked great.

Cornwallis House, and all the other houses, were built two stories high and in the shape of an H. One side was the junior side and the other side belonged to the senior boys. Each side was identical, with a large day room, a boot room on the ground floor and a large dormitory that ran the length of the building upstairs. Each dorm had thirty-plus beds, and there was a wooden locker between each bed. The wooden floor shone from daily polishing. "I wonder who does that," I asked. Silly question really. The part of the building that made up the cross section of the H downstairs was the housemaster's flat, and Matron's accommodation on the junior side. There were matching reception rooms on each side between the quiet room and the day room.

"Hello New Jacks," beamed one boy. "I've been here a couple of terms. My name is Polson, but you can call me Peck." This kid had a large nose, hence being called Peck, his nickname. He sat down with us and tried to answer all our questions. "Matron is Matron to her face, or you can call her Sister Chamberlain, but we all call her Fluey."

All the junior boys wore short trousers and so did the seniors unless they were Badge Boys, a sort of prefect, and they wore full uniform all the time, gold embroidered corporal stripes on their arms. Next were the Petty Officers with two stripes and each house had two or three of these. And each house had two or three Chief Petty Officers with two stripes and a crown. These were called Chiefies, Peck added; watch out for these as they had the power to punish you big time. If any of the Badge Boys wanted your undivided attention, they would walk in and call 'house'. The boys in the room would stand to attention and keep silent as the Badge Boys gave out the announcements. I listened to Peck intensely, and just as he finished the Badge Boys called the house to tell us to get our coats and shoes on and to fall in.

"Fall in, fall into what?" I asked.

"That means we're going to march to supper," explained Peck. That was going to be fun, no-one had said anything about marching. I'd seen it on the telly, how hard could it be? In the muster yard outside, and each house had one of these too, the whole house, coated and booted, stood around talking until a Chiefy shouted at us to 'fall in'.

Very quickly the senior and junior boys formed themselves into two squads, three boys deep. "Attention!" thundered the Chief from the standing position at ease: with their hands behind their backs the whole house snapped to attention, their heels snapping together in silence. Us New Jacks had been held to one side of the yard and then a leading boy added us to the junior squad and told us to follow the others as best we could. "House right turn." Us New Jacks were facing the wrong way. "By the right, quick march" – thank God we were at the back otherwise we would have been flattened. Arms swinging – some boys were swinging their arms together which made me giggle only to be yelled at, and by the time we marched into the dining hall, everyone was laughing at us.

"We were just the same as you," Peck later explained. "You'll be laughing at the New Jacks next term after Christmas." We muddled through the meal and thankfully the journey back to the house was a gentle walk; at least we could do that.

While the rest of the juniors played snooker or table tennis or wrote letters home, us New Jacks were taken upstairs by a leading boy and shown how to make our beds the following morning. Then Fluey posted the lists for our cleaning stations for the morning, before breakfast. I was on the dormitory, so after a small bottle of milk and a few biscuits, we went upstairs and changed into our pyjamas and got into a regulation single naval bed, with regulation naval bedspread with blue anchors all over it. Then Mr Burbage, our Cornwallis housemaster, came in. He was a medium-height man, in his mid-sixties, with a white balding head and a large moustache. He reminded me of Mr Pastry, but something told me that he wasn't going to be as funny. He barked his questions. "You, boy, where do you come from? What do they make in your town? Is your father still in the service? What rank is he?" When I said my dad had died, he just asked me something else: "When did he die? Did he die from his injuries in the war?" I didn't like Burbage, not one little bit. Thank God for Fluey.

The next morning at 6.45am the school bell chimed. Not quite the same as Big Ben, but just as loud. At that moment, the dorm was alive. Each boy was out of his bed in a flash and emptied his whole bed onto the floor. Next, they dropped their pyjamas and put a bit of toothpaste on their toothbrushes and went into the showers. The shower room was huge, covering the same area as Mr Burbage's and Fluey's flats. The whole room was a wet room for the showers, with a small space for towel hooks, towels and toilets. The initial rush into the shower room was for the urinals, I learned later, not for the showers. Mr Burbage was there in his dressing gown standing by the water control lever. Brushing your teeth, washing your face was all you had time for; no soap was handed out. Then you dried yourself quickly with your towel and folded it back onto the hook, and back into the dorm to get dressed and put your tooth gear back into the locker. Making the beds the way we had been taught the night before, we stood at attention at the bottom of the bed and asked the nearest Badge Boy if the bed was OK, with its special hospital corners. Given the OK, it was off to the cleaning station.

The whole operation since the bell had rung had taken fifteen minutes. I was put in a party of eight that would be cleaning the dorm. The beds were placed into four sections, each taking a quarter of the huge room. There was a wide-open section in the middle opposite the double-opening doors. Each quarter was taken by two boys. One would dust the lockers, skirting boards and window frames, the other was on the broom and swept the whole of his quarter. The last ten minutes of cleaning time, we all came together, eight of us on our hands and knees in a tight row, each having a thick duster, and were given a signal by a Badge Boy that we would be polishing the floor in a figure of eight motion towards the back of the room, turn and then polish it back again. No shoes were allowed on this floor, and rightly so, I'd just polished it. Cleaning stations took half an hour, then shoes on, ready to fall in line and march to breakfast.

Once inside the dining room, we'd stand between the tables and the long benches which sat five boys each, and the rules were that we'd stand in silence until the duty master and leading Chiefy shouted attention; clap of the heels, attention, gave a short prayer and then it was controlled by the red lights around the enormous room. When the light came on, it was the signal for the boys to sit down without talking. The sitting down bit was noisy enough. The light would flash as the signal for one boy from each house, called the trolley boy, to run into the kitchen to collect the large trolley carrying the food for each house. Each house had three lines of two tables, the Badge Boys sat at the top of each. Then it was age and seniority in order down to the bottom where the New Jacks sat. Cornflakes, buckets of milk and very little sugar, the portions started from miniscule to large as they started to be passed down the table. Then the trolleys were returned to the kitchen by the trolley boys and the red light would go off for two minutes for eating and talking, with spoons and mouths going ten to the dozen, and the noise was bordering on deafening. Red light on… finish eating. Red light flashes, dirty plates and cutlery passed down to the New Jacks who had to stack the dirties. Red flash again, trolley boys ran into the kitchen to collect the next course which was always interesting. Boiled eggs one day, beans on toast on another and even kidneys and tomatoes. Sundays, Peck said, were always great: egg and bacon.

Once delivered, the trolley boys would push the trolleys round to the New Jacks end to collect the empties, eat and talk quickly, red lights flash, talk again, pass down the plates to the New Jacks, flash, stand up, flash, attention, a quick prayer, then after any notices or announcements, we could walk back to house. How to feed 600 hungry boys in twenty-five minutes, that's how. The operation worked for three meals a day, seven days a week and never changed.

Also, during breakfast, each boy was handed down a mug of tea, and at each table was placed four complete sliced loaves of white bread and a small knob of butter on each boy's side plate. For some reason, this butter was called flop, God knows why. Nobody knew.

School was from Mondays to Saturday mornings. After breakfast, we would collect our books, plimsolls, etc. and fall in ready for a march to church. Just before that the Badge Boys would give out any mail that had arrived. The school chapel again was enormous and made the church I'd been to once in Boxmoor look like a garden shed. We would be there for fifteen minutes before classes started. A hymn, a short biblical story and a prayer, then out. We walked to our classes. With a short break at 11am when we were handed out buns and cakes, then back in the classroom until 12.35. Then back to the house, drop the school stuff off, fall in for lunch. Walk back to the house, time for a short rest, time to read your letters if you had any, and then around 2pm, change for sports.

In the winter terms it was mainly football and rugby, and in the summer it was cricket, athletics and tennis. Boys could choose what sport they wanted but every boy had to do something. There were no letters from mums asking to be excused, Fluey had the power, but never gave them out, unless one was on his deathbed. One afternoon, just before we ran out onto the playing fields, a Badge Boy and a Chiefy asked if there were any New Jacks interested in representing Cornwallis at the inter-house boxing tournament. I was the smallest, but had always loved a bit of a scrap, so my arm shot up together with a couple of the others. The following Sunday the Chief and Mr Burbage showed us the rudiments of the sport and it wasn't long before we were skipping and ducking and diving against imaginary opponents in the Muster Yard. In the school gym we had everything, wall bars, trampoline, and even a junior ABA boxing ring. This was the 1950s and gloves were old-fashioned brown leather, and we had no headgear or gum shields at all. As we had no other boys as small as me in the school, after a win in the first heat I found myself going to the final. I would be fighting someone called Rivett from St Vincent House.

Andrews, another Cornwallis New Jack, found himself in the finals too. He was much bigger and heavier than me and he was a tough kid from Whitstable in Kent. We decided to train together.

Four

IN THE RED CORNER, TOMMY FARR!

Mr Burbage procured two pairs of gloves from somewhere and we would spar together. I knew he would hold back from knocking me flying, but I tried as hard as I could to knock his block off. He was a quick learner and looked like he had boxed all his life. The afternoon of the final came, and the gym was alive with the whole school. The headmaster and his wife were there. She loved a good punch-up, she told me later. All the masters were sitting with their houses. The naval PTIs looked the part, in white plimsolls, dark naval trousers, and sleeveless white vests with the Royal Navy Signature on their chests. Being the lightest weight, Rivett and I were up first. We stood to attention when our names were called out and we faced each other. The school was completely quiet during the announcements and during the rounds of fighting. Between rounds the volume of support for each fighter was deafening. A naval PTI called us together to the centre of the ring. "Now then, this is your first final, right? Do yourselves proud, box properly, no slapping like girls and when I say stop, stop immediately. Now shake hands and fight like men." If only Mum could see me now.

I was a bloke, albeit a small one. Three rounds of jabbing, punching, heads knocking together, and I could feel my teeth bleeding. Rivet had a bloody nose. At the final bell we shook hands and waited for the judge's decision. I won, and my supporters in Cornwallis went bananas. My heart nearly burst out of my chest. I was so proud. That evening at the house gathering Chiefy congratulated me and Andrews, as he had won his bout too. Commiserations to the senior boy who had lost his fight. A British professional fighter who had fought for the title against Joe Lewis, the world champion, was a fighter called Tommy Farr. Chiefy said from now on my nickname had to be Tommy, and that was how it stayed for my entire time at the RHS.

During that first term at school, I was also chosen to play for the first under-twelves football team. I was making good friends but in the classroom it wasn't so good. I was slightly older than the other New Jacks, so I was put into the older class, 2B. It was a comprehensive type of system at the school. The first three classes in the second year were 2X, 2U and 2A. Grammar school standard of learning languages, Latin and advanced maths for the really clever boys. 2B and 2C were secondary modern streams and we did metalwork, woodwork and technical drawing along with the main curriculum. In each boy's school tests, the whole class would be moved up and down on a leaderboard, something like a professional football team league placings. At the end of each term the top three were promoted to the class above, the bottom three demoted. So in each of the classrooms, the rivalry was fierce.

At the end of each month, pluses and minuses were handed out by the teachers. If a boy got one plus, it was well done, two pluses, very well done, three or more and it was tea in the housemaster's flat the following Sunday, with sandwiches, chocolate biscuits and cake. The added bonus of the treat was that you could watch television for an hour. It was another story for those who got minuses. One minus, watch out, improve on that subject. Two minuses, in free time extra lessons were for you, and three or more minuses, it was the stick; the punishment was to be beaten on the arse up to four times only wearing pyjama trousers. The welts could clearly be seen in the showers the next day, and these were known as the 'cuts'.

In early November of that year, the tailors had been, together with a team from Clarks Shoes, and it finally felt that I had the kit. It looked just like the uniform I had worn for the Coronation Day fancy-dress competition. But when all the New Jacks stood in the Sunday parade there was a feeling of camaraderie at Cornwallis. Every Sunday there was a school march parade, together with a marching band, the School Guard in their full uniforms with their white ankle gaiters, white gloves and real live rifles across their shoulders. This was proper naval. You wait till I see Mike and tell him, I thought. After the parade, it was church again. This time, the service was longer and then after we could all walk freely back to the house, change back into our day wear, and after lunch the afternoon was free time, unless you were in the house sports team. Then it was practice, practice, practice.

One morning, the New Jacks and first year boys were called together by the teaching staff. In a couple of weeks, it would be Remembrance Sunday, and those boys whose fathers were no longer alive could wear their dad's medals if they were sent from home. That meant me. I wrote home to Mum, and in a few days I received a package, with a note from Mum, saying that she would be so proud and would be thinking of me that morning. They never did anything like that at Eton with Mike. The housemaster took the medals for safekeeping and gave them back to me a couple of days before the ceremony. "You are to go to Petty Officer Walker, and he will explain the medals and how to wear them," explained Mr Burbage.

I knocked on the Petty Officer's door and was called in. I didn't know the man; I'd seen him around the school, he was quite elderly. He had medal ribbons on his jacket and looked like he'd had a very busy war years before. He took the box of medals and explained what each one meant, and where in the world they had been won, and he showed me how to pin them on my tunic. He then started to ask me about Dad's war and about the ships, and then he explained what had happened to them and whether they had been sunk or not. "Christ, your dad must have been a brave man to go through all of that," he said. At that moment, with pride in my chest, tears started to roll uncontrollably down my face. I was sobbing. I wanted my dad back, not to wear his medals.

I didn't remember shedding any tears the night he died, or afterwards, I was kept well away. Perhaps Mum had thought that best. I hadn't really said goodbye. The Petty Officer looked at me. "I'm going to leave you to grieve for a few moments, son," and he left the room. When he returned, I was dry-

eyed and smiling at him. "That's better," he said. "We won't say any more
about this to anyone, after all, you're supposed to be a boxing champion,
aren't you, Tommy?" He knew my name, God bless him. I wore Dad's
medals for the next seven years, and each time, I remembered Dad under fire
and that good old Petty Officer, who had brought me out of my grieving.

Going home for Christmas leave was the best feeling. The day before
there was no school, but there was work to be done cleaning the house
from top to bottom. The evening before supper, if you had pocket money
left over, it was given out together with your train ticket. Seeing that boys,
past and present, had a name for every special day, it seemed that this day
was called 'Leave Cash Day'. Early next morning, we dressed in our No. 1
uniforms, best shoes, and raincoats. No luggage, we didn't bring anything,
and boarded the buses back to the small country station called Bentley in
Suffolk to meet the RHS special train taking only us boys to Liverpool
Street station. Boys who lived in the north of England left independently
of us, much earlier. Excitement was high, and so was the volume on the
train. The Chiefs were keeping order as best they could, but even they
wanted to get home just as much as the rest of us.

Mum was waiting for me as I got home. She hugged me and said how
smart I looked. Sasha was jumping up to get in on the act, too. She said
that she had a surprise for me and gave me a bag. Inside was my first pair of
long trousers: I was thrilled. She laughed when I said that boys who didn't
make Badge Boys were still in short trousers at school until they were at
least sixteen or seventeen years old.

It was great to be with my friends again from The Anchor pub. They
said they had all sorts of Christmas events planned, including parties where
there were going to be wall-to-wall girls. Mike was home for Christmas,
too, with his first car, a Singer. We would explore the area as it was still
very new to us and we found a zoo, and some beautiful Hertfordshire
villages. Each time we went to Hemel Hempstead, the town attached to
Boxmoor, we noticed something new had been built and it was starting to
look very good.

The three-week break went by very fast. My holidays were longer than
Pete's and Paul's. They went back sooner, but they had a half-term break,

I didn't. It was almost as exciting going back to school to see all my friends I had made there. It was spring term and there were a few changes. The sport we played this term was rugby. I had never watched or played rugby in my short life, but it looked good, a bit like scrapping with rules, and I couldn't wait to get started. So all of the first year students, and me of course, were instructed on the rules of rugby, including how to tackle, pass and kick the weird-shaped ball. After a couple of weeks, we had it and teams were made up and we played each other. Flemwell (his name was Victor, but no one used Christian names, but nicknames were allowed however), was a Cornwallis New Jack who had joined the same day as me. He'd been pretty quiet during the first term, not really interested in football and didn't talk much. He was put in the same rugby team as me and we were laughing when we couldn't catch the ball.

The master, trying to keep order, got annoyed and blew his whistle. "This game is not funny, now get serious or there will be some trouble." How were we supposed to know he was Welsh? "Right," he said, he was going to join in the game, so watch out. Play resumed and it wasn't long before he had the ball and was running full pelt down the side of the pitch, boys bouncing off him as he pushed them aside. Then from out of nowhere, this small figure launched himself at the master, tackling him so cleanly round the ankles that he went down and so hard that he broke the halfway pitch flagpole.

He lay dazed for a moment, but Flemwell said nothing, he jumped up to his feet, shook his shoulders and ran back to us. We were cheering, jumping up and down, patting Flemwell on the back as if he had scored a winning goal. Flemwell was a natural at this game. He was immediately dubbed Flogger. He went very quietly through the house team, school team and became the most feared full-back in the county. There was nothing or nobody that would pass Flogger on a match day; thank God he was a Cornwallis boy.

On Sunday afternoon, houses took it in turn to be allowed to go for a free swim in the indoor school pool. The pool had a water slide, diving boards and even a pair of trapeze swings over the water that we could use on these free days. So the free-swimming party would fall in, towels around our necks and march to the pool. Our housemaster had to be in attendance. We were halted outside the pool.

It was as if Mr Burbage was looking for trouble that afternoon. He picked on a senior boy called Pearce Senior. His brother, Pearce Junior, had joined the school a year before me and they were called Piggy One and Piggy Two. Piggy One was holding a plastic football. Seniors were going to get a polo match started. "Stand up straight, boy," he barked and gave Pearce a sharp push in the chest, the ball flying out of his hands. Mr Burbage went to kick the ball, missed and kicked Pearce in the leg. The ball bounced across the path. Pearce reacted instantly and punched Burbage back. "You bloody bully," he shouted.

His mate, a boy called Watts, broke ranks and picked up the ball and shouted, "Go on, Piggy, give him another, I've got the ball." The junior and the senior boys hardly ever marched in a squad together, a free-swimming party being one of these times, and I was only two places behind Piggy Senior and had a ringside view of the whole event. My heart was pounding, what was going to happen next? This was going to be the talk of the school for weeks. I expected old Piggy One was going to get expelled. Nothing happened to Pearce Senior and Mr Burbage never mentioned it again. They had given their explanations to the head, and it was announced at the end of the term that year that Mr Burbage would be retiring as housemaster of Cornwallis but would still keep his senior teaching position. A couple of years later, he met Mrs Burbage and became a much nicer person.

The whole house was convened one spring day and our house Chief introduced Mr Neville Long to us, our new housemaster. He taught history and was a short stocky Welshman, a rugby man. What did we call him? Shorty Long, of course! He was young, enthusiastic and had a very pretty wife called Betty, but best of all he had a sense of humour, unlike Mr B. Almost immediately, the house started to improve, both in sports and in the classroom. All the boys were trying harder, even me. All the sports and classroom results were collated and the winning house at the end of the year would win the Kings Banner, the royal standard flag that had been presented to the school by royalty years before. With Mr Long driving us forwards, with his wife at every inter-house competition, it wasn't long before Cornwallis were the ones to watch. Our football teams rarely lost, our rugby team didn't – of course we had Flogger Flemwell – and after games, in the showers Shorty Long would be there grinning from ear to ear.

My fourth term, the autumn of 1960, I got a promotion to 3A, more points for the house. Boxing, I did it again and so did Andrews, and the Loveday twins excelled at running and I was part of the Cornwallis junior cross-country running team and that year the Loveday twins came first and second; I was third and I think we had another one in the first six, lots of lovely points.

Another thing that happened that year was that I was given the job of being the trolley boy in the dining hall. It happened after supper. All week, I had been running into the kitchen, grabbing my trolley laden with plates and hot food, and racing out again against a lad next to me, the trolley boy from Collingwood house. Prayers said, and the school was filing out to evening prep in the classrooms. I was in the kitchen, revving up my trolley ready to go. It was my job to collect all the dirty plates and bring them back to the washing-up department. "Go boys." We were given the order and I thundered down the walkway like a greyhound on a Friday night at Watford Stadium. All I felt was a thud as Fluey shot across one of the tables. I'd run down my own house matron. There may be trouble ahead, I thought, as I ran to her. She was on her feet, but hobbling a bit, she certainly wasn't very happy. I don't know how many times I said sorry. What was Mr Long going to say?

"You could have killed the woman," he screamed at me. Up to now we'd got on very well, but a single detention was not going to be enough for me. He seemed to calm down a bit.

"I've been looking at your file," he said. "It's your thirteenth birthday today, isn't it?"

"Yes, sir," I replied, looking for special leniency.

"Well Farr," (he wasn't going to use Tommy in this situation) "it's unlucky thirteen for you – Happy Birthday by the way. Now go up to the shower room and change into your pyjama bottoms."

The next morning in the showers I was showing off my four cuts neatly spaced across my bum. I didn't cry but did something equally stupid; when the beating had finished I stood up and said, "Thank you, sir."

"Thank you? For what!"

I could only think of one thing; I was thankful I was not going into detention, and that in my opinion was much worse than the cane. For a start it was held every Saturday evening after supper, in the school block for two hours. The rest of the school sat in the assembly hall, and it had been made into a cinema with a huge screen, full-sized projector, just like being in the Odeon or Gaumont theatres. We were allowed to take a can of pop and sweets and we all cheered when the lights went down. First it was always the Pathé News, and we would see short clips of what was going on in the world, finishing with the cup final or major sporting event. Next up was a cartoon, always Tom and Jerry, which I loved. The producer of Tom and Jerry cartoons was a man named Fred Quimby, and when his name came up on the screen, six hundred voices shouted in unison, "Good Old Fred!" I still do it today with my grandsons. The main feature film was either comedy, war or adventure. We never had love stories or horror movies and always walked back to the houses re-enacting our favourite scenes.

Another master that I got along with was Mr Cairns, our PE teacher. He was Scottish, so he was dubbed Jock, and he was also my boxing teacher, now I was in the school team, with Andrews of course. This was a teacher you didn't mess with. In class swimming lessons, he had caught me doing something stupid in front of the rest of the boys. We'd have to strip off naked, go through a freezing-cold foot bath and sit quietly and wait for him to come through. He caught me bang to rights being a clown and immediately sent me to the top diving board. He followed me with a plimsoll in his hand. The class sat in silence ready to witness my fate. On the top board, he bent over me and pushed me off, and I fell into a tangled heap in the water, a bit sore, but thankful I hadn't got the slipper.

Inter-school boxing was on Friday nights normally, and I had to go into the classroom in my number one uniform with a bag with my RHS tracksuit and boxing boots, etc. Friday afternoons was the only day of the week that we had to go back to school after lunch, and I would put my hand up to leave and my master would say, "Best of luck, Tommy," as I walked out with the others. Mr Cairns would drive the minibus and we would go to another school in Suffolk somewhere for an evening's boxing. On the way home, we'd all laugh with Jock about the silly moves we'd made against our opponents, and a favourite was to stop for fish and chips on the way back to the school. Jock always paid; he wasn't that bad after all.

I wasn't doing so bad; Andrews, on the other hand, wasn't losing to anyone. I always fought before him because I was lighter, but always made sure I was showered and back in my uniform or tracksuit to watch him. Jock was always delighted with him. At a training session, Jock announced to the team that this coming Friday there would be no inter-school boxing tournament. We had been invited to take part in a boxing event against HMS Ganges, a little way down the River Stour, at Shotley. Boys at HMS Ganges, a shore-based naval training camp, were there from the age of sixteen to become naval ratings. These lads were from rough areas and were starting right at the bottom. Andrews told us that his dad was an instructor there and he'd said the lads were hard, and for us to expect a hard fight too. Our team was fighting well under our age weight, but Jock had insisted that weights were pretty even, except me. I was to fight a boy from Ipswich Boxing Club, who had already won a junior ABA title. "Well, no pressure there then," Jock said.

The local paper was going to be there to cover the evening. This lad's name was Hart. We arrived late in the afternoon at HMS Ganges. At the entrance we passed through a patrolled gate, and we could see ahead a tall ship's mast at the end of their parade ground and a party of boys climbing the rigging. This we were told was done when they had open days or when they had a special parade. We watched as each boy climbed the mast and then along the outriggers to music. One boy climbed right to the top and stood there with a bar between his knees and saluted. "Bugger that for a game of soldiers," said Jock, and I was right behind him.

The gym where we were boxing was crowded, noisy and smoky. All the lads watching were allowed to smoke and did.

41

"There will be more noise throughout the rounds, too," said Jock. "You must listen hard to me."

This was going to be impossible, as when Jock raised his voice in class, his accent got stronger.

Guess who was up first? The MC had a microphone and introduced the fight to big cheers. My heart was pounding.

"From RHS, our neighbours, and the new young talent at special midge weight, Tommy Farr." The place exploded; perhaps they thought the real Tommy Farr was my dad!

We came together. My opponent was a little taller than me and perhaps a little heavier too. At the first bell we circled each other and after a few jabs, not much to say for the first round. At the end of the round, I went to the corner. Jock had plenty to say.

"Don't be scared of him. He's heard how good you are, so bloody well knock his block off."

Second round, different story. I went for him, and he looked a bit worried. I hit him on the chin, and he went down like a sack of spuds. The crowd erupted and I went to the neutral corner whilst the referee gave the compulsory count to nine. Jock was waiting for me, shouting from the floor, "Finish him off, Tommy, finish him," and I went forward again then BANG! The next I knew I was on my back and the crowd were on their feet. This was turning into a real fight. During the final round I cut my lip and ear and he blacked my eye and we clashed heads more than once and at the final bell I knew I'd been in a scrap. My body ached everywhere. The judges deemed that he had won. It was my first defeat, but Jock didn't care; he was proud of the way I'd gone for the champion who had more experience than me. I even had a talk with John Hart afterwards, and he was a really nice bloke who said that he'd never been knocked down before.

Later that evening Andrews stepped into the ring. The noise level went up another notch. The crowd knew he was Chief Petty Officer Andrews' son and they knew he was unbeaten as his dad had told everybody. I pitied his opponent. Andrews fought his way tirelessly to another victory. Back at school in the showers the next morning, I showed my blackened eye like a favourite tattoo.

Five

THE ONE AND ONLY SHOW

At home, Janny and John now had two babies and were moving to their own house, which they had bought in Berkhamsted, the next town and train stop down the line to Hemel Hempstead. Mike had passed out of Dartmouth as a young officer and his first posting was on a minesweeper, keeping an eye on the Russians and their fishing fleets. When they crossed the territorial line, it was Mike's job to board their vessels and confiscate their catches. He could now speak fluent Russian, but that didn't make him or the boarding party any more popular. He also had another serious problem. Even during the slight swell, he would be seasick, and as the weather worsened so would he. The Navy didn't want to see a new, young, gifted officer suffer, so gave him a chance to become a pilot in the Navy's Fleet Air Arm. He didn't pass the stringent eyesight test so that was the end of that.

"There's only one thing for you, laddie," the PTI had said to him. "It's submarines for you."

Mike went to sea as a guest in a submarine to see if he liked it. He loved it. From the moment the sub dived, it was quite still, no seasickness at all, although the old diesel submarines got quite smelly with the fumes. Mike didn't care, he was going to make a name for himself beneath the waves, and he did. As second officer on a submarine, he won his first medal in the 1962 Malayan crisis. In a few years, he captained one of Britain's nuclear submarines. The UK only had four of them at the time and Mike had one. We were so proud; it was a great conversation piece for me, especially when the girls' fathers asked me about my family.

Merry had left secondary school and worked as a telephonist at the Berkhamsted and Hemel Hempstead Telephone Exchange. One day, she announced that she was off to the Navy too, as a Wren, and she did very well in the job and the posting she was given was ending up in Scotland where she met David, her husband. Mum still worked in the pub, making lots of friends.

On one of his leaves, Mike drove up to see me at the school. When a relative or parents would visit, we would dress in our No. 1 uniform and we were allowed out from the school perhaps for Sunday lunch or tea or on a Saturday. He drove me to Clacton and on a dreadful windy cloudy day, we sat talking whilst looking at the sea.

"Steve, what would you think if Mum wanted to get married again?" Mike asked.

My thoughts flashed back to the nights when Merry and I could hear Mum sobbing through those thin walls at Caldwell Road. She'd been a widow now for some twelve years. It was time she had happiness, perhaps with a new partner again. I was all for it, and during my next holiday, I was introduced to Stan Pitham. He seemed OK, he had a daughter slightly older than me and slightly younger than Merry. She seemed nice. Everything seemed to be going OK, then all of a sudden Stan wasn't mentioned anymore. Years later when I'd left school, Mum explained that it was off when Stan wanted his old, very old mother to live with them. Mum had said no.

At school, I was doing well. In class I had been promoted again and now I was in GCE O-Level classes, and if I did well in those exams I'd go on to take A-Levels and perhaps go to Dartmouth like Mike. In sports, Cornwallis House were unbeatable and had been each year. Also, each year we cleaned up in the Kings Banner stakes and the prize was ours again and again. Even our New Jacks were doing well. I had done my time in the junior side of the house and now I lived on the senior side. The rooms and furniture were identical; the only perk that I could see was that we stayed up a little later in the evenings.

During weekdays, the school returned to the classrooms after supper to do their prep (homework). The work had been set by the teachers and we were left to get it done without any of the teaching staff present, except one. All the Badge Boys from the school had a form each and had to look after them; the more senior Chiefies looked after the older forms. If caught talking or misbehaving the Badge Boys would send the offender to one member of the staff patrolling the corridors almost looking for trouble. It was instant detention. That meant no film, no sweets next Saturday night. Some masters took it into their own hands to dish out other punishments. It was one evening when a Scots boy in my class was caught trying to be an idiot. He was told to go outside the class, put his face against the wall and stand at attention, wait for the master to pass. It wasn't long before Mr Seacombe, a tall lean man, burst into the room, dragging the boy with him. He said that he was going to beat the boy there and then (no pyjama trousers then!), and the lad was sent to go and get the stick from the master's office and the book where the punishment details were logged down. This was the first time most of my class were going to witness a beating, as normally it was one boy, one master in a shower room or a study. When he arrived back, Mr Seacombe placed the boy by the window and told him to bend over. Then he walked back ten paces to the door. You could have heard a pin drop in those few seconds. Then he ran full pelt towards the boy and hit him with so much venom that he screamed as he sent the boy flying.

"Get back there!" shouted the master and the boy obeyed the order. Another run, another cut, this time harder than the first. The screaming stopped as the boy gulped back tears, begging him to stop. "Get back!" ranted Seacombe. I felt terrified and sick to my stomach. This should not be happening; this should not be allowed. Thankfully the masters were only allowed to give four cuts and by the time the fourth one had been administered the boy was barely conscious. The master left the room and the Badge Boy helped him up and sent him back to his house. Somebody asked what we could do about this and what we'd just seen. The Badge Boy, who I think was just as shocked and upset as us, said he would try to talk to someone, but I don't know if anything happened.

I loved the Royal Hospital School, but this had left a bad taste in my mouth. I was beginning to question authority and when I did speak out, Mr Long wouldn't stand for it and said I was getting tiresome. Worse than me was Peck Polson, often speaking up for the defence of much younger boys when he thought they were being bullied or accused of behaving out of turn. He looked a bit like a lawyer, even at fourteen. He didn't know it then, of course, but he later became a very successful lawyer in Portsmouth, even successfully defending a pair of Royal Hospital School students who had been accused of shoplifting in Ipswich, the nearest town to the school. Peck also had a limp, which was my doing. In an inter-school rugby match I had the ball out of the scrum and went for the line to score. I could feel the breath of my opponents on the back of my neck, and they were just about to stamp on me when I passed the ball to Peck running to my side. I flipped the ball to him, and he tried desperately to get to the score line. Just then four of them jumped on him and there was a chilling breaking noise as they snapped Peck's leg as if it was a small branch. He spent months in different hospitals and was left with one leg shorter than the other. Never a cross word, though, and even now, when I meet him, I still say sorry.

At the beginning of the next school year, I was surprised to see a boy called Flexman being allowed to bring his drum kit to school. It was a beautiful blue Premier kit with chrome stands and symbols and he teamed with a lad called Toaze from Drake House, who played electric guitar through a small amplifier. They were allowed to keep their gear in a small room off the kitchen block, so it was not disturbed, and I liked to sit and listen to them. I had a Spanish acoustic guitar back at the house, so did Flogger Flemwell, and we played badly together sometimes. I was talking to Toaze one day.

"What we need is a bass player in the band, like the professionals," he said.

"I'll do it," I said immediately, and that Christmas, Mike bought me a bass amplifier, while I spent every penny I'd saved on a Vox bass guitar. How hard can it be? I asked, it only has four strings and I play one of those at a time. A few weeks into rehearsals I was still struggling; still they couldn't sack me, I was the only one. We all decided what we really needed was a singer to make the group complete. The day I first walked into Cornwallis I'd heard Piggy Pearce junior singing. He knew he had a great singing voice, and he did it to let everyone else know. His favourite at that time in 1959 was "She Was Only Sixteen" and we heard it again, and again and again. But now we needed him, and he was thrilled to have the job, and Toaze had a microphone which Piggy plugged into the guitar amp. If we rehearsed a harmony song where Toaze and I were singing along, everything was turned down so we could hear ourselves. Flexman wasn't so keen, but he kept hitting the drums though. Week by week we improved, encouraged by the kitchen staff who were always looking on.

As we were getting older, so were the activities the school planned for us. One such scheme was the CCF, the Combined Cadet Force. It was designed to give us an insight into what life would be like in the forces. Everybody had to do the first year with the army and then choose to stay with the soldiers or cross over to the Navy, as most of them did. One afternoon per week we dressed out of our blue day uniforms and put on khaki trousers and army boots. The top half stayed blue. We would be taken out into the woods or to the nearest army headquarters to get a taste of army life. All I got was a taste of cigarettes again and tried to sneak off whenever I could for a quick smoke. My pals at home were smoking regularly too, I liked the taste of tobacco but at school I had to be very careful, God knows what the punishment was for smoking. You got hung for murder, so it couldn't be that bad. A year later, I didn't get caught, I told the truth. We'd been for a weekend at some military establishment and had travelled to London and back by train. Everybody was smoking and when we returned to the school Mr Long called me into his office, saying he'd had reports of people smoking on the train to Ipswich last weekend.

"Were you smoking?" he asked

"Yes, sir," I said.

"OK, if you have nothing more to say, go upstairs and change (into pyjama bottoms) and wait for me in the shower room."

I was the first. As I sat there, I was expecting the shower room to become crowded; old Shorty Long was going to be a bit knackered after beating us all. I was joined by Flogger Flemwell in his pyjama bottoms.

"They're all denying it downstairs," he said.

Most of them by now were Badge Boys and if Badge Boys were in for a beating, then they would also lose their stripes. Chiefies were demoted. No wonder they were all lying. So it was just me and Flogger that took the cuts. Years later when I went back as an old boy, Mr Long told me that the truth had come out about the smoking weekend and that he'd felt so ashamed and let down by the Badge Boys that he never looked at them in the same way ever again. It still didn't make me give up smoking though.

That summer term we were to go to Lark Hill on Salisbury Plain to have a week with the Scots Guards. They laughed at us as they thought we were kids and we laughed at them because we couldn't understand a word they said. The young corporal who was taking everyday care of us would scream at us for not doing our marching drill the army way which was much more exaggerated than the laid-back style of the Navy. One morning we witnessed a tank practice firing live rounds onto a target half a mile away and watching an Honest John missile being launched, fabulous! Another day we went to war. From the stores we drew a rifle each, a camouflage-style jacket and an army-style tin battle hat. We were put into squads and given an assignment to do. Half the squad were attacking the other half defending hills with flags on, and we weren't the only school taking part, so we wore coloured armbands to show who was on our side. My squad was going to try to take a flag stuck in the ground. It was in the forest over there somewhere, and we had to be quiet and do exactly as our babysitter corporal told us. We sat in a ditch waiting for the off. He told us to put dirt on our faces and ferns in our hats just like in the war films. He handed out the cigarettes.

"I've got one request, Corporal," I chirped up, just as the first thunder flash went up, indicating to everyone that the war had started.

"What's that, laddie," said Jock (they were all Jock).

"If you have to give orders, can you shout bloody slowly, so we can understand?"

"Oh aye," was the reply.

Through the smoke and now thunderous bangs set off by the war marshals, we found the hill and saw our objective. Another ditch, another fag as the corporal explained what the next stage was. Split into two groups, the first were to charge the hill, straight up, and the second group attacked from the side. He said the defenders would be distracted with the charge of the small brigade and by the fireworks and more bangs. The second group had to grab the flag and that meant success and victory as part of the war. I was put in the first group, charging.

"Corporal, that makes us cannon fodder," one lad said.

"Aye laddie, that's right!"

On the given bang, we charged through the bracken, yelling, trying to sound like soldiers and not girl guides. With my rifle in the charge position, I moved up the hill. I didn't get very far. The tin hat, that was far too big for me, slipped down over my face and I ran straight into a tree. As I fell back down the slope, my rifle fell and I tripped another two boys and we landed in a heap at the bottom of the hill, still rolling around laughing when they came and told us that the war was over, and we had won. The corporal's plan was successful, hoorah. So it was back in time for tea and a hot shower and just enough time for another quick fag though.

After breakfast the next morning we fell in on the parade waiting for the coaches to take us back to East Anglia and the Royal Hospital School when from behind came a sound of tight snare drums being beaten in a rhythm. The pipes and the band struck up and the full glory of the Scots Guards band came around the corner, marching in rehearsal. The sound of the bagpipes made my head swim and I'd only seen them on television before. The music was magnificent. They were magnificent. Although they were not wearing their kilts, I could quite understand that through the years, their enemies had fled when they heard the Ladies from Hell coming over the hill into battle. God, what a week.

And so it was back to school; revision time, as exams were getting closer. It was about that time I was made a Badge Boy. Thank God, at last I was in long trousers. It felt as if I was growing up a bit. Letters still came regularly from Mum, Mike, Janny and now from girls! During holidays, Peter and

Paul Robbins, Pip, Bruce and I were still together. Football, cycling and now playing cards. There was a new block of flats being built across the road from The Anchor pub, whose wall we all used to sit at. Bruce found a manhole to a huge sewer not yet in service, so we could climb down for a long card-playing session. The sewer was quite big though, enough for us to sit around to have a few guest players. It was named Ricky Pong Bend. It was easy to find at night, just look for a manhole cover pushed to one side, beams of candlelight and fag smoke drifting up into the darkness. On Sunday evenings we all got dressed up in our modern clothes, coloured socks and back-combed hair and went to the local under-eighteens' dance hall. There was a live group every week, but it was only cool to do the slow dances with the girls, although at times I wanted to jump up and shake myself silly to the rocking songs. I'm sure though if I'd done that, I would have been walking home alone.

Local girls loved us because we were hip. I kissed and cuddled as many as I could. I was only home for a few weeks at a time and they always promised to write. Even their mums made me parcels of cakes to take back, I was in heaven. The letters kept up for a couple of weeks, and I'd think this is the one for me, as they'd say how much I was missed and how I'd get more kisses and a lot more when I got home next time. In nearly all cases, after a few weeks at school, the 'Dear John' letter arrived.

"I met him at the bus stop, and he walked me home in the fog."

It wasn't just me, all my housemates in Cornwallis were getting similar letters and the timing in Portsmouth and Chatham was very similar to that of Hemel Hempstead.

The pain in our hearts had subsided about twenty-four hours later and the letters were pinned on the noticeboard for all to read. I told Mum and Mike just before my GCEs that the Navy as a career wasn't for me. Mum was disappointed but perked up a bit when a commission in the merchant navy was mentioned. At that time, in the mid-1960s, Esso, BP and other oil companies had massive tankers sailing all around the world, and when I got tired of oil, there were lots of cargo vessels, keeping people busy and making them rich. The first thing in a potential merchant navy officer's life was the stringent eyesight test. I went, but it was so hard to see the tiny pinpricks of light in different colours, that I failed miserably. So that career was out of the window. So was a pilot officer in the RAF, another avenue I tried. So, putting the career on the back boiler, I headed headlong into the GCE O-Level examinations. Over the next two weeks, there was nothing but last-minute revision, exam after exam. With that over, I could get on playing with the group. All rehearsals had been put on hold. Piggy Pearce was a level-headed intelligent boy and was expected to walk straight into Dartmouth Officer Training College. And he did. Toaze wasn't interested in the Navy and I'm not sure what happened to old Flexman.

One afternoon, a piano teacher came into our practice and announced that he was going to put a show on at the end of term. He wanted us to play. Another boy in Cornwallis, Ruffle, an excellent trombone player, had formed a jazz band. They were in, and we were to play together with the school choir and some talented piano players on the last Sunday afternoon of term.

"If Pearce wants to sing into a microphone, we'll rig up the school PA for you," he said.

We were thrilled. This was going to be our first proper gig. For a while now, we'd called ourselves The Volskys. A history master had come up with the name; apparently there was an ancient Egyptian tribe called the Volskys known for their beautiful music which they played to the pharaohs. Fluey had seen in the pop magazines in the day room that most of the nice-looking groups were wearing the same thing and got to work making some sleeveless V-neck tops out of some old blue curtains. I hurriedly wrote to Mum to send my dark blue trousers and Beatle boots, so did the others. We practised about six songs, my favourite being "I'm Alive", by The Hollies. We worked hard on the harmonies and by that Sunday we were ready. At the dress rehearsal, the assistant headmaster came in. We were interrupting his lunch and scaring his dogs making such a racket. Racket! We were doing this live in a couple of hours, we couldn't change it now. Another, younger master approached us on stage.

"First show, boys?" he asked.

"Yes, sir," I replied.

"Well then, I'm in the right place at the right time. I'm taking your pictures on stage now, and when you're famous, I'll sell them for a fortune."

He took the only pictures of The Volskys. It was to be our first and last gig. As we were going to be the loudest act on, it was decided that we were going to play four songs to finish the show. Piggy sang well and the rest of us kept together. We went down a storm. We had to. Most of the school had never seen a live group.

It was the end of another year at RHS. This end of term was different as many of my close mates were leaving, most to join up and do other things in the Navy. The Loveday twins were joining the Navy, Burton was going to a bank, but it was the sixth form for the rest of us.

This holiday was going to be different, too. I was going to get myself a job. Hemel Hempstead in the 1960s was a new vibrant town with more and more people leaving London to live in council housing with good schools and green parks. On the outskirts they were continuing to build the M1 motorway and that's where they put all the factory estates. Unemployment must have been at an all-time low, there were hundreds of jobs. It was so easy, even for me, to get a holiday job, everybody seemed to be hiring.

The town centre was a long road called The Marlowes, with a small square called Bank Court. They called it that because the planners had put all of the banks together. Opposite there was a new eating place called the Wimpy Bar. The building was up a ramp, and made of glass, bridged between two buildings, with a large water garden taking up the pavement below, and the restaurant always seemed to be busy. I walked in and asked about holiday jobs. Mr Lee, the restaurant owner, took me on immediately as a washer-upper, and in the next few weeks I worked every hour I was offered, and I earned more money than I had ever had before. When it was time to return to the Royal Hospital School, the staff, all women, and Mr Lee, bade me farewell and a promise of more work on my next leave.

By the end of my last year at school, I had saved up enough for a scooter. The Mod movement was well underway, with Hemel Hempstead being one of the meccas for the Mod scene. I was now the proud owner of a 150cc Vespa. It was turquoise green in colour. That was OK I thought, it would go well with my green parka, an essential part of the kit if you were going to be one of the in crowd, especially with a scooter.

In the late summer of 1964, the GCE O-Level results dropped through the letterbox. I hadn't done too badly, passing seven subjects, Maths, English Language, English Literature, Geography, Woodwork, Technical Drawing and Physics with Chemistry, so I had made it into the sixth form, but still had no idea of what I wanted as a career. Piggy and Peck Poulson had both done well and we were all promoted on the Badge Boy ladder to Petty Officers. The next step up was to be made a Chief. I never made it, but the others did.

The sixth form to me was a different type of learning. O-Levels had been much easier, each boy receiving typed pages of notes, easy to read and digest. In the sixth form we were expected to make our own notes, visit the library in our own time and produce countless essays and opinions, and I was struggling to keep up. Mr Long saw through my bad results and suggested that perhaps, with all of my outside interests, music, clothes, my scooter, dancing and Mod mates, it was time to move on. So after only two terms in sixth form, I made an immediate decision to leave the Royal Hospital School. Mum was furious, Mike was disappointed, then John and Janny who lived in Berkhamsted suggested that as I liked music so much I might try the BBC. Brilliant. Soon after the application letter was sent, I was requested to present myself to Broadcasting House in Portland Place in London. A week after Easter, I was to start work at Bush House on The Strand for the BBC, and it was at the news information department. Mum was again suitably impressed, and Mike approved, too. Nowadays we saw him very briefly every six months or so as he would get home from leave after sitting for months under the ice cap monitoring what the Russians were up to. To fill in time before starting with the BBC, I went back to help out at the Wimpy Bar. Mr Lee taught me how to cook hamburgers, benders, fish fillets, and everything we offered on the Wimpy Bar side of the restaurant we offered on the posher side too. We got on very well together and he understood that I wanted so much more, so he never asked me to stay on permanently. I would be there from nine in the morning and I would still be there at 1am the next morning, tired but very happy. It was the women working there who started to take an interest in me. The younger women, still at least eight years my senior, would talk to me about music and make jokes that it wouldn't be long before I would lose my cherry.

The restaurant was open from ten in the morning through to midnight and I can say that I never saw it completely empty. Business was steady, building to 'rammed and frantic' through the lunch-time period every day including Sundays. At around 7pm Mr Lee would close his side of the grill and go home, leaving me to cook the late-night Wimpy menu. During the day there would be ten women serving and six would stay for the evening shift. They were a cheery bunch, not one of them was over forty. When I took my break, I would sit in the staff room with at least three of them and they took great pleasure in seeing me blush. We sold a long frankfurter sausage called a bender. It was nicked with a knife across its body every 20 centimetres and when cooked in hot water the cuts allowed the sausage to bend almost in a circle. Great to have in a burger bun with a fried egg and pickle. The women laughed when they asked me how long was my bender and did it bend up when it got hot? Did I know how to use my bender? I didn't say much, just laughed and smiled back. At closing time, we spent an hour cleaning the grills, the ovens, tables and floors with the music loud. Somebody was always singing along. I finished my chores and went into the changing room to get out of my chef's whites and trousers.

She slipped into the room without anybody noticing. She was about six years my senior, attractive and one of the leading jokers. Undoing her Wimpy overall from the top, showing off her ample bra housing very ample tits, "I've come to see your bender for myself," she said, smiling.

In a second, she had hold of my bender, which, by the way wasn't bending anymore and we were kissing furiously, my fingers finding her bra fasteners and then with her overall completely open my hands were down into her panties. Just then another girl came walking past the changing room door but didn't enter. I suddenly thought of somewhere we wouldn't get disturbed, the men's toilet; I was the only bloke. So we raced across the hallway, locked the door and were at it again. She sat me on the toilet, dropped her pants then dropped herself onto me and my bender. I knew her name, of course, but only that. Was she married, living with someone, any kids? Right now, none of that mattered, and still didn't for the next few minutes. I came, she giggled and climbed off me and bender, who was now back to bendy. Dressed again we left the toilet. Now we were both smiling ear to ear. Most probably she did it for a bet and was now triumphantly collecting her winnings from the other girls. I felt triumphant too; I could now tell my friends at the pub and at the Royal Hospital School that I, Stevie (Tommy) Farr, was now cherry-less.

Six

SCOOTERS, SAXOPHONES AND ANGELS

With a new suit for my new career sorted out I was now able to update my scooter to a Lambretta. It was an LI150, a beauty in blue with chrome bars and mirrors and a shiny spare wheel which made up the back of the dual seat. As I was still a learner driver it was decided that the train was a quicker and safer way to get to London every day. The main line train would take about thirty minutes into Euston station and then a few stops on the underground to Charing Cross and, after a five-minute walk, I was there. On my first day I was introduced to a Mrs D'Arch Smith in charge of the News Information Centre at Bush House, a friendly lady past middle age and a chain smoker. As I sat in her office, she smoked two cigarettes. She explained how it worked. In her part of the office were the readers. All these middle-aged people sat every day and read every article of every newspaper and wrote in pencil where each article was to be filed. Every BBC News bulletin was typed and labelled. Through the day the newspapers were delivered to a small office next door, that's where I was to be working. I joined five others, all about my age, and we had our own desks. The leader, a lad slightly older than the rest of us, was Chris Crouch. He explained to me our part in all of this. We were to cut each article, label it and add it to the pile then after lunch took these enormous piles of cuttings into the information library, an enormous room full of filing cabinets, and spent the rest of the day putting cuttings into their categories. Programme researchers would then use the library for information and ammunition in some cases. That's what the job was. It wasn't quite what I had in mind. Where were the cameras, the lights, the music? Certainly not here. On the train home I wondered just how long I was going to stick with this. It wasn't going to bring me down; I was in London, the heart of British music and the fashion scene and I wasn't going to let that pass. Chris, my news information leader, was also nuts about music. His passion was the Beach Boys and I had become a great Who fan. Every lunchtime we would race out and spend the hour in a record shop, sometimes a guitar shop for me, and occasionally a clothes shop, perhaps in Carnaby Street a short one-stop tube ride away. D'Arch Smith would always frown and mention that she had noticed our late return, Chris ought to have known better, but never took it any further. I always thought had she been our age she would have been there with us.

One of our girls, Margaret, was the daughter of an army officer and enjoyed talking to me about the Royal Hospital School and compared her upbringing military style and mine, suggesting we spend a weekend together at a place she'd heard of in Hampshire. I agreed. She had tits even bigger than Wimpy Woman's – I couldn't wait to get them out. Alas, though, it never did happen. Soon after I had walked in, an Indian girl was introduced as a new addition. She was going to be with us for a short while, she was waiting for her university course to start. She was the most beautiful girl I had seen to that date, with a smile that would light up the room. Chris, myself and the other males in the room went to putty when she spoke to us. Military Margaret stepped up her game, not to be outdone, inviting somebody else from the office to her Hampshire hideaway, although actually who was never announced.

A motorcycle or, in my case, a scooter, driving test was very easy to apply for. The waiting time was just a couple of weeks, no lessons were taken and only because it was the test did a rider wear a crash helmet. St Albans was the nearest test centre because Hemel Hempstead didn't have a set of traffic lights at the time. I reported in and an elderly man was to be my examiner.

"Drive up to the next corner, turn right, turn right again, come back round the block to me. Pull in with the correct hand signals. OK then."

"Yes, sir." I checked the traffic, looked in my side mirrors then turned, pulled out, turned right, followed the instructions then back to him.

"Good, son, now do it again and as you come back to me this time, I will raise my newspaper and drop it down like a flag. This will be your signal from me for you to do an emergency stop. Having done that, come round to me and stop in front of me."

"Yes, sir," I said. Round the block, emergency stopped and started going back to him, plenty of hand signals and mirror glancing.

After a few questions on the Highway Code, "Well, son, you've passed." Another first day in the history of Stevie Farr. He went back inside the test centre, and I promptly lost the crash helmet, put on my black beret and my dark glasses, singing at the top of my voice all the way home. Pete Robbins was thrilled when I told him the news. He'd just bought himself the most beautiful full-length dark blue leather coat; with me with my beret and very dark glasses and new black parka, him on the back, we were Kings of the Hill, taking envious looks from the girls and the guys alike.

I first saw her standing at the platform of Boxmoor station, waiting for the same train as me to go to London one morning. She had short, bobbed hair and wore a brown suede coat with a face like an angel. I couldn't take my eyes away from her. Day after day she was there, not with anybody in particular, and when I was feeling braver than normal, I would stand close by so we could get into the same railway carriage. That's as far as it went. She even went on the same Underground platform at Euston and got off at Oxford Street, the stop before mine. I didn't see her on the way home. I thought she was a nurse or somebody that worked late shifts. Scooters were free to park at Boxmoor station so I took the advantage of having my transport there for a quick getaway home and the house was only just a few moments away. I was in my suit and carried my parka as my coat to work. One evening the heavens opened a couple of hours earlier and wasn't giving up at all, then when the train stopped at Boxmoor I jumped off, ran into the now empty waiting room, slipped on my parka and black beret – glasses were a waste of time. It was then my mystery angel from the mornings walked past me to the station exit. From the station scooter park area, I watched her as she crossed the road and stood by the bus stop in the pouring rain. Now's my chance, I thought. There was hardly anybody else standing with her so it would not be so depressing if I got a 'Fuck off' as an answer to the offer of a lift. I stopped by her and asked the question.

"It's really nice of you," she said with a fantastic smile, "only my dad is meeting me here with the car, thanks for asking though."

I was speechless she had spoken to me. I bet the words "Fuck off" had never entered or passed her lips never, ever. Another important day. I could now say good morning to her, knowing even though she might be thinking oh fuck off she would be too nice to say it. Oh happy days.

Although still enjoying my company cruising round on my scooter, Pete had found himself a girlfriend called Maureen, a real beauty – this town had hundreds of them. It was Maureen's birthday and Pete asked me to go with him into the town to the best handbag and leather shop, as that's what he wanted to buy Maureen, an expensive handbag. I went along as I was the driver; I certainly knew nothing about handbags. The young shop assistant came to our aid. Christ, another beauty. She smiled, laughed out loud at my jokes and Pete took ages choosing and changing his mind over the bags. It gave me time to check the pretty girl out. She had short, bobbed hair like the station angel and her clothes were well-cut and modern. I would have to work fast if I was to get anywhere as Pete had made his final choice and the assistant, whose name I had found out was Sue, was wrapping the parcel.

"Would you like to go out on Saturday?" I asked.

"I can't this Saturday, but I will next week." She smiled.

So a date was fixed for a week's time. A week to clean the scooter, clean myself, I even helped Mum clean the house just in case she came home with me. Even the boring work at News Information seemed to fly by that week and I was a little nervous as I rang on the door. Some weeks before I had met a nice girl called Hilary and after a few simple evenings out I was invited to tea to meet her mother and father. He worked in the City and was a high-ranking officer in the Royal Naval Reserve. Hilary had told him about me and the naval school, and he seemed very interested in meeting me and talking to me about the Royal Hospital School. I presented myself to their lovely house, and Mrs Todd opened the door, showed me through to the lounge where Mr. Todd sat smoking his pipe. I sat on the sofa making polite conversation. Hilary, explained Mrs Todd, would be down in just a moment. I heard her bounding down the stairs, the door flew open, and she launched herself at me, plonking herself heavily onto my lap. At that moment every molecule of air that was in my stomach and bowels was forced out and the largest fart I had ever done fanfared from my bottom. I wanted to laugh out loud, cheer in fact, it was a Brahma of a fart and was to be celebrated. I looked at the Todds; they clearly weren't amused. I looked at Hilary – thank God she burst into laughter. I had to join in, I would have died trying to stifle the huge laughter that always followed a fart of that magnitude. The parents were not that keen on Hilary seeing me after that incident. It didn't break my heart or hers, but we did remain friends for years though.

As I stood at Suzie's front door, I had a feeling I was going to like the pretty handbag girl. The door opened and my jaw hit the floor. It wasn't Sue at the door, it was my station angel.

"Hello, you must be Stevie. Come in, my sister isn't quite ready. I'm Linda, by the way."

I followed Linda into a small front room. I couldn't think of anything to say. The silence was broken by a short woman with a Liverpudlian accent calling Sue down.

"Come on, Sue. Stevie-weavie is here."

In walked Sue's dad, another small person, and they welcomed me with open arms as if I had been going out with her for years. She walked in looking even lovelier than I had remembered, flashing that beautiful family smile that could warm the coldest of hearts.

Over the next few weeks, we went everywhere together. My mum and the family loved her instantly. Life was going to be perfect. Something had to be done about the BBC though.

In November of 1965 I had my eighteenth birthday. British Rail took my junior status away and from now on I had to pay a full adult ticket rate to London. Hang on, I was still on junior wages. So I went to D'Arch

Smith, and explained the problem to her. She tried to get me some more money to cover the extra cost but with no luck. So by the New Year I had given my notice to Auntie BBC. Over that previous Christmas I had gone back to Mr Lee's Wimpy Bar to help out and I stayed on for a couple of weeks, grateful for some real wages.

One of the largest employers in the town at that time was a paper manufacturing company called Dickinsons, famous for their Basildon Bond writing paper and envelopes. I answered an ad in the local Hemel Hempstead Gazette to become the assistant export manager at Nash Mills, their cardboard-producing factory. The work was more interesting, and I enjoyed the challenge of getting tonnes and tonnes of cardboard on ships going all over the world. The office, though, was a dark miserable place and so it seemed were the rest of the staff who worked there. So as soon as the day's work was done, I would sit at my desk devising and organising fortnightly trips for the staff.

One of my big successes was ice skating. I would organise the coaches, collect the money from everybody. Once inside the ice rink (our nearest rink was Silver Blades in Streatham, South London) we would go to the group counter to collect tickets and boots, then spend the next two hours hilariously trying to get round the rink like everybody else. The music was provided by a live band. Nursing sore arms and bruises didn't put the boys off who worked with me in the factory trying to get off with the secretaries. At work they wouldn't have had any chance of it at all. But the following morning they were walking around smiling and so were some of the women, so I like to think that I did some good during my short time there.

Since leaving school I hadn't done much playing, so I decided to look around to try to join a young local group. After several auditions it was clear that I was not the great bass player I thought I had been at school; at the Royal Hospital School I was the only one. One evening I met some lads who were playing together at the church hall. Their leader was a good-looking kid named Dave Stow. We were enthusiastic but the practice didn't go well. One of his mates, another guitarist, insisted on building up the folding chairs that were at the side of the hall into a pyramid and attacked them one by one whilst he played his guitar. Pete Townsend of The Who did a similar thing to his amplifiers at the time – wasn't the same though. At the end of the evening Dave and I ended up in his kitchen being given tea and sandwiches by his lovely mum, impressed that Dave had brought a friend home whose elder brother was a naval officer. I met Ernie, his dad, a hard-working heating engineer, and Dave's younger brother, Jeff. Jeff was still at school, only just. Dave was the Mod in that family, he was saving desperately to get his own scooter. Jeff fancied motorbikes like his dad. As we talked that evening over many machines it was clear that, with Ernie's tuition, they both knew much more about scooter and motorbike engines than I was ever going to know. I came home that evening with two new mates to go around with and two new friends that I have kept forever.

Sue met my friends and liked them. Jeff had a pretty girlfriend also called Sue and the two got on very well together. One evening we went out as a foursome to see a soul band in Aylesbury. American soul music was getting more and more popular, and it wasn't long before Britain was copying the American style. We went to see Geno Washington and the Ram Jam Band; just the name told us the evening was going to be great. The place was packed with young Mod kids hungry for the new music. The band were introduced and played a couple of numbers before they introduced the singer and leader, Geno himself. During the whole performance my eyes were trained on just one thing: the two guys playing the saxophones. I'd never heard saxophones played that way; the way the guys swung them when they weren't being played, I just had to get me one of those and learn to play it. I couldn't believe it when Jeff said he'd love to play one and be in a band like that. So, it was decided on the way home that we would go to the nearest music shop and ask about saxophones.

Seven

HELLO NEW WORLD!

Hammonds at Watford was the nearest music store and as a well-established shop on three floors had plenty of them for us to look at. Close up they looked even better. We decided to buy a tenor saxophone each and get started right away. The young helpful assistant would willingly take my bass amplifier and guitar as part exchange and my savings would take care of the balance. Jeff wrote down the hire purchase details, guessing his dad would sign the forms, although having only a few weeks more left at school, he had a Saturday job and planned to make the payments that way. Ernie, Jeff's dad, didn't see it that way at all and flatly refused to sign the papers. What now? Disaster! The next Saturday I walked into the shop with a very disappointed Jeff to collect my new second-hand instrument. We told the young assistant of our plight.

"What else could go with a saxophone to play soul music?" I asked.

"Why not try a trumpet?" he answered. "We've got a really good one downstairs."

Jeff looked at the instrument, and after a few hints on how to blow the thing, he put it to his lips and blew immediately a continuous steady note right across the shop.

"There you go," smiled the salesman. "Not many can get a note out of it the first time, you must be a natural. Oh, the price – I'll take £6 and give you an instruction book, showing you how to play each note."

So, we left the shop a hundred times happier. Each with an instrument, each with a book of how to do it. And now we needed some songs to play so it was straight round to the record shop where I bought Geno Washington and the Ram Jam Band's Funky-Butt Live album. Our plan was clear, if we could play along with Geno and his men from one end of his record to the other then we could walk straight into a soul band.

The first rehearsal sessions were awful! Luckily for us Jeff's dad had seen his son's determination to play and allowed us to use his cellar under the house to practise. Dave helped out by playing the right note on his guitar and, with the aid of our How to Play books, tried to play the same note as him together. Very shaky to start with but with three full evenings a week improvement was evident. Within a month we had the notes down and put the album on track one; it was almost exactly the same tunes as he played on a live show. So when we weren't playing, we tried to dance in time with each other as the Ram Jam Band had done. A couple of months later we could play the brass parts on every track, the dancing was good too. We were ready for the next part of the plan – to find a soul band. This was going to be hard; there weren't many as the music was so new.

At Jeff's school there was a band called Eve and they were Jeff's mates. They were playing the hits of the day, which included some soul and Tamla Motown numbers. The singer, a slightly older lad, called Ray, was out of school and worked in the offices of a large building firm. Mack played the drums, Stewart was the bass player, and Perk played guitar. We went along to the local youth club to see them play. No wonder I hadn't managed to get a bass-playing job in civvy street after school! These guys were great, the Volskys wouldn't have stood a chance. We put it to them during the break. How would they like to play like a real American soul band with a brass section for one night to see how it went? Ray was the keenest, the others weren't but went along with the idea that it was just for one night. Eve were regulars on the Hemel youth club circuit; the town had at least half a dozen clubs so kids could dance almost every night of the week. A date and a venue were chosen. Warners End Youth Club was the most hip and it should go well there. Any doubts soon flew out of the window after a couple of rehearsals. Jeff and I insisted that we play songs from Geno's album in Geno's key and Geno's way. Changing things around a bit didn't seem to bother them, especially Ray, who was loving what was about to happen. On the night, Eve played as Eve for the first half; the rumour had gone around the schools saying that a full soul band were playing the second half. From the moment the second half started the audience were up dancing, cheering, shouting and even screaming. Christ! This is just like it was in Aylesbury at Geno's gig. We came off stage eventually after two encores.

"Right," said Ray, assuming the leader of Eve. "I want these guys in the band."

Mack the drummer was keen, just Perk and Stuart weren't.

"OK," Ray said, "you're sacked or I'm leaving. I'm gonna be with these guys."

Oh dear, we hadn't planned any of this – Jeff's mates had fallen out badly with one another and we had successfully split up a great little band. Now what? It wasn't long before Jeff, me and Ray were getting together planning the new band.

In the real world, things were going through some changes. Jeff had left school, his father insisting there was a great future in heating and air-conditioning, and he was to go to college. Dave, his brother, was already doing very well as an apprentice electrician. Being an assistant manager at Nash Mills was becoming a little stale and boring. The actual export manager wasn't an old man, so his job wasn't going to become vacant for ages. I had managed to brighten up the lives of the people that worked there a little, but as a future career for me – no, sorry, not for me. I couldn't think of an office career, now all I could think of was the band. As a little job at the weekend, I'd been doing some car cleaning on the local car lot in Hemel Hempstead, and I bought an old Ford Anglia for £50 from Mr Macintyre, the boss. Racing around with L-plates for a month or two, I passed my driving test. There was no stopping me now.

Sue was still the great love of my life, we still loved going to Mod places and seeing Mod bands. The night The Who came to Hemel Hempstead we dressed as Mods to see them but they came on stage wearing clothes we'd never seen before. Roger Daltrey, their singer, wore hipster trousers with big checks, while Pete Townshend, the guitarist, wore a jacket made from a Union Jack flag. A couple of weeks later Sue presented me with a present; she'd found a piece of material similar to the large checks that Roger had worn and made me a pair of hipster trousers. This angel could do no wrong, after all, she came from a family of angels!

Mack, Eve's drummer, had decided not to stay with the band after all; he was a close friend of Jeff's, so it was important we stayed friends. He wished us luck and we wished it back. Ray, on the other hand, had been busy; he sang with great volume and spoke like that when he wanted to get his point across or tell jokes that everybody must hear, but for a young singer he was very gifted. There weren't many who could sing like him in this town, and we were very lucky to have him. He introduced the new guitarist, bass player and drummer to us. Andy Powell was on guitar, a good-looking blond kid and he and his drummer mate Terry Finn had come from the local grammar school, as had Dave Casey, a new tall dark bass player. I was amazed just how well that these guys played. It wasn't long before the band, still nameless, had a programme and we were ready to go. Transport was the next problem. I was the only driver with a licence. I soon found an old Post Office van for a bargain and painted it blue. We needed a name like Geno Washington and the Ram Jam Band; whoever thought of the Garnet Clark Sugar Band was a genius! It was just right. I knew it wasn't me or Ray, it must have been one of those grammar school kids. The next time that we drove up in the van the name had been added in coloured letters all down the sides of the vehicle. We were ready. Ray was to be Garnet.

Starting with the Hemel youth clubs we quickly started to play regularly, and it was at a crowded gig in Chaulden that we met Joey Johnson for the first time, a tall very dark guy with a mop of black hair and an infectious grin showing a mouthful of busted teeth. He jumped up on stage and asked if he could sing a song; we agreed, and Ray introduced him. He went to the wings to make his entrance. On his cue he ran out to the microphone; in those few seconds he'd slipped on his headgear – black stockings over his head, where his mouth was a white taped hole. We were on stage with one of the black and white minstrels! He started his number 'Mockingbird' and moved around the stage. Great dancer, lousy singer.

At the end of the evening, he talked to Ray.

"I wanted to look like a proper black soul singer," he said.

"Didn't work," Ray said, "you looked like a prat! Bloody funny though."

"I'll give you a hand with your gear," he said.

There must be other bands who have had strangers come up to them and said those same words, I guess that's how roadies are born. Joey was to be with us for a long while and in all that time I don't think that he ever had his own driving licence.

I had taken on the job of finding gigs and taking bookings. We had already moved away from the small youth clubs of Hemel, and we were doing better-paying gigs. The American air bases paid well, and we had moved into the London club scene, playing the Valbonne and the Bag O Nails regularly. The work rate stepped up and we were working some weeks five nights straight through. Joey was tireless and kept us amused when we were tired and hungry. We changed the old Post Office van for a Ford Thames van, bought scruffy and given the Dave Casey makeover. Our bass player seemed to be a master craftsman; he made his own guitars and Marshall speaker cabinets exactly the way Marshalls made them for a fraction of the cost. He also took this Ford van we'd bought and painted it with a roller and when it was finished it looked brand new. With a row of bus seats behind the driver and a partition between us for the equipment we were ready to go anywhere.

At a hall in Cobham by the River Thames we first saw our name at the top of the poster, the Sugar Band. We dropped the Garnet Clark bit as Ray had had enough of "Hey, Garnet, do you do requests?" or "Oi, Garnet, that girl fancies you." Ray was happy now just to be Ray. In the dressing room there was a rack of second-hand clothes, ready for a jumble sale we were told. But in the break Joey had selected a dress and asked Sue, Jeff's girlfriend, to make his face up with lipstick and powder and to put his hair up. Losing his boots he stood in front of us – our very own go-go dancer, that's exactly what he wanted to be. When we were well into the second half of the show Ray introduced Josephine, our own go-go girl.

The band kicked off and Joey sidled onto the side of the stage; he danced well even in the girly go-go seductive way. With his back to the band, he lifted his short skirt to show the band his white pants. Andy Powell saw it first; he stopped playing as he fell to his knees laughing. As Joey swayed his arse, still facing the band we saw for ourselves the back of Joey's white pants were covered in skid marks, or in his case, tank tracks! There wasn't time to stop him. With a flick of his body, he spun and wriggled his bum to the crowd. The reaction was mixed; mostly all the women made that 'eurgh' face, while the boys fell about laughing and they cheered when it was over. Joey wouldn't have it that they were laughing at his skids and said he'd done so well we ought to keep it in the act. No way, Joe!

Every so often we would do prestigious gigs. Not far from Hemel Hempstead was another town, Dunstable. The California Ballroom there was the largest one in the area and attracted top bands. On this particular Saturday, the Sugar Band were sharing the stage with Status Quo and The Who. Joey had been working on the van, trying to make it quieter in the cab. This Ford van had its engine between the driver and the passenger seats, and it was noisy, so when Joe said he was going to fix it he had the band's full approval. He found lots of papier-maché egg trays and fitted them into the engine cover; it worked. On our way to Dunstable somebody smelled burning, so we stopped. Joey lifted the engine cover. The egg trays were on fire and the flames shot into the cab. He threw the cover down, giving us enough time to get out. Ray and Andy ran to the back doors of the van to get the gear out. The front of the van now totally in flames. The coach came screaming to a halt behind us and the driver jumped out brandishing his fire extinguisher and after a few hectic minutes the fire was out. With the help of lifts from dads and friends we played the show but that was the end of our beautiful Ford van. Never mind, Dave would do his magic again very soon. But things were changing. In a few months it was quite clear that Andy Powell, our guitarist, was improving at a faster rate than the rest of us and he wanted to push his abilities further. Guitar bands playing the blues were becoming popular, so we put a few in our music set. On his guitar solos he lifted the band to another plane.

A local band competition in Watford was the beginning of the end of the Sugar Band. Without breaking into a sweat, we won it, hands down, the prize being a recording session in a studio just outside of the town. We decided to record some blues, trying to write our own song as the second recording. They turned out well, but we did nothing with them. Jeff, by this time, was under pressure from Ernie, his dad, to knuckle down and get serious about his college work. Ray also wanted to do well with his building company and announced he was leaving. Andy had gone for an audition with Dave to a London management company that wanted to form two new bands. The girlfriends too breathed a sigh of relief as for some time now my Sue, Jeff's Sue and all the other girls had been complaining that they hardly ever saw us. Perhaps it was time for me to knuckle down.

Eight

HORSE FARTS AND HANDSPRINGS

I had left Nash Mills as the assistant export manager and was now working weekends in the open air with Mr Mcintyre, my car dealer mate. Wanting to work outside all summer I took a more permanent job delivering bread. Mansbridge's Bakery was in my village and two minutes from my house. It was a family business run by Dad Mansbridge, Reggie and David, his sons. David was a little older than me and delivered bread from a horse and cart, that's how I knew him. He delivered to my house maybe two or three times a week. He'd asked me to help him on the cart, then when I got used to everything, I would have my own round in a small Morris Minor van. It felt a bit odd standing on the bread cart, Dave with the horse's reins in his hands like a stagecoach driver going along slowly, the heavy traffic getting very close as they passed by. The horse, a large black handsome beast called Trigger, didn't seem to give a monkeys; he knew the round anyway, and could almost do it by himself. But we travelled along, standing there eighteen inches from the horse's arse, singing cowboy songs.

"A farting horse can ruin your day," Dave said, and it often did. The smell would get into your clothes and make your eyes smart; the singing stopped immediately just in case it got on your tongue. On a bad day Mum wouldn't let me into the house until I'd stripped. Dave told me he was used to it and he and Trigger smelled like that the whole time.

"His poor wife!" Mum would say. It wasn't long before I had my own round and van – thank God. On a sunny summer morning there weren't many better jobs than driving round the Hertfordshire country lanes, the smell of beautiful warm bread in the van. I would jump out, whistling, offering a selection of fresh breads and rolls in a large wicker basket to all my mums, grandmas, some blokes and a few nuns. I would be finished in the afternoon which gave me more time to plan my next band. There was a downside to this job though: dogs. There was a Jack Russell who would have ripped my throat out had he been able to dive through his kitchen window every time I left bread in a tin on the windowsill by his back door; other dogs would growl, some wanted to lick me to death, some even wanted to shag me. On one particular occasion, I walked to the back door of a large country house and was met by a huge Great Dane. He ran up to me, jumped up and pushed me against the wall next to the door. Christ, this dog was taller than me! Just then the lady of the house opened the bedroom window above me.

"Get down, Major!" she said. Nothing from the dog. "OK, kick his balls, he likes that." I didn't need that instruction twice. I lifted my foot and gave him a softish boot in his three-piece. With a sort of half bark, half whimper he scurried off. "No, no, no," she said. "His balls over there on the lawn, you silly man." Great job – didn't last long though.

I had always fancied myself as a writer so when a junior newspaper reporter position came up at the Weekly Gazette I sat up and took notice. Hemel Hempstead was to have a new daily newspaper called The Echo. The Echo chain of newspapers was pretty national, popping up in other towns as well. I immediately got called for an interview and, wearing my best suit, I sat there and gave them my brief history, school details, GCE O-Level results and got the job. I was overjoyed. I was to be part of a team when the paper got started. "At the moment," one of the interviewers said, "there seems to be a bit of a problem with the print union and the shopfloor workers, so we don't exactly know when we want you to start. It shouldn't be too long, though."

I flew home on the scooter and couldn't wait to tell Sue and Mum. "I expect being a reporter you'll have to travel a fair bit," said Mum. "Why don't you learn about car engines in the meantime, then if you have car trouble you know how to fix it." Great idea. Mr Mcintyre had a mate that had a much bigger car dealership than his; I met Paul Lambert.

"I've got a vacancy in my Bognor Regis garage," he said. "I buy the cars up here and it'll be your job to drive them down to Bognor, stay the rest of the week helping my lad do the servicing and get the cars ready for the resale."

"OK," I said. It sounded fun.

"You can take a room above the garage – there's a bedroom and a shower room. Any questions?"

"Yes," I said. "Can I use any of the cars that haven't been valeted in the evenings?" I had planned to visit some old Royal Hospital School mates that lived in Portsmouth down the coast.

"Yes, of course," Paul said.

I was set. I was looking forward to this, albeit short, garage career. I arrived with the first car, met Kenny the mechanic and settled in my sparse accommodation. Next day I worked well with Kenny. He didn't mind answering the, sometimes stupid, questions I asked but I wasn't sure about his boss, Brian. On day three I went to see Brian.

"Paul said I could get one of the unprepared cars if I wanted to go out, if that's OK? I want to go out and see a friend."

"He said nothing to me," said Brian. "So no, you can't use a car."

"Well, let's phone him up," I said.

"You can't, he's away for the day. Anyway, I still wouldn't let you as it would be my responsibility."

"Is Paul the governor of the company?" I asked. "He said that I could. That was part of the agreement of my coming here," I said.

"I don't care," replied Brian. "The answer is no."

This Brian was pissing me off.

"OK, well I will leave a message with his wife and if I don't hear from him or you by six o'clock to say I can use a car I'm off. All right?"

I told Kenny about the conversation.

"I'm not surprised," he said, "that Brian's a stubborn bastard. If you go, how are you going to get home?"

I hadn't been paid a penny.

"I don't know, I'll thumb it home."

I'd only been hitchhiking once before. Bruce, my Anchor pub and Ricky Pong Bend card-playing mate and I, had, on a whim on a Friday, thumbed rides to see his granny and aunties in Cardiff. Some rides came quickly, other times we were walking for ages.

Six o'clock came with no message. I packed my suitcase. Kenny's mum promised to Red Star it on to my house, so I was travelling light. I was out of Bognor Regis quickly and the lifts went well until about nine o'clock, then by luck a truck stopped for me, he was going North up the M1. Junction 8 on that motorway was Hemel Hempstead, thank God! He dropped me – I thanked him and then walked the three miles into town and then onto Boxmoor, my village.

I was knocking on Mum's door at 2am. My keys were with my scooter keys, and I had left them with Mum. Nervously she asked who was there through the door. With the story told, a cup of tea and a bacon sandwich I went to bed and slept for ten hours. In the morning Mum didn't mention it. Still, who cares about this job? My reporter job was going to start soon. Jeff and Dave came to my rescue. They would teach me the rudiments about cars. Ernie, their dad, offered to take me on for a short while till the paper started – thank God for the Stow family!

I started to work with Ernie, Jeff's dad, going to London every day in his van. I helped run out iron plumbing pipes in offices and banks and then as the final straw at an old men's nursing home. As soon as I entered this home in Harrow my stomach turned. These old men were sitting in chairs in corridors half dressed, nobody seemed to care for them. Now and again a male nurse would push a patient past me while still sitting up in his chair covered with a sheet, obviously dead. This wasn't for me, and Ernie quickly saw this. I didn't last long in the plumbing game. I hoped it would be better for Jeff.

The next day Mum showed me an advertisement in the Hemel Gazette advertising positions for junior reporters for the Evening Echo – that's the job they had offered me, and I had accepted. Perhaps they were ready to start. I called the numbers I had been given by my interviewer and asked about the situation.

"What's happening?" I asked.

"Well, it's been a while since your interview and the paper has taken so long to start, due to the union problems, that we thought all the successful candidates from last time had found alternative employment."

I told him that I had been working anywhere just marking time for this job.

"If you like I'll take the interview again," I asked.

"I'm afraid the junior reporter team is now full and we're not taking on anymore – sorry."

I was devastated and my mum was clearly not happy. She told me later that she had become so afraid that I would drift from job to job as I had done over the last six months or so, not getting any more qualifications.

Seven GCE O-Level passes wasn't going to carry much weight when I was in my twenties going for a job. Sue had changed her job as a shop assistant and was now an up-and-coming window dresser. Her wizardry with fabrics and attention to the finest details made her windows eye-catching and it wasn't long before the larger department stores were after her. Mum sat us both down and lectured me on settling down and at least finding a proper job.

The idea came to me one evening when Sue and I went to the local cinema. The B movie showing before the main feature was an old film starring Fred McMurray. He played a touring jazz musician, always on the band bus touring and living out of a suitcase. One day the band folded up suddenly through lack of gigs and money and he found himself in a small working town with no job, so he became the Scout leader and with his experience of life on the road he straightened out all the wayward kids. I sat up in my seat. "I could do that!" I said to Sue, and I was still full of it on the way home.

Mum thought the idea was good and asked, "A teacher! What are you going to teach?"

"PE, swimming and games," I said. "I'm a born natural."

So, letters were sent in a hurry, the new college year was approaching. I just hoped I wasn't too late. I'd chosen a college only a few miles away from the house as it was important that Sue and the band weren't far away. The band was going to help fund my three years there.

Newland Park College was just outside the village of Chalfont St Giles in Buckinghamshire, about twenty minutes' drive from our house. An old-worldly pretty place, so old-looking they chose to film the movie Dad's

Army, the popular wartime television series, there. I sat in front of two lecturers on the day of my interview. There was to be a formal interview, this was it, and then an aptitude test in the gym. There was nothing formal about the first part. The two gents who were in the physical education department immediately put me at ease, and they first asked me what was in the headlines in the papers that day. Easy for me; I read the newspapers every morning, front to back, so I was able to give them politics and crime, pages one to three, and the sports details including football league positions on the back pages.

I changed and followed the older lecturer into the gym, not so big I thought, the last gym I was in had been enormous at the Royal Hospital School. Having been in the school gymnastic display team I could do all the gymnastic activities he asked for – a handstand, a handspring and even hopping through the loop I made by holding my left foot with my right hand. I thought everybody could stand on one leg and hold it without wobbling over, these were silly games I had played in the playground. The secret is to focus on something on the floor about 2 metres ahead of you and I came through that afternoon with flying colours. When my place came through the post a couple of weeks later, Sue and I shopped for the list of gymnastic gear that they said I should have; I even had to buy a blazer with the college badge on it. I'd never had a blazer before.

For the first year I was to live in the college so there was a list they suggested I buy for my room. I suppose for the normal young men that were going there this was their first time being away from home. And the next year I would spend learning how to teach. I had to choose a secondary teaching subject as well, so I picked geography. By the time I had to report in I was ready and fully equipped. I had changed my car, too; a year earlier brother Mike had bought a Renault Caravelle, a sporty-looking car, characteristic, I thought, and I loved the metallic deep red machine from the day I first saw it. Imagine my surprise and delight when he offered it to me as he would be leaving, off with the Navy to the Far East and America for quite some time.

After I had registered at the main office, I went down to the gym to meet the other guys on my course year, a mixed bunch I must say, nearly all of them younger than me. They'd come more or less straight from school. We sat around drinking tea and just talking. Most of them had chosen the better-known PE colleges like Loughborough and Exeter, failed their entrance examinations and tests and had been sent by the education college clearing house to Newland Park. They'd never heard of Newland Park College and had had great trouble finding it. I put it as my first choice on the application forms, no wonder they loved me.

Most of them were horrified that they were to be in the countryside and had to depend on the college bus to go into Chalfont St Giles for the nearest shops and pubs. Word soon got around that little London bloke had got a Cadillac and they tried to latch on to me. We were shown our rooms in the long wooden structured buildings, I'm sure that the film crews had used them in wartime prisoner of war camp scenes – remember The Great Escape? Our huts were a dead ringer for them. Inside was slightly better, each room had a single bed, a side locker, small chest of drawers and a single wardrobe. Each room was exactly the same. I was placed in the middle of the corridor so on my left was a lad from Nottingham, Roger Ferne, shy to start with but a brilliant gymnast; how he failed at Loughborough I'll never know. To my right a Welshman, Dickie Evans, who I became great friends with and a few years later I was his best man at his wedding in Ebbw Vale. Dickie's family were very strong Labour Party and Michael Foot, the future leader of the Labour Party, was there with his wife. He congratulated me on my speech. I'm glad I decided to leave out all the rude jokes.

Just inside the entrance of the huts was a kitchenette with a kettle in it and opposite that was the TV room, all in all a tidy place to live in. Over the next year the small bedrooms would become stores for car bonnets, bicycle wheels and frames, old TVs, record players and disused sport equipment. Also during that year, we were raided by the college security department, looking for stolen or borrowed parts of other Nissen huts or bits of the local women's college, and to top it all the cleaning staff mounted a demonstration, stating it was unsafe to enter and do their work. Mr Shaw, head PE lecturer, would come in, smile slowly shaking his head. Girlfriends were banned from staying at the weekend and we as 'the Great Escapers' had a drill when the security arrived to check, that the head of the escape committee would have been proud of.

In each year of the teachers' tuition there was a period of six weeks when each student was given a school to do his teaching practice. I would turn up at the school in Rickmansworth at 8.30am and be a teacher for the day. Most of my time would be in the gym and I noticed right away that the older difficult kids in a normal classroom were busting to get out either onto the playing field for some sport or onto the street where they could impress. So, with school approval I was allowed to take the older students ice skating (lots of experience there) climbing on a climbing wall, roller skating, canoeing and it had a profound effect on their school behaviour and classwork. I came away from my first teaching practice with a Distinction – it was a great job having fun and making fun for them.

Year two was quite different. We were put out of the Nissen huts and into digs in Chalfont St Giles and Chalfont St Peter. My landlady was a very sweet elderly lady called Mrs Upham, whom I saw very rarely. On my gig nights she always left the tea-making things and a sandwich out for me and I never saw her in the mornings before I left for college. It didn't seem right to sneak Sue into this house, so I didn't. It was only twenty minutes to home anyway.

My second year's teaching practice was early that year and this time it was at Juniper Hill Junior School in Loudwater near High Wycombe, a beautifully run happy school with a great headmaster, Mr Ferguson. He and I got on immediately. He said he liked the way I taught and often used to sit at the back of the class observing. Thank God he wasn't there on a particular day when I was taking the class of nine-year-olds. I had set the scene of a story, often doing this with very bad acting skills but good jokes, and the class had to write down what happened next. While everybody was quietly writing I took the chance to hear the children read one by one and they came up and read to me from their favourite books. This one kid, a chubby little lad, didn't like me much and I didn't care for him. I called his name. He brought his book and stood close to me as I sat at the desk. I whispered for him to start. He looked at me with an evil sort of quirky look and read; seconds later I got it. The quirky look was 'take that' – a silent fart, that smelled like a nine-year-old's, wafted up around me. He could hardly get his words out; he wanted to burst out laughing with a 'gotcha'. He wasn't going to get away with that. I had a beauty in the departure lounge ready to go, perfect timing. Without a change of expression, I eased out the return fire without sound. Well, it was much better than his. I watched as his expression changed.

"Go on now, a couple more pages," I said. He never did that to me again.

That summer I announced to the band that I was having a holiday for a month. I, Roger Ferne and another gymnast mate, Ian McDonald, had made plans the Christmas before to take a trip to Greece and we were going to take our girlfriends. How were we travelling? By road. I planned to sell the car and buy a van with windows as we were camping all the way there and back. So, tents, stores, sleeping bags all had to be bought.

It was Eastertime, I was on my holidays from college, and I met up with Jeff, who was on his break too. We wandered into Hemel Hempstead and noticed some men clearing out the famous Water Gardens. Some years before, when they had constructed Hemel Hempstead as a new town, they had diverted the River Gade with concrete sides and bottom to flow through the back of the town with bridges and gardens opening up to a small lake behind the Co-op. Seeing as both of us weren't doing very much we asked for a job.

"Yes," they said. "When can you start?"

"Now."

The job was to get into different sections of the river, which was drained, shovel out the shit and rubbish and occasionally bike wheels and supermarket trolleys and put it all into a skip. The money was great, and Jeff and I worked hard. I even volunteered to be the one that did the river draining. This meant I had to get up around about 4am and open up and close all the different bungs to let the water in and out of each section. I was about to draw out part of the lake early one morning, it was still dark, and a police car came round the corner, his headlights picking me out. They stopped, wondering why this young bloke was standing in the middle of the lake in waders and pyjamas. When I explained they thought it very funny – they were certain to get a free breakfast when they told the cook the funniest thing of the night. They left but returned five minutes later with a camera and a cup of tea for me.

At the end of the Easter vacation there was a promise of further work in the summer. I explained my holiday plans. "No matter, work as long as you can," they said. Great, Sludge Gulpers Incorporated took us everywhere to clear messes up. In Basildon we were shown a pond square the size of a public swimming baths all about 2 foot deep. It was full of purple-looking sludgy clay stuff. Jeff and I had a fire hose; our job was to empty the pond into the sludge tankers the size of petrol tankers. The heat of the sun had dried the surface of the pond to a crust. Underneath the purple stuff had the consistency of thick custard – that was the task.

"Leave it with you, boys. Pick you up tonight," said our boss as he got into his car.

The weather was lovely, the job not so good. We had to break through the crust, somehow dilute the purple stuff with the water hose and suck the goo into the tanker. Jeff and I soon had it sussed. We both stripped off, got into the stuff and marched up and down in it to mix it all up. That done, it was loose enough for the pump to suck it up into the tanker. One diluted while the other marched up and down pushing the goo towards the sucking end.

The boss showed up just as we were finishing. He was very impressed that we had done the job in one day. He was the sort of man who would have got in with us, I know, but he refused to let us back into his car. We stank from head to toe and had to stand our ground while he put the hose on us. The next day the job was in Dagenham. It was an enormous concrete sewage tank that needed cleaning. The tank was 80 foot high. The good news was it had already been half cleaned out, the bad news was that Jeff and I had to do the lower half. A hole had been cut through the concrete just above the shite level; Jeff and I had to crawl in with the fire hose and mix it up with water to be pumped away. My partner in poo soon had it worked out; Jeff suggested that the fire hose pressure needed to be increased. This was done at the hydrant valve but the hose at this pressure was way too hard to hold so we sat in the tank one behind the other. The man in front held the hose nozzle and did the washing down while the other sat close behind him sitting on the hose, to stop it kicking back, and having a smoke. The sewage had been treated, I must say, but it stank almost the same. We were doing very well until a well manoeuvred change round went wrong and the hose got free of the both of us and whipped and kicked like a demented python. We were both getting completely covered in shit as we tried to tame it. We gave up, laughing, and went out into the sunshine to have a smoke. We were covered in it, even in our ears, eyes, mouth and hair – no wonder the money was good!

By the time I was ready to start the holiday, I was loaded. Sue had saved hard and was flush too. I just hoped we wouldn't be bailing out the others after a couple of weeks from now, but I needn't have worried. I bought a Commer van with windows and quickly made a second row of seats from an old studio couch. We loaded our stuff. Sue and I drove to Nottingham to meet Roger Ferne and his girlfriend, Lynn, then about turn down to Worthing to meet 'Mack', Ian MacDonald, and his girlfriend. We left on a Saturday morning and journeyed across the Channel through France. France was completely different to Germany, and Germany was different to Austria, Austria was nothing like Yugoslavia and by the next Tuesday we were entering Greece. Our plan was to have enough time to visit Athens and some Greek Islands and then it was back home. The weather was gorgeous almost all the time, we ate foods and fish we'd never even heard of and swam in waters so clear we thought we'd reached paradise. Those few weeks flew by and then we returned to college to face our final year. The fuel bill for that holiday was £34!

I had decided I would commute now from my house to college everyday as I didn't have to be in all the time. The band was still together and well up for a busy autumn into Christmas. It was then that our guitarist, Andy Powell, went missing. His father called to see me one evening saying he had gone to London a few days earlier and had not returned – could I help? His school mate and our bass player, Dave Casey, knew that Andy had gone for an audition with a new band that was forming in London. He'd got the job and decided that he would stay in the flat the management had let for the new band to get to know the others and rehearse as much as they could. This was the formation of Wishbone Ash. A few weeks in and I got the call to collect Andy to get him home to a doctor; he had pleurisy. Dave had been keen to join the management's other band and he'd been employed by them in another line making all the speaker cabinets for both bands.

The Sugar Band had started to fall apart. Ray needed to study more, so did Jeff; Mack, our drummer, had his sights on a university course in Manchester. It was time to form another band quickly. Sue had thought that, with the demise of the Sugar Band, the music thing would be out of my system, and we would now settle down to be a proper couple. When I explained that the music thing would never leave my system, she gave me the final ultimatum. "It's the band or me," she declared, and in a day or so she got the answer she dreaded.

I cried that night. I hadn't done that since the medal episode at the Royal Hospital School. I was losing the first girl I had fallen in love with, and she and her family had been so supportive through these last years. I'm glad that when we met years later, we could laugh and joke about those times.

So in 1968, the Ashley Ward Delegation was formed. The name came from the new-born son of our new Hammond keyboard player, Neil Reynolds; the guitarist was Paul Green; Jeff was still playing with me on the brass; the new drummer was a guy called Ian Gabriel and he came together with Mickey Atwood on bass. Paul didn't last long, but he did share a flat with Ian and me in Rickmansworth. A new guitarist came in with his singer mate; Bill Roberts played amazing guitar even then and Dave Bedford, his singing mate, had a fine Joe Cocker-type voice. Right from the start Dave was full of enthusiasm and said he could get all sorts of gigs and even TV slots. In the meantime, I plodded away getting more and more airbases and fair-playing gigs. Then Jeff made the announcement that he was finally going to give up playing and concentrate on his college work. A sax player new to the area was looking for a band, so I went to see him as he only lived up the road from me. I knocked on his door and met Stuart Blandamer.

He stood a fraction taller than me and had a thick head of hair that looked a little different; he had a very high polo-neck sweater which gave the illusion that he had no neck. Even Bill, when he first met Stu, asked me later, "Where's his neck gone?" He agreed to join the band and came to watch us at the gig at the village hall not so far away from Hemel Hempstead. It wasn't the best night for us. The band were getting fed up with all the bullshit we were getting from Dave, our singer; he had repeatedly walked in with fictitious gigs and appearances, none of which came to fruition. There were always fantastic stories of let-downs and excuses – it was time for Dave to go and tonight was the night. We played the first set and sacked him in the interval. He stayed for the rest of the gig although he needn't have bothered. A massive punch-up started just like a bar brawl in a Western movie and the promoter closed the gig down. Bill and I would now do the singing. Stu immediately fitted in, making up the third harmony when it was needed.

Stu was to become the stalwart of the band and my best friend in the world; his wife Diane and our children all got on very very well. He had a day job; he was an electric adding machine engineer and made good money changing old pounds, shillings and pence machines into decimal calculators. He knew all about electrics and motors and just about everything important. The band was going well, Bill was starting to write his own songs as well as Stuart – I expect it was the same for all budding songwriters. Sometimes the titles were a bit off the wall and the lyrics were everywhere; Stu was writing about strawberry jam. The day came when Stu announced he was quitting his full-time job towards becoming a professional musician.

I had been working as an evening cleaner for British Home Stores from Monday to Friday, leaving the weekends and daytimes for rehearsals and gigs. It was my last year at Teacher Training College and I didn't go in much, preferring to revise for the final exams at home. I did have to go in for my last teaching practice, six weeks in a secondary school in Rickmansworth, which I loved. In the gym and on the athletics track that summer I really gelled with the more difficult kids who hated the classroom and wanted to excel outside. That year we had a sprint champion and a pole-vaulter who had never entered a competition before. I would drive them to the meetings, and we would all have fish and chips on the way home. (I wonder where that idea came from?) Earlier in that final year, just before Christmas I had come into college to go to the library when I saw a woman struggling with her scooter, which was refusing to start.

"Can I help?" I said. "I had one of these once."

She explained that she knew nothing about them.

"Leave the keys with me and I'll fix it," I said. I promised I would return them to the office, she worked for the bursar in the college.

I spent an hour on the machine and by then it was starting first time with a much cleaner spark plug – a piece of cake for me. I walked into the bursar's office and put the keys on the table. There were about five women in the office all giggling to themselves. The woman with the scooter problem laughed and explained, "We all had decided that the next male student to come into this office would take Anne here to the Christmas Ball tomorrow night and guess what? It's you!"

I looked at this young dark-haired girl, obviously embarrassed, but she had a great smile.

"And do you want to go?" I asked Anne.

She answered, "I don't know – do you?"

I was up for it, so it was set, we were given the tickets and we made arrangements for me to pick her up the next evening. I turned up in my changed car (a Mini) at her address in the local village on a filthy night that was getting worse. As I knocked on the door, I realised I knew absolutely nothing about this girl apart from her Christian name. I was asked in by her older sister, Irene, and met her mum and dad and younger brother, David. Her dad looked very much like John Wayne, a cheery man with a wicked sense of humour.

We arrived back at the college hall for the ball and sat at a table. The conversation was stunted and a little awkward. Every time there was a silence I piped up, "Would you like a drink?"

"Oh yes please," she said, "a vodka and lime please."

So every time I went to the bar I bought a vodka and lime for her and another for myself. She said she didn't really dance so we sat most of the night drinking vodka and limes. By now the conversation was at full flow and so were the vodka and limes. I hadn't drunk this spirit like this before and I was having trouble focussing on my date. Anne, on the other hand, hadn't changed one little bit – her speech wasn't slurred, she didn't repeat herself; it was almost as if she had been pouring the drink I had been buying her into the plant pot. There were calls now for the last dance which we did, thank God! It was a slow dance so I could hang on. We made it back to my car. The fog was now really set in, and it was to be my saviour. I drove, God knows how, very slowly back to the village through this pea-souper and eventually arrived outside her house. I declined going in for coffee, gave her a peck on the cheek on the doorstep, back to the Mini, I drove round the corner, parked up and threw up, and settled down for an uncomfortable night's sleep in the car – great first date! Later that week I called into the office to see if she was OK, silly question really. I later discovered Anne had been drinking like that since she was fourteen. We laughed about that night; she knew I was gone when I couldn't lift my head to speak, but she said that she'd enjoyed being with me and the ball and we started to see a lot more of each other. We would drive back to her house on her lunch hours to be together and soon we were inseparable.

Nine

BIG BREAKS AND BREAKDOWNS

1969 had been a good year for the band. Some months earlier a couple of the guys called Jack Winsley and Bob Seger had seen us playing one of the London clubs and asked to see us. Stu and I went to London. Bob Seger was a very successful session singer and Jack was quite posh, wanting to get into the management side of the pop world. He explained that his friend, Maurice Gibb of the Bee Gees, had written a good little pop song and would we be interested in covering it? So, I went and put the vocal part on the already finished track and it was called, "The Rhythm of the Big Bass Drum". Bill, Stu and the rest of the band didn't like it much – we needn't have bothered as it wasn't even released. We still had a very busy Christmas ahead of us and I was warmly welcomed by Anne's family at the numerous parties and gatherings; so much better than last year.

Exactly a year before, Christmas Eve 1968, the Ashley Ward Delegation had a gig at a club restaurant in Eastbourne on the south coast. We had played there before, and we were always treated well. The governor there had been a singer in a big band in the fifties and he knew all about touring and one-nighters. Ian, our drummer, had a new car. As a watchmaker, in his day job he did well and showed up in this bright shiny new Vauxhall Viva. Immediately Stu asked if he could get a faster ride home so he could be home when Nathan and Emma, his two young children, woke up to open their presents. It was decided that myself and Bill, the smokers in the band, could have the van to ourselves and drive the gear back to Hertfordshire, as neither of us had any kids. However, I had planned to spend the night at Sue's with her family as Mum was off to Hong Kong. A few days before she was very excited, having never flown anywhere before. Mike was with the Royal Navy over Christmas. Mike could speak fluent Russian and had been very useful to the Navy on fishery patrols in the North Sea a few years earlier and now the powers that be in the Admiralty had chosen Mike to go to Hong Kong to learn Mandarin Chinese. The special forces had sent their man for the same task; he was Paddy Ashdown, later to be the leader of the Liberal Party. He lost his pants some years later.

With Sue and her sister Linda, together with a very jolly Mrs Hibberd and family, it was going to be a fabulous few days. A good gig well done, the band loaded the van with Bill and me and we said our Happy Christmases and they were off. I was the driver and well up for getting home. We'd been going for a while when we lost all power and the van came to a halt; we had plenty of fuel, it just wouldn't start. Just off the road a couple of fields away we saw a light on in a farmhouse. We knocked on the door and a cheery young dad opened up, his young kids already charging around with their new toys. He gave us hot tea, which was badly needed and we explained the problem to him.

"Right," he said, "after breakfast" – that his wife was working on – "we'll get the tractor out and should get it going with a strong tow."

Bugger me, it worked after a while, so we disconnected from the tractor, said grateful thanks and were off once again. Not for long though, as within half an hour the same thing happened. By now it was light, and we had stopped alongside a very grand house with a long drive. We weren't members of the AA or RAC, and no garage would come out to us on Christmas morning, so Bill and I decided to ask if we could leave the van through the large gates of the large house somewhere down the drive and try and hitchhike home. The owner of the house was just as nice as the farmer.

Of course the van could stay there, come back when the garages were open. Would we like to bring any personal instruments into the house for safety? We did that. Bill, however, wasn't going to be parted from his beloved guitar. Hitchhiking on Christmas Day wasn't a good idea and I eventually knocked on Sue's door around about eleven o'clock that Christmas night. They had kept dinner for me, and the girls desperately wanted me to open presents, but I could hardly keep my eyes open and had to go to bed to sleep. After the holidays I went back to the big house by train and a garage took a few hours to find the problem. A leaf had got into the fuel tank and intermittently covered the fuel inlet pipe. A great Christmas!

When the New Year came it was head down, revising for me; I had to catch up with my reading as I had let my college work slip a bit since the start of the third year. By Easter I was needing a break, so Anne and I decided to have a quick camping trip to Cornwall. The Mini was quickly loaded, some very quick goodbyes and we were off for six days. The weather was good, food was great and all of a sudden, it was over and it was back to exam revision. Exam dates loomed ever closer and by the end of June they were done.

I didn't stick around at Newland Park and took an evening job at a plastics factory, MMA, in Amersham. The hours were six in the evening till six in the morning with a dinner break around eleven o'clock and plenty of tea breaks as the working conditions were bloody hot! MMA was a plastic moulding factory that made all sorts of Bakelite plastic tops for bottles and containers. I was shown a large press where I would be working, and my job was to load the pellets into the press moulds and then when they were full a large handle brought down the enormous core which started the moulding process under extreme heat. A few moments later the covers were lifted, and the bottle tops were emptied and thrown into a bin. Twelve hours of that every night – God I hope I pass those exams! Everybody who worked there was from either Pakistan or India; only me and a huge fat man with a walking stick, called Ken, who was the night foreman, were English. It was obvious that Ken had no time for the Asians, and would shout at them nearly all night, but luckily he took a shine to me. He insisted that we take our dinner breaks together, often cooking eggs and chips, sometimes fish, sometimes ham – always with bloody chips!

It was a shame really; the Asian guys were willing to be friendly and often invited me to eat with them. They would all bring a different dish, put the pots to heat on the presses as they worked and at dinner time sit in a circle on the floor eight or ten in a ring and put the food in the centre circle and they would each dip their naan breads and eat to their hearts' content. I tried to explain that I had to be with Ken; I'm sure they understood, and they often used to slip me a couple of naans filled with delicious Asian fillings. One night one of the men came to me with a piece of paper and a pen.

"Stevie boy," he said, "how do you write 'fucking bastard'?"

I smirked, wrote it down and asked him why he wanted those words.

"I want to write on foreman's car!"

A few more weeks of that and suddenly it was time to go into college one final time to say goodbye to the tutors and some very good mates and, more importantly, to get the exam results. I wanted this badly, I wanted this adult qualification more than a job, although to become a fully qualified new teacher I had to complete a year of teaching in a school. The music thing in me was as strong, though, and I would lie awake at night tossing the arguments for a career in bands over one in the classroom. It didn't help much when I got my results. I passed in all subjects and got a Distinction in my teaching practices, with great words of praise from the headmasters I'd worked for during those six-week periods. My friends on my course had been applying for teaching jobs in their hometowns and were already attending recruitment meetings and interviews; I hadn't done a thing. Anne and I took another short break to discuss my future.

I carried on working in Amersham and even took a third share in a flat with Ian, our drummer, and Paul, the guitarist. The landlord didn't like us much, accusing us of having parties and playing our loud instruments in our large front room – something we never did. Perhaps it was the loud music from the fabulous sound system that we had wired up to our record turntables? Across the hall lived three very nice girls, one of whom got with Paul and later that year we had our first mate's wedding. I was stunned a few weeks later when, arriving back to Anne's house and sitting in the Mini, Anne told me she was pregnant. My first terrified reaction was to tell her not to tell anyone – too late, she had told her mum but not her dad, thank God! The last thing I needed was a head-to-head with a pissed-off

John Wayne. From the car where I had just received the news I went into Anne's house to speak to Marge, Anne's mum. Margery King was that sort of woman who didn't panic, she was quite unflappable, especially over something like this, and she worked as the personal secretary for a top London gynaecologist at the Central Middlesex Hospital; she had years of experience dealing with this sort of problem, if it was a problem. As I sat there, she explained that she had spoken to her boss and he, of course, because it was Marge's daughter, had offered the best private treatment to whatever we decided to do about it. Were we talking about a termination? Christ, that was quick; I had only known half an hour before that I might be a dad. Anne wanted me to make the decision. I said I needed time to think about it. I liked Anne a great deal and her family would stand by us whatever happened. As for my family, I wanted to keep them out of the loop for now. During the next few days, the thought of becoming a dad grew on me rapidly. I would have to be a proper dad, a married dad. With all that laughter and love in the King household, bringing up the baby would be a piece of cake. The thought of my first baby being terminated made me shudder; there was no way that was ever going to happen. When I told Anne the next week she was delighted and so was Marge. Of course, Anne's mum had known from the start when she had noticed small changes in Anne's behaviour, I later learned. But now it was time to face John Wayne.

"He's in the shed," Marge said. "Pop down there and you can have a few moments alone." I stepped inside the large garden shed and started to explain myself to him, getting in very early, that I would always stand by Anne.

He stood there listening, with a hacksaw in his hand. "You stupid bastard!" he said. "You've done that to my little girl? Right, put your dick in this vice," he said pointing to the metal vice bolted onto the work bench.

"You're not going to cut my dick off with that?" I said.

"No," he said, "you are. I'm going to set the shed on fire."

We both fell about laughing. He explained he already knew and wanted to see me sweat a bit; he'd always wanted grandchildren. I liked him from the start, and he liked me, and we would be great friends and it would last for the rest of his life. Over the next few weeks, the conversation was 'baby' at the King household. I still hadn't mentioned it to my mum. The 'let's get married' conversation was a quick and happy one, nothing big, register office ceremony and a reception party at Marge and John's. The date was set for Saturday 17th October 1970. Anne and I had only known each other for ten months.

The Ashley Ward Delegation was starting to fray. Some of the musicians were progressing faster than others, some preferring to hold on to their steady day jobs rather than strike out for professionalism and a complete music career. I desperately wanted to play but now had to think of baby and Anne instead of just me. I was getting pressure from Mum and Mr and Mrs King to make up my mind fast. October was only a few months away and I had asked Stuart to be my best man. Of course, the band was invited. Mike, my brother, had annual leave so he and Mum would be coming together. Of course, Janny and her husband John were coming. John was fast becoming a very successful accountant and had a brand-new car, a big shiny Austin 1800 which he offered as our wedding car. Mum wasn't at all happy, saying she couldn't understand why we wanted to rush into marriage. I still hadn't mentioned that Anne was expecting although she got it in the end. Jan and Merry had already given her grandchildren – she smiled at the thought of another. No dramas there then.

Mike had come home from China now an excellent Mandarin Chinese speaker, a talent that the Navy put to use some years later. He loved his new submariner job. Under the raging waves it was quiet and calm – perfect. So in 1971 he took command of his first diesel submarine, HMS Finwhale, as the captain, and from there he never looked back.

Meanwhile Bob Seger and Jack Winsley from the Maurice Gibb pop song thing were back on the phone with another song and were we interested? Stu, Bill and the boys weren't; I was, though. Ashley Ward days were numbered.

There were wages, and rehearsals were to start soon, but was this the big break that I had been waiting for? The Ashley Ward Delegation boys were my special friends, and they would stay that way forever. We did our last gig and parted. It wasn't long before Stu, Bill and a new very young bass player mate, Kelly Cantlon, found their first professional job playing with a guy called Pete Saunders in Wild Wally's Rock 'n' Roll Circus. Some of their first gigs were to play for the troops in Northern Ireland when the mood on the streets was very tense and violent. Other mates also popped up on this gig. Joey Johnson from Sugar Band days was the roadie and a drummer I really liked, called Mike Dolan, was to join too. I went to London to join a new band. We were to be called New Horizon and our first single was called "Lucy's Lovin'". I did the vocal track, and everybody seemed pleased. The driving force of the band was Frank Clark, the drummer; he had as much club experience as me, having worked in the successful London band 'Aardvark'. The record was to be released on Saturday 17th October, my wedding day, and Jack had asked Noel Edmonds to play it around 11am and to mention my celebration. Sure enough, on Radio 1 at that time Noel played the record. We sounded good on the radio, was it going to be a hit? I doubted it but it was good to get the wedding mentioned, both families heard it, realising that maybe there was a budding popstar in me. The pressure was off for a while. The wedding day was sunny, and I was getting married around 2pm at Amersham Register Office. I was dressed in an off-white suit, cream-coloured shirt and tie. Stu, the best man, was with me of course, and we were the first to arrive. Problems. The registrar said that we hadn't completed some of the paperwork, so it was hurriedly done and Stu paid for late entry charges, as I hadn't brought a penny with me.

All the guests filed in; Anne followed, with her dad John looking as pleased as punch. Anne had on a cream-pattern short dress, white knee-length tight-fitting boots, really modern and chic for that time, and her hair was tightly curled into southern belle ringlets. So after the ceremony it was back to Marge and John's for a lively party that seemed to go on forever. Mike and Mum stayed much longer than I thought they would. Mike, although very well-spoken, talked for ages to John King, another Royal Navy man, the two getting on very well together. Alas, they were never to meet again. My sister Merry did not make the wedding but heard the record; she had got married for the second time and had just had her third child. Her husband was working in construction and money was tight for them living in Goring in Berkshire.

Luckily, we had sorted out our living accommodation. Neither of us wanted to live at our parents' houses and at the flat we boys were always under the threat of eviction from the grumpy landlord. Neil, our keyboard player, came to our rescue. Neil Reynolds played great Hammond organ; we had first met at the formation of the Ashley Ward Band. He worked as the plumber in his dad's building company and he was married to Fran, a chubby cheery girl always with a smile on her face. I called to see him, with Ian, the drummer. Fran showed us into his lounge, and he was sitting watching television with a loaded twelve bore shotgun across his lap. To save us asking the question Neil said, "I saw a mouse pop his head out of that hole in the skirting board and if he does it again, I'm gonna blast him!"

That's what we wanted in this band: a normal level-headed guy – just the job. His firstborn son was to be christened Ashley Ward Reynolds. Ian suggested the Delegation bit and that was that. He had since moved, finding a deserted farmhouse in the middle of a wood, doing all the renovation work with his dad. Hearing that Anne and I would be looking for a place, he offered us a share of the house. The timing couldn't have been better, and we moved in a few days before the wedding to deliver sheets, bedding and clothes. After the wedding party Anne and I were keen to get away to our first home. The lane though, through the woods, was pitch black, you wouldn't want to walk it at night. When we pulled up outside, Neil's dog, a large Alsatian, would not let us get out of the car. We sat there until the barking roused Neil and Fran. During the forthcoming weeks the dog was always a problem for us. We either had to make a run for it or wait for Neil to put the dog away while we came in. Once inside the dog would come in and sniff us in a friendly manner – this was odd, I thought. Our room had no heating, so we bought ourselves an electric bar heater which we put on an hour before we came to bed. It was getting close to Christmas and the weather had turned very cold. With the heater just turned off we hung onto each other for warmth in bed. When we first heard the noise, I thought it was a rat running round the room; Anne hid under the bed clothes. I cautiously went to the light switch to see what was running around the room – I silently prayed it wasn't rats. It wasn't. The sound was coming from the wallpaper unsticking itself from the wall and rolling down the wall; the heater had dried the paper and it was detaching itself from the damp wall. I explained to Neil what had happened and after that Anne wasn't all that happy there. I told Mum about the wallpaper on the next visit, and she demanded that we move into her house in Boxmoor, Hemel Hempstead, saying that damp was no good for a new baby when it came. Neil and Fran understood completely, and we were still firm friends when we moved out the next week.

New Horizon kept on rehearsing. We had appeared as a guest band on the Jimmy Young Show again on Radio 1. We recorded five songs including "Lucy's Lovin'" and Jimmy played a different one each day. Christmas 1970 was approaching, we had no band to play local gigs with, New Horizon had one show in Manchester and that was that. I stayed rehearsing with the band until our daughter, Joanna, was born. I planned to leave and find something else. I was disappointed that New Horizon hadn't been the dream start. I missed playing with my mates at home and New Horizon was a band of strangers put together to fuel Jack Winsley's dream. My leaving the band wouldn't put him off; he'd just find another kid dreamer like me.

Anne's waters broke around seven o'clock in the morning on April 16th. Mum and I put together what she needed, and I was off to the Central Middlesex Hospital within twenty minutes. I wanted to drive fast but Anne had her sensible head on and slowed me down to a hurried pace. They took her into her room and got rid of me, saying that it would be hours yet. I phoned Marge before I left. Breakfast was next, then on to the rehearsal room for 10am. I couldn't stand it much longer than twelve o'clock so I made my excuses and left, back to the hospital. I walked into Anne's room, and she looked at me, saying nothing.

"Hello love, are you in any pain? Don't worry, it won't be long now."

"What are you talking about?" said Anne. "I had the baby two hours ago!"

Still laughing for being a stupid prat I was shown my daughter, perfect in every way – all new dads say that. Down the corridor Marge had her office and she told me that everything had gone perfectly and both mother and daughter were quite healthy. Anne would stay for a day or two. I expect Marge had arranged that so she could have as much time as possible with Jo, her new granddaughter. My mum would welcome the baby a few days later; she was very experienced when helping out as this would be her eighth grandchild.

While Anne was away, I took the chance to go and see Stu, Bill, Kelly and Micky do their rock 'n' roll circus thing. Pete Saunders as Wild Wally was an enthusiastic band leader, among other weird characters, while the band pumped out the rock 'n' roll tunes interspersed with stupid weak jokes. Joey was at the side of the stage with me and explained that one of the highlights of the show was a great thunder flash going off at a specific crescendo at the last song; he had the flash powder already panned out onto a metal plate. It was Joey's job to ignite the flash at the special moment with a match. I watched as he knelt by the dish half a minute before ignition time. As the music pumped out, he suddenly realised he didn't have the matches – there was no time for him to go and look for them. All he had was a newly finished stub of a cigarette in his mouth, the end of the cigarette had to be burning red to set the powder off. So Joey looked at me, smiled, "Watch this," he said, closed his eyes and drew on the cigarette until it glowed, and lowered his head into the dish. Oh, the flash went off all right, but Joey wasn't so good. Some of the powder had blown into his eyes and he fell back yelling as the blood ran through his fingers that were covering his eyes. The band and Wild Wally hadn't heard Joey's screams but Micky the drummer had – he turned his head to see the blood coming from Joey's eyes and promptly fainted, falling backwards off his stool. I didn't know who to help first. I chose Joey, getting water and a band towel to rinse his eyes; Micky would come round soon enough. The music came to an abrupt end – I expect half the crowd thought that the show always finished that way. Joey was OK. His eyes were very bloodshot and sore, the rest of his face was singed, eyebrows and the front of his hair burned off. I don't suppose he ever did that again! Wild Wally came up with another way to do the thunder flashes. He bought a metal dustbin and lid, and the flash was ignited electrically hence no more burning hands or faces. The first time it was tried the blast turned the dustbin lid into a giant frisbee and it skimmed slightly over the audience's heads, spinning at great speed and crashing into the wall at the back of the hall. I think that idea of the whole thunder flash thing was soon dropped.

Ten

GOOD OLD NORTHWOOD HIGH STREET

A few weeks after that incident I met with Bill, Kelly and Stu at Stu's house over a cup of tea; they explained they were getting fed up with Wild Wally. They wanted to be pro musicians but not playing rock 'n' roll in a show like that. They wanted to play their music and asked me to join them in a completely new band. Of course, I was up for it, but I still needed to work to feed Anne and Jo. Just prior to this meeting I had answered an ad in the local paper. A heating and plumbing shop, Sanheat Supplies, wanted a delivery driver, mornings only. Right up my street, I thought. I got the job easily. The main boss was Roy Farr, no relation to me though, and my shop manager was a friendly man called Dennis Scott. The money was fair, and I found the job interesting. Besides driving I had to learn all the different plumbing fittings and pipe sizes to help make up the orders and soon could take orders over the phone and do the follow-up paperwork. This left me completely free to rehearse with the boys in the afternoons. We decided to call the band Curly. Bill's dad had a foreign stamp collecting shop in Watford so Bill worked there with Andy, his brother. Two doors down from the plumber's shop, Sanheat Supplies, in Northwood was Harry Brand's shop, Northwood Electricals. My manager, Dennis, and Harry were good mates, and they were always to be found together in the pub at lunchtimes. It turned out that Harry wanted help in his shop

– someone who could mend irons, toasters, and the occasional vacuum cleaner – which was right up Stu's street and he readily agreed to join me each morning in the car to Northwood from Hemel Hempstead. It wasn't long before we found a job for Dave South, our new roadie, too. There was another plumbing merchant just around the corner in Northwood, STC Plumbing Supplies, and they wanted a driver to do the same job as I was doing. He went for a trial day and fell right in. Half of Northwood High Street was now sponsoring Curly – I loved it!

We would try and get together most afternoons to hear Bill's and Stu's new songs and start work on them straight away. One morning when I wasn't working the phone rang. It was Bill Clayman from the London Clayman Agency and they had given me lots of work in the London clubs with the Sugar Band years before.

"Stevie boy, are you free tonight?"

"Yes Bill, what's up?"

"Have you ever heard of Jimmy James and the Vagabonds?"

I had, everybody had! He was a household name, a major player on the English soul scene. His big hit was a cover of the Neil Diamond song "Red, Red Wine" long before it was covered by UB40.

"Well, he and his band have parted, and he needs a band tonight at the California Ballroom in Dunstable – can you do it, do you think?"

Well between me, Stu, Bill and Kelly we just about knew every soul song there was.

"Yes Bill, we can do that."

Minutes later Jimmy James was on the phone. He gave me a list of songs he did in his show, he didn't know what keys he sang them in, no problem for us though. We arranged to meet at the church hall for a rehearsal at 2pm – oh Christ I had just taken the job on, and the boys didn't know yet. I phoned them and they agreed; after all it was more money and I called in our old Sugar Band drummer Pat McInerney who was home from Manchester University. By the time Jimmy drove up to the church hall we had most of his show down. He brought two guys with him. The Count Prince Miller was part of the Jimmy James Vagabonds show and he was like the song introducer or a bit of a rapper, and Freddy

Fredericks, a tenor sax player, was going to show us the soul riffs that he, Stu and I would be playing. Christ, this soul band sounded good! Jimmy and the Count were over the moon and at 6pm we stopped, loaded up the van for a short trip to Dunstable just in time to pick up a change of clothes.

At the California Ballroom the promoter, a young Mickey Roker, was starting to pull his hair out having heard that perhaps Jimmy James wasn't going to show. Imagine his delight when we walked in. We quickly set up on the small stage, no time for sound checks, and on the other live stage were the Small Faces, with top of the bill The Who – oh yes this was going to be a night! We were the opening act. We went out on stage and played an instrumental to warm ourselves up. We knew the 'Philly Dog' from Geno Washington's album; Freddy knew it well and went into a great soul solo. The music went down very well, and the place erupted when I brought on Jimmy James and the Count Prince Miller. This was our first pro gig together and when we came off stage our faces were beaming. I knew then that I could never go full-time back into a school. Jimmy came into our dressing room to say how pleased he was and how well it had gone. He had quite a list of gigs for the forthcoming year, and would we be the new Vagabonds? I told him about us being signed to Circle, but we appeared as the Vagabonds for Jim. My first pro job... yeah!

Stu surprised us the next week: he had gone out and bought a Ford Transit with double wheels at the back, all the small pro bands were buying them. Ours was light blue and had sliding doors in the front and at the side. We quickly fitted it out with some bus seats and the band put up a wooden partition to keep the equipment from falling on top of us. Jimmy loved it, saying we looked like a professional act as we drove up. Dave South loved it, loving to drive it and took it upon himself to keep it looking great inside and out; the band paid for the monthly payments. We didn't include Jimmy as we knew that we wouldn't be with him forever. The van was ours and besides, he liked to turn up in his own car with the Count. Freddy wasn't with us any more after that first show. Jimmy was a great guy, the shows always went well, but there was one thing I hated. I dealt with the money and wages for the band and Dave, so I had to deal with Jimmy's management accountant, a nasty Nigerian bloke who always stalled on paying, always paying late. We always shied away from hotels, preferring to drive home afterwards. After all Stu, me, Dave, Kelly and Jimmy, when he was with us, could drive. Often we didn't have time to go home, with the schedules being so tight. Often it was Margate, Edinburgh, London in three nights or very similar – we were tired but very happy. Dennis and Roy at the shop were very accommodating and I went in when I could. I even took some local supply teaching at a local junior school. Often the band would be waiting at the school gates for me to join them with a briefcase containing books to mark and we would hightail it on to the next gig, back home in the early hours to be at school by 8.30am – that couldn't and didn't last long.

In the north of England, the club scene was much bigger when it came to cabaret acts: they were huge and well attended, with big stages, great facilities and lots of good-looking waitresses. The Fiesta at Stockton was a big favourite of ours. We always stayed in a big theatrical digs called Elsie Laidler's. Elsie was very laid back, would have very late breakfasts-cum-lunches and we would eat at the club just before it opened with the girls in the evening. The early part of the evening was a guest DJ playing his records and giving out birthday, wedding messages and congratulations. Then a house band with a singer compere would take over. Around 10pm a guest comedian would do his act and the main act, Jimmy and us, would top the bill at 11pm to 12.30am, the house band again with compere singer and the DJ would finish the night off around 2am. All this time the punters could eat and drink at tables tiered around the stage that lowered to a dance floor when the cabaret had finished. We hardly saw any of that, though, as Jimmy's management always had us booked into small clubs in the Teeside area to do the early show around 9pm. That done, it was a race to get the van loaded and back to the Fiesta for the late one. These doubles were great because of the double wages but the band and Dave were usually knackered by the end of the evening.

It was a seven day a week entertainment club thing. I will always remember the great comedians Dustin Gee and the very infamous Lenny Bennett both honing their acts to the people of the north-east; if they didn't like the act then they would let you know in no uncertain terms. Both these comics did really well and went on to become TV household names. Lenny was staying at Elsie's with us, so we drank often back at the house after the show. On one occasion Lenny challenged the band to a pool competition. Elsie had a table in the front room; the losers would always have to get the drinks in and face a forfeit. Lenny, of course, was a past champion and wiped the floor with us. His forfeits always followed an undressing theme – streak to the butchers and back was a favourite, I remember. Mine, when I lost, was to sit cross-legged on the floor in my pants and ice cubes were poured down the front all around my three-piece. The pain after a few moments was excruciating – where's the fun in that, I thought. Lenny thought it was hilarious.

One evening Mack the drummer and Bill had met a couple of girls and brought them back to the house for a late drink. Lenny had met an old mate of his in town; Derek Quinn, of Freddy and the Dreamers, and he had stayed to see the whole show. They both came back to the house and seeing the lads with the girls asked if they could get some snacks in; they disappeared into the kitchen. Ten minutes later they both appeared completely naked, each holding a plate of beans on toast. They held the plates low enough so that their cocks lay across the middle of the beans and both plates were offered to the girls, who shrieked and ran out. The next day a pissed-off Bill beat Lenny at pool and sent him outside naked where he was to stand in the bus queue and wait for the first bus to come – well done, Bill.

There were days when our wonder van wasn't so wonderful and we needed Stu's mate, a young garage mechanic, to do his magic on it. We were doing hundreds of miles a week and generally giving the van a real pounding. The band had a gig supporting Mungo Jerry at a college in the wilds of Oxfordshire and I wondered how we were going to get there. Kelly had bought himself an old London black taxicab so the band's transportation was taken care of. I still needed to take care of the gear. Most days after driving Roy and Dennis would let me take the van home for the afternoon if I promised to be at the shop by 8am the next morning, so I promised that and quickly emptied the van of delivery straps and trolleys and Stu and I loaded up the Sanheat van to go on its first gig. By the time we reached the college in Oxfordshire we were running really badly behind time. The van kept stalling and it had taken hours longer than we had planned to arrive. Still, no time now, a quick set up and sound check and it was almost time for us to kick the evening show off. While Mungo Jerry went through his paces to the agricultural students, Stu and I pondered on how we were going to get home. Stu lifted the bonnet and opened up the van's distributor; inside there was a rotor arm that turned and distributed power to each spark plug in turn. As he lifted the arm off to inspect it, it fell into several pieces.

"Now we're fucked!" he said. "We won't get one of those here tonight."

The thought of making the call to Roy and Dennis in the morning, letting them know where their van was, filled me with horror. "Oh and by the way the van's full of our band gear. No chance of me keeping the job then, is there?"

Stu was quietly thinking. "I reckon I can make one," he said after a few minutes. We had a few tools with the gear so we saw what we had and what he could use. "Steve, go find me a girl's hair grip and make sure it's a metal one." I returned with the grips and the girl, who had come with me as she was interested in what we were going to do with it; I'd explained it was a matter of life and death. Stu fashioned the hair grip into roughly the same shape as the rotor arm and then with chewing gum made a base for it so it stayed in place. Put together, he tried to start the van. Oh, sweet joy! It started. I could've kissed him. We went home very slowly back to Hemel Hempstead, unloaded the gear, and went straight to work. I explained by saying that the trouble had started yesterday afternoon and Stu had fixed it – no lies there then.

My mum sat me down around this time and explained that my grandma had died. She was the last of my grandparents from both sides of the family to go; she had died peacefully in her beautiful old rectory house in Somerset. We always called her Granny B on account of her surname, Brierley, and also my mum's maiden name. She grew up in a very grand house in Lancashire, her parents being very wealthy, but had fallen out with her father when she went against his wishes and married Eustace

Brierley, a short, skinny, very unwell man suffering from chronic asthma. From that day she never received another penny from her family. Eustace had died way back in 1951. I had only seen Granny B at Christmas when she came up to visit Daphne, Mum's sister, in Ickenham near London Airport. Daphne's husband and my Uncle Norman was an airline pilot, one of the first to fly jumbo jets. Mum took us there every year. She had left my mum a fair sum of money and she explained what she was going to do with it. All her sisters, apart from Daphne, lived in Somerset and she told Anne and me that she planned to put the money down on a deposit on a cottage down there. Mike had given her the idea, as he offered to pay the mortgage payments for the rest of Mum's life. At last, my mum's dream of owning her own house was going to come true. I was thrilled with the idea. It was good news for me also, as I would be taking over the rent at the house at Boxmoor, Hemel Hempstead, a large three-bedroom property with a large garden in a small cul-de-sac – a great place to bring up kids.

With Mike away, Mum, with the help of her sisters including Auntie Daphne and Uncle Norman soon found a place in Chardstock, a pretty Somerset village. The thatched cottage needed some work. The thatched roof had been done and she eagerly waited for Mike to come to the surface somewhere in the world to sign the mortgage papers. Of course, Stu, Dave and I did the move for her in our van, but she didn't really take much from the house, leaving Anne and me all the curtains, carpets, kitchen stuff and the beds. She was very thankful and talked to us about the band; she had never seen me play in any of my bands so far. In later weeks I helped her replace her bathroom.

I was getting on very well with this plumbing thing. During the afternoons, when I wasn't rehearsing, I often used to help plumbers when they came into the shop, ordered some stuff and asked me if I was free to give them a hand. To me it was a piece of cake. I was also learning about boilers and central heating systems. I turned up at a large house in Hemel Hempstead to help one plumber remove a bathroom suite and install a new one. He only really needed me to help get this very heavy cast-iron bath out of the house.

"There's a good few quid in this scrap," he explained. "If you can collect it in the van later you can have it."

I said, "OK," and completely forgot about it until one day Stu and I were completely skint, wondering where we could lay our hands on some money for fuel for the van. "Wait a minute, I know where there's some money!" I exclaimed. We drew up to the house to find an enormous removal van outside. I knocked on the door.

"Hello, I hope you remember me. I was here a couple of weeks ago to change your bathroom. I've come remove that great heavy bath from your garden."

"Oh good," sighed this young woman who I hadn't seen before. "You're a plumber, right?"

"Er, yes," I said, looking at Stu's smirking face.

"I very nearly phoned you but great that you are here. We can't seem to light the boiler. You see, we are moving in today, could you light it for me before you take the bath?"

"Er yes, of course," I said. How hard could it be?

This large out of date Potterton boiler stood in the kitchen, out of place against newer more modern kitchen units and a cooker. I'd seen how to light these boilers before with an igniting spark switch; you had to turn the gas on and hit the switch, a spark ignites the boiler pilot light then if called for from the thermostat on the kitchen wall the boiler burners would glide into action. So, gas on, switch the switch watching the pilot burner – nothing, no spark. This meant I had to get a match instead of the spark to light the pilot. Trouble was that the pilot light burner was very low and halfway back along the boiler burners – I see what I had to do – no match could reach it so I quickly made a paper taper out of a newspaper page. I lay on my stomach so I could see where the pilot was positioned, lit the taper and pushed it towards the pilot light gas jet. There was a massive bang! The lady's dog ran howling down the garden path closely followed by Stu and the lady. Everything was still and quiet.

"Are you OK?" shrieked the woman.

"I'm OK," I replied. "That's done. That's got the boiler alight."

I stood up; both of them were laughing, the dog still unsure. She stood me in front of the mirror. Have you ever seen a Tom & Jerry cartoon when Tom gets his face blown off from a Jerry hand grenade or bomb? Well, that was me, I looked just like Tom, bright eyes, no eyebrows, blackened face, no hair. When I was cleaned up and the bath was on the van ready for the scrap merchants, I said goodbye to the lady, who pressed a fiver into my hands.

"That's for the boiler. I'll be able to dine on that story for weeks," she smiled.

I was getting pissed off with Jimmy's accountant. He still would not pay us for shows played weeks before and I could tell he was getting pissed off with me. He stopped taking my phone calls and I was complaining bitterly to Jimmy. We drove to Crewe one day, only to wait for Jimmy to show – he didn't, and we knew then that this gig was finishing badly. A few days later the accountant told me that Jimmy had found another band that wasn't so much trouble and could I return Jimmy's PA system. Stu, Bill, Kelly and I were livid too; all those gigs done and no wages. We decided to say bollocks to the accountant bastard and sell Jimmy's equipment in lieu of wages. Now it was Jimmy and his manager who were livid, threatening to sue us. We replied with the one-word answer, "Bollocks."

We were still together as Curly and Circle Management. Mind you, they weren't coming up with much lately. Thank God for Sanheat Supplies, Harry's electrical shop and Bill's dad.

One day Bill showed up at the rehearsal with the local paper under his arm. He showed us an ad in the music section beside electric guitars and drums. A guy was wanting the services of a local band or musicians that would listen to his songs and play them their way with a view to recording them, just so he and his wife could listen to them finished.

"Let's call him," said Bill. Stu and I agreed with Kelly that the recording experience would do us good, so one evening we called and later went to see Ken. Ken and Vera Holway lived in a beautiful house in a village called Bovingdon Green, a few miles from Hemel Hempstead. He welcomed us into his lovely home and after a couple of drinks played us the first two songs he wanted us to give the treatment to. He had played the piano and sung the songs into a cassette machine; Ken was no singer, that's why he had placed the ad. The next week we returned, Stu and Bill carrying their acoustic guitars and playing the first tune, called "Vera". I sang the verses in the way that Bill and Stu had smoothed them out, and when we hit the choruses in the middle eight in perfect harmony the tears welled up in Vera's eyes. I knew immediately we had the job. Ken said he'd seen and heard other groups and musicians' versions, but nothing came close to ours. The second song, "Dimensions" – same class of musicianship from us – same reaction. A studio was booked a few weeks later in London, but not just any studio. Ken was a wealthy man and wanted the best, so he had booked Morgan Studios in north-west London. Many a hit had been recorded there and Ken, a very successful property developer and fantastic businessman, soon met the owner of the studio, Barry Morgan, also a very successful drummer from the hit band Blue Mink. Very soon the two were great friends, he warmed to us boys as well, especially my jokes. What a lovely man he was.

As a band, though, we were struggling for work; Christmas was coming. We decided to forget asking Circle Management for gigs and I got on the phone to my local agent mates. They soon came up with pubs and local clubs. Money wasn't a patch on what we had earned as the Vagabonds, although it would get us through Christmas. On the Watford bypass was a very large roundabout with an equally large pub on the corner, The Red Lion. The stage was not a stage but an alcove in a large bay window and after the first gig there the response was so good that Ken, another Ken, the landlord, wanted us there every week because he knew that the place would be rammed. Friends who had watched us when Curly first started could not believe the improvement in our act and the material Bill and Stu were now writing, so all that playing time with Jimmy and our countless rehearsals was paying off. It was like playing in our own front room, we had a big regular following that loved our music and often my jokes, too. Ken, Vera and their friends were there every week. When the gig was finished, we would stand around and talk to our audience until Ken the landlord kicked us out, but he didn't rush either. Stu was talking to a dad and his son, both of them loving the band.

"We've seen this competition that's going to be run by the Melody Maker and the New Musical Express this summer. There's equipment, a recording contract and a TV slot on The Old Grey Whistle Test as the prizes. We filled in the forms because we know that Curly can win it."

At a quiet time later, Stu told us what he knew. Hell, we knew we were good but were we that good? The competition would be thrown open to bands all over the UK. It was a 1973 X-Factor for bands.

Circle Management gave us a gig at the University of East Anglia to support the Pretty Things in Norwich. The night before, a Saturday, we had played The Red Lion, and on the way home our windscreen had shattered. In the morning I, Stu and Kelly figured out a way to make a makeshift windscreen. I cut up some half-inch copper tube, flattened the edges and stuck the vertical bars across the windscreen opening with gaffer tape then clear builders' plastic was stretched over the bars and taped down. The plastic wasn't that clear so Kelly had got some cling film from his mum, Frieda (a big Curly fan), and the part the driver would be looking out of would be much clearer then. When Dave saw it, he went off to get a big coat just in case the windscreen didn't hold. We also put in some big gauntlets, motorcycle goggles and a few blankets, just in case. It started to snow outside Norwich on our way in; we should have known the windscreen wasn't going to hold. The wet from the snow was already making the gaffer lose its sticky. Dave and the rest of us got ready for the long journey home. There was only one road from Norwich back to Hertfordshire, through Thetford, and at that time of night there was only one filling station, one café at Red Lodge on the A11. Our speaker cabinets, all of which had canvas covers, were loaded into the van naked; the covers were going to be for us to crawl into. We started off and it wasn't long before the whole window repair project slid off the van onto the road. We all laughed and shouted bollocks to the weather that was getting progressively worse by the minute, wrapped in our coats, gloves, woolly hats and speaker covers using the hand-hole cutouts in the canvas to see out of. We thought we would be all right – we weren't.

Eleven

CURLY'S YEAR

The snow, now very, very heavy, was settling on Dave's goggles, hat and beard. The van was filling up with snow, too, and we were getting very cold. Soon the joking stopped and then the conversation, everybody huddled together, Dave sitting in the driving position alone looking like an Arctic explorer. The van had a heater that was banging away. It wasn't until the next day that Stu confessed that, as he was sitting next to Dave, he had pulled the heater tube from the vents, stopping any warm being wasted, and put the tube up his trouser leg. A couple of hours passed, and we reached Red Lodge for fuel and hot coffee, hot tea, hot anything!

Kenny Ball and his Jazz Band were having late food in the café that night. When we pulled into the car park, they told us later, they all stopped eating and came to the window to see what was getting out of this bandwagon. Dave had to be helped out of the driving position. He was very nearly frozen solid and the rest of us crawled out from the snow that covered us. We stayed in the café for a long time, thawing out, and Dave was relieved as driver. Another two hours of miserable existence and we were never more glad to get home. The abominable band driver stories circulated round the industry for some years after that.

We heard from the Melody Maker competition in the early part of 1973. There were to be heats locally, a semi-final in London and the grand final was to be at the Roundhouse on June 10th. The winner's prizes and TV appearance on The Old Grey Whistle Test were to be announced later.

We were told that our first heat would be in Harrow, not too far away from Watford. On the day we showed up and set up in a space around a hall, a space for each band. The place was mobbed with family and friends and we, on the other hand, had hardly told anybody. It seemed everybody in a band from Herts to Middlesex had entered. The standard wasn't that good, and I just knew that we were going to walk it – we did. When we finished our song even the wives, families and friends of our rivals stood up and applauded us.

A fortnight later another venue in Kenton, Middlesex, and the heat this time was for bands from Buckinghamshire and Essex and once again we had a great night and a great result. There were no nerves from us; I knew that we were that strong. The band had found our permanent drummer in Dave Dowle from North London just before the journey up the Melody Maker ladder had started, and he was fabulous in my eyes. He was still taking lessons, although fully accomplished, studying rhythm and the many different sounds you could get out of a drum. He had fixed rubber tubes to his drums and when he blew extra air into them and then let the tube fall from his lips the tone of the drum would change dramatically.

The semi-final was a different kettle of fish. Large stage, big sound system, big lights and the top bands from the South of England and Wales. Each band played and then there was the long wait. When the name Curly was called out as the winner the Royal Festival Hall erupted. I had no idea that we had so many friends and family there that night, the Hemel Hempstead lot had hired a coach for Christ's sake – brilliant! For the final we were to play two songs. We decided to play Bill's upbeat song "I'm Just Taking It Easy" followed by Stu's great harmony ballad "High Flying Bird". Next, we discussed our stage act, which at the moment was nil. Bill, Stu and I needed to be standing behind a mic stand each and there was another mic stand set lower for Stu and me to share our saxophone playing. The only thing which we thought might be different was that once we were all ready, instead of Dave clicking his drumsticks together or shouting the opening count, "One, two, three, four," I would take four steps towards the microphone and that would be the introductory count for the first song, the brass and the band would hit together with great strength.

On the night we were second from last to go on stage and do our thing. The Roundhouse in Camden, the venue for the grand final was rammed with hundreds yelling for their bands. I didn't know the numbers, but the Curly crowd certainly knew how to crank up the volume when we walked on stage. We were introduced through howling cheers, and we stood like statues and waited for the noise to subside. We were all ready, a quick glance and I started to walk. Dave had told me the count he wanted so he started "I'm Just Taking It Easy" at the right tempo – it worked like a charm, and we were immediately off, a great sax intro, great harmonies and Bill playing and singing the verses. After enormous applause Stu quickly had to change his alto sax for an electric guitar while I confidently explained that these songs had been written by Bill and Stu. I sang the verses to "High Flying Bird" at the end of the song, rising to a big finish with big harmonies. Job done. We couldn't have done that any better; it had certainly gone down very well.

Jab Jab, a band from Leeds and favourites to win, took the stage as the final act, then there was the wait; it seemed forever. The judges on that day were Roger Daltrey from The Who, Bob Harris, radio disc jockey and presenter of The Old Grey Whistle Test for the BBC, and Chris Welch, the lead journalist from the Melody Maker. There was also someone there from Warner Bros Records, the label the winners would be signing to. Bill Shepherd even turned up, our local newspaper was there; yeah, the same ones who had advertised the junior reporting position (given to me and then taken away). I'd have something to say to them if we won and I got interviewed. When the result was announced, third, then second Jab Jab, I knew it was ours. A second later, when Curly was crowned 1973 champion of the Melody Maker National Rock Competition, we hugged each other as if we had scored a winning goal at the World Cup, our fans and friends went crazy and the rest of the night was carnival night for Curly. There were no TV cameras there that night, but we didn't care; we had The Old Grey Whistle Test to look forward to.

A week later we were called to the offices of Brian Morrison, a music publicist in Knightsbridge, later to be heavily involved with George Michael. Bill Shepherd was there. We were congratulated on our success and a publishing deal was given to each of us. When we signed, we received £40 each, then the drinks came out. Bill Morrison's secretary walked in with a message: could Stu and I possibly get our saxophones and ourselves to a London recording studio where Status Quo were recording a new album and they needed some brass on two of their tracks? Stu and I jumped at the chance, bugger the drinks. So at around 11pm we arrived at the recording session.

A few weeks earlier Curly had supported Status Quo in St. Albans and backstage we immediately made friends, with jokes and general London banter. We entered the studio to be hit with two things, one the music being played back was so bloody loud we had to shout our hellos, the next thing was the central control room was so bloody hot the boys were sitting laughing and joking and their studio engineers were wearing nothing but T shirts and shorts – boy were they going to get a shock when they walked out into the night air. The sax parts were dead straightforward, only on one part of a song called "4500 Times" they wanted the saxophone to be played with no interruption as they played the track to us through the earphones, which were so loud we put them down as transistor radios and could still hear quite clearly. I took great gulps of air as if I was going to dive down to the bottom of a deep swimming pool. When the moment came, we delivered, and everybody was happy. In later years they became friends, often coming to the gigs, and some years later, when I worked for the British Army I was instrumental in helping bring Status Quo to do an Army gig in Germany.

The next few weeks were worrying and confusing. Bill Shepherd had taken our £20,000 prize money and given £5000 to the publisher, £5000 to Ian Ralfini of Warner Bros Records and taken £5000 for himself as future management fees. Next thing he wasn't reachable at all; even his small office staff didn't know his whereabouts. We told Ken what was happening, and he immediately took over. He managed to get the remaining £5000 from the Circle Management bank, threatening them with legal action. Ken was now our new manager and that pleased us all no end. His first job was to offer our booking agent at Circle Management a job working just for us for now, keeping the gigs already in the diary. His name was Steve Parker, and he did a good job getting us out there as 1973 Melody Maker champions.

One of the more memorable gigs was at a college in Egham, Surrey, where we were opening for Queen, a band who had just released their third single, "Seven Seeds of Rhye". The students loved our stuff but jeered Queen, asking for us to come back onto the stage. When Queen had finished their show they went into their dressing room, shouting and arguing; their drummer scolded them individually as if he was a football manager. He must have licked them into shape, as their sixth single which followed shortly after was "Bohemian Rhapsody". Next Ken procured the everyday use of Gaddesden Hall, just outside Hemel Hempstead, for full-time rehearsals. Next, wages for everybody, including Dave and his new assistant, Steve Winkworth. Our new minibus and the equipment would now be taken to the shows by Dave and Steve in a hired truck. Dave and Ken had been shopping for a new PA system, finally choosing a local manufacturing company called RSD. The large sound system was state of the art with a fabulous mixing desk and full monitoring system so we could hear ourselves on stage. The Kinks sound engineer, Pete Coggins, was a local man and Ken offered Pete the job to teach Dave how to mix the music as we played it. So we were complete, with full-time rehearsals, plenty of gigs, even new stage clothes, and Dave the drummer was moved to be closer to us. I didn't know how he did it, but Ken had an enormous mobile caravan placed in a field opposite to the hall at Gaddesden; the caretaker of the hall, Mr Goddard, knew the owner apparently. Each day we would be at the hall going over new material from 10am to 5pm. Ken would come over later in the afternoon and listen to our new stuff and then take us to the Gaddesden pub, The Red Lion, for a pint and a game of darts.

Stu had written a really catchy tune called "Darlin". We rehearsed it and found some great harmonies (as we always did). Ken sat there, listened to it and then, "It's a bit of a cowboy song, isn't it, boys?" We didn't put it in the set at gigs; shame really, as years later it went to number six in the record charts with Frankie Miller and Stuart earned a small fortune from the royalties when it was covered by over a hundred artists. Frankie Miller had recorded it, not liking the song, and later, when we met Bonnie Tyler, she said she would have died for it – funny world really. Ken was having problems with Warner Bros Records. Ian Ralfini, head of Warners UK, wanted to put us with Warner Bros America; they, never having heard of us, weren't having any of it so Ken said it was like beating his head against a brick wall and gave up on Warner Bros. A short time later he walked into our rehearsal hall with a face we had seen many times on TV: it was Russ Ballard, guitarist and songwriter with 'Argent'. He had just signed his new solo recording deal with CBS UK. He was invited to play at the annual CBS convention. This time it was to be at the Grand Hotel in Eastbourne, and he needed a band so he could play live to the bigwigs there. He liked us and we liked him, and he was a regular visitor to the hall to rehearse his music before the convention. Ken had asked if we could have the stage before Russ came on for two songs. Ken wanted CBS to hear Curly doing Curly so that there might be a chance of CBS picking us up for a record deal.

At the convention everything went perfectly to plan. We played the same two songs we had won the Melody Maker competition with, and they went down very well, then on came Russ and they loved him as well. While we were at the bar talking to CBS secretaries Ken made a beeline for Maurice Oberstein, the head man at CBS UK. By the time the weekend was over, we were the boys to work with Russ Ballard when he needed us, and we'd have our first single released by CBS. Russ and the band became great mates, playing football together in a team of musicians which included some young lads looking for a break with their band – they got it too. They were to become the band Kenny, having a hit with their first record, "The Bump". I loved those guys and we remain great friends to this day. They were good-looking lads too; I remember talking to Stu, saying that they would have no problem pulling women at their shows.

More rehearsals for Curly and Russ; this time Russ and Colin Blunstone, who were great mates, were doing a music variety show for Granada TV in Manchester. We played with Russ, and he stayed on with us to play for Colin Blunstone. There were some great names that night; Neil Sedaka from America, a new group who had just won the Eurovision Song Contest called ABBA and not forgetting the Bay City Rollers.

On the Curly front, trouble was looming: Jimmy James and his manager had taken on the services of a solicitor and were threatening legal action against us for taking and selling his PA system. Perhaps we had been a bit hasty – no we hadn't – bollocks, he owed us far more than the equipment was worth. Ken sorted it out and paid the solicitor working for us himself.

The CBS signing was not as smooth as we thought it would be. The A&R department was headed by a Dan Loggins, brother to the American recording artist Kenny Loggins, and he wasn't happy with the way that Curly had been signed through the orders of Maurice Oberstein, head of the record label, and not being discovered by his A&R department. It was clear that when the single was released we weren't going to get any help promoting the record from them. We were in the studio for three days. Our producers were Tony Rivers, a one-time singer – a very good one at that – and a classical producer, Michael Gore, brother of singer Lesley. They didn't really get on that well: if one said that particular piece of the recording was a take the other would say no, do it again it can be better. Through the bickering and moaning they produced a fine single, Stuart's "High Flying Bird" and equally on the B side, Bill's "Break Out".

On the release they had reviewed it in the Melody Maker.

Curly "High Flying Bird" (EPIC)**** School of Barclay James Harvest really – but very well done. Curly have changed considerably since I first heard them – in those days they were a second division soul band roughly – but now they are operating at the pop end of what used to be called the Progressive Scene. This is an excellent song and the band give it a comparable reading, their vocal harmonies are superior and the record builds steadily with brooding guitar and a course of sustained 'ah's' fading briefly into a moment for piano before they go all in for the big finale. A tip of the cap to all concerned.

We were thrilled but without the record company's support the single wasn't going anywhere. Ken called us together to say that after trying to get the record company to cooperate he was at last defeated. He was letting us go with the hope that a new more experienced manager would come along. The Curly boys and I were stunned and went away to think about our future.

Twelve

FIRST EUROPEAN TOUR

The first bombshell to land was Bill's resignation from the band. Russ Ballard was going to America, touring, and Bill was going to go with him. He left quietly and to this day nobody has seen him again, although years later I spoke to him on the phone. Ken would leave us, and he said he would need to take back the minibus and the PA system. Dave and his new assistant, a more experienced guy called Tony Bowen, arranged to take a loan to buy the RSD system from Ken. Their plan was to amalgamate with RSD, form a hire company and earn good money getting the RSD name out there – they did very well.

Stu, Kelly and I wanted to stay together. Dave had had an offer from a new rock band called Whitesnake which he joined with great success. Our new guitarist was Stu's friend Brian Marshall, a good songwriter with a great sense of humour. I thought how lucky we were to get a replacement for Bill so local and so soon. We had to get Curly out there as soon as possible before the name was forgotten as Melody Maker champions.

On the home front Anne was very pregnant again. It was any day now and because everything was healthy, we elected to have the baby at home. My mum had come to visit and help out in any way she could. It was a lovely day on June 5th when Anne's waters broke, and I called the midwife. Stu's wife, Diane, was taking Jo to the park for a picnic and a swim so she was out of the way, hoping for a sister to play with later. The events of that day were somewhat hectic, and I told everybody at Zoe's

wedding breakfast in my father of the bride speech years later. The story
was in poem form and went like this.

"It was a hot day in June, I can't remember the tune
That was top of the pops at that time
Our baby was due, we knew what to do
When Anne sat down and gave the first sign
"My waters have busted!" and I looked disgusted
It was as if she had peed on the floor
My mum then walked in and said with a grin
"No problem, I've done this before"
Through the chaos and din, Joanna went for a swim
And the dog was put out in the yard
Then as if out of thin air the midwife was there
Looking old and grumpy and hard
She opened her bag then lit up a fag
And told Anne to stop making that racket
"The baby won't come and then you'll be done,
'Ere have a smoke from my packet"
She turned to my mum and said "You're the one
Who will make tea for me through the day.
I don't want to see you at all, just come when I call
And leave biscuits and tea on a tray."
My best mate Stu arrived and took me aside
"I know this old girl from before.
She delivered my son, smoked ten fags when she's done
Then sent me to the shops for some more."
She then gave a shout "The gas and air's just run out
Steve, go to the clinic for more.
Be as quick as you can, you go in your van."
And she pushed me out of the door
I had no shoes on my feet, I was out on the street
I couldn't go back and face her.
So I drove in my socks, put the gas in a box

At least I was breathing fresh air!
A good few smokes more and then she was sure
That baby was a beautiful girl.
I suppose she had done a good job with a fag in her gob
Now Zoe had entered the world
But when Zo' was a tot she would sit in her cot
And pretend to smoke like her mum
My warnings and fears just fell on deaf ears
By then the damage was done.
This story is true but as Zoe grew
She gave up and now won't smoke at all
When she has another, whether sister or brother
There's one person she'll definitely not call
When her next baby is due, she'll know what to do
Get a birthing pool and then when it's time
Zoe and Dean will climb in, there'll be no chaos and din
Because the pool will be filled up with wine.

Ladies and gentlemen please charge your glasses and join me ready to toast the marriage of my beautiful little girl and her very handsome groom. Zoe and Dean, the very new Mr and Mrs Cataneo."

We answered an advertisement in the Melody Maker for bands to go and play in Holland at the government-sponsored youth clubs. Not knowing what was ahead, we applied and were invited to do an audition in London. We got the job immediately and then were told the details. We supplied our own gear and transport, they paid for accommodation and paid a fair price for each show which we were to be paid in cash each night, we paid for our own food, they paid travel and expenses including ferries. Curly's first European tour – wow! Our route was from Harwich to the Hook of Holland overnight and we were staying in Den Haag.

We went to the youth club representative and we followed him to what we thought was our hotel. The hotel turned out to be a flat above a wallpaper shop. Once in the front door and up the stairs the living room and kitchen were open plan and beds were one floor up and there was another floor after that with more beds; this was going to be for the second band staying there too. We were to share the cooking facilities and everything else in the day room. There was a toilet and a spare room. Our man explained that we would be spending very little time in the flat, as every gig was a drive away and when we got in it would be highly likely that the other band would be either in bed or later than us arriving home. We had just settled in, having chosen our beds, and we were having coffee and cake. There was a loud noise downstairs. It was the other band arriving.

Six or seven very large blokes walked up the stairs, grunted and nodded their hellos. They were from London too, a rock 'n' roll band, they were greasy and dirty-looking. Their leader was the biggest of them all and his name was Killer; he said nothing and just scowled at us. Thank God we hadn't got to see much of them, best not to say I was a Mod on a scooter several years before!

The next morning, we were up early as the first gig was on the German border a good few miles away. When we arrived in good time and ate before setting up equipment, we were pleased that the Dutch youth clubs were more like clubs selling beer. The youth leader was very helpful, loads of free beers and in the first show we went down really well. After that the word must have got around as we played to packed houses, lots of beers and even a night's accommodation in a lovely Dutch youth leader's home way up north of the country. We arrived at the show in Eindhoven and were told that a few nights before, a rock 'n' roll band had played there. They swore a lot and bullied the young Dutch into liking rock 'n' roll the way they played it – I'd had a feeling they would be like that.

One morning, later that week Stu and I were having an early cup of tea when two of the rockers came down into the kitchen. They made themselves a drink, not even acknowledging that we were there, and started a conversation.

"Last night's gig wasn't so good, was it?"

"Nah," answered the other.

"What was wrong with Killer last night when we got back?"

"Dunno, why do you say that then?"

"Well, he went to bed without his cocoa!"

I caught my breath, I wanted to burst out laughing. I quickly looked at Stu – there were tears in his eyes. I prayed that neither of us would make a laughing sound or we would both take a pasting. I turned away from looking at Stu and pushed some of my jumper into my mouth, then left moments later. Any longer and I would have passed out or pissed my pants. We fell about and told the story to the boys on the way to the next gig.

During the next twelve days we were there we had one day off. This particular morning the rep came bounding up the stairs with great news. Bill Haley and the Comets were playing at a gig in Luxembourg, and could we be the support act? If the truth be told they had planned to give it to the rock 'n' roll band before the tour started but they had changed their minds – I wonder why? Luxembourg was a fair distance away, so we had to leave early. Expenses were, of course, being paid, together with a small hotel, as it was too far to drive back that night. It was going to be one of the biggest audiences Curly had played to. I wasn't sure that we were the right choice for the show – I couldn't have been more wrong.

Bill Haley was from the fifties and that was twenty years before and now his fans were twenty years older, well dressed, well mannered, thirty to fifty years old, sitting waiting politely. We played using Bill Haley's sound system. The sound man on the desk and out front was a Dutchman who I was to meet years later and he did a really good job on us. We went down very well and boasted to ourselves, that's another country we have conquered.

Backstage was another story. The local Hell's Angels were doing the security and there were a lot of people lingering around the dressing room corridor, press, TV, other VIPS. This was a massive gig for Luxembourg. Suddenly the largest Hell's Angel shouted for everybody to shut up and later spoke in his own language and English. He ordered everybody, VIPS, TV, camera crews, the lot to put their backs against the dressing room corridor wall. That done, he told everybody to remain silent until Bill had passed onto the stage. This is a bit odd, I thought. The door to Bill Hayley's dressing room opened and the largest Angel walked slowly out, closely followed by Bill, both his hands on the Angel's shoulders. Two smaller Angels were close behind him. To me Bill Hayley didn't look all there; for one he looked like an old man covered in make-up. Was he pissed or was he on drugs? Difficult to know, certainly not one hundred percent.

I saw a few acts like this years later, looking like that until they walk out on stage and suddenly take a transformation and be the stars they are meant to be. Poor old Bill; in my opinion he should have given up a good few years before – a legend of rock 'n' roll shouldn't have had to go through all that.

Thirteen

GIRLS FROM AMERICA, NEW BOYS IN THE BAND

We came back to the UK without too much work in the diary. Steve Parker, our booker, had moved on when Ken had called it a day and we couldn't afford to keep him working for us anyway. By the end of June 1974 Melody Maker and the New Musical Express had a new national rock competition champion and although we still had full houses at the last gigs, I had to think about going back on the tools again, still thinking of what to do musically. Stu and Brian had formed a local band together, trying out their new material, so I decided to promote myself with their help. I formed Steve Farr and the Sobs, a large band, with brass, of course, and two girl backing singers. I would front the band, racing around the stage and performing somersaults and twists and turns off a trampette. Oh, what else could I have? Oh yeah, I made my own dry ice machine. My first gig was at a school, and I invited everybody I knew. The local paper did a pre-gig interview (Life After Curly) and even my mates from Kenny showed up now they were rising handsome popstars.

Anne and I decided to have an after-show party. The show went OK, the party was fabulous. A couple of shows followed but I wasn't going to set the music business on fire, so it fizzled out. Now what? Out of the blue, Clayman, Jimmy James' agency, called me one evening.

"Stevie boy, what are you up to? I've got three black girls coming over from the USA to do a club tour. They are called The Flirtations, have you heard of them?"

Of course I had – who hadn't!

"Want the job?"

"OK, thanks."

Next, I had to put a band together. Stu and Brian were up for it, Kelly was missing; he'd got together with a few of his mates and decided to go to France and Italy, camping and busking. He bought himself a double bass and his friends played guitars; the street act came together very quickly, and they had a great summer, even being asked to play on private yacht parties. So I asked another bass player mate of mine, Bob Morledge, and his friend, the keyboard player Sparky Ian Harrison, to play. We took a rehearsal room in London before the girls arrived in the UK, to get the music down, but first had to audition a drummer as none of my local drummer pals were available. On the second day I was beginning to get nervous that we hadn't found anybody who was going to cut it. In the afternoon a very young black kid walked in and when he started to play everybody stood up and listened. After playing with us for a few songs it was obvious that this young boy was super talented – his name was Mel.

"Great Mel, that was really good. How old are you?"

"Sixteen."

"Are you still at school?"

"Yeah, but I leave on Friday."

"Do you fancy the job?"

"Oh yeah."

"Have you got your own drum kit?"

He didn't. I turned to his dad.

"Is it OK for him to come on tour with us?" (I wasn't sure whether we needed some sort of special permission).

"No problem," his dad said. "And he'll have a kit of drums by Friday. Do you think he's that good?"

"He's awesome!" said Bob Morledge. "I'll keep my eye on him, don't you worry about that."

Mel was beaming. He'd wanted to do this ever since he'd first seen a drum kit and we were pleased to help him to get started. Welcome Mel Gaynor, later to be a star with Simple Minds. By the time The Flirtations girls arrived from the States we had the music to their show down. Mel was a fast learner and had a great sense of humour, almost as crazy as our own. After the first rehearsal any fears the girls might have had when they saw a sixteen-year-old boy getting behind the drum kit quickly disappeared. The only thing that went wrong at rehearsals was that Shirley, one of the girls, told Bob to put his shirt back on – it was a hot studio and Bob was almost down to his knickers! Sparky Harrison said he had enjoyed the rehearsal time but didn't fancy doing the tour. We were going to carry an electric piano anyway and Stu could always accompany the girls on the slower sexier songs. To keep costs down we doubled up at the hotels.

One night, Bob, who was sharing with Mel, put talcum powder in Mel's bed, and when he jumped out of bed in the morning he was white from the neck down. "That's because you are playing with us white boys," Bob explained. "You're turning into a honky." Mel saw the joke and later paid him back, no doubt. Those club tours only lasted a few weeks at a time, and we soon had to say goodbye to Mel; we had nothing to keep him for.

It was at a club in Solihull that I invited an old girlfriend to come and see the show. My mum had bumped into her mum, Mrs Borman, after not seeing her for years and had a good old catch-up there in the street. Pauline, once the love of my life, was living with her new partner up in that area. Mum knew that I was going to be playing there and immediately invited them to the gig. Once I knew, I made arrangements for them to have a good table and a dinner at the club before the cabaret started. I explained to the band that this was the girl I had fallen hopelessly in love with when we were in junior school and I was ten years old, and I hadn't seen her since. I also told them that she was the prettiest girl in the class, a great sports girl and good fun to be around.

On the evening of the show, they came from the box office to tell me that Pauline and her partner had arrived and had been seated at their table. The band were jeering me up saying at last my lost love was here. I went to meet them. The band had taken a table almost next to them to witness this love reunion. I walked up to Pauline; we hadn't seen each other for sixteen years. She was still very pretty but it seemed since I last saw her in junior school in 1959 that she hadn't grown an inch. Her partner was a bit of an oddball; he was albino, white hair, moustache, beard, very pale skin with blue eyes and he smoked a Sherlock Holmes-type pipe. I didn't dare look across at the band; they were going to give it to me later and they did.

On the home front family things were jogging along. Jan and John had moved to Pangbourne just outside Reading and John was rapidly moving up the accounting ladder; he'd been made company financial director for British American Tobacco and they were making plans to let their large house and move to Mexico. They were to be there for four years, living a great life with plenty of golf, tennis and sunshine. Merry wasn't having such a good time. A few years before she had married a submariner, had two kids, Catherine and Mark, and they had settled in Helensburgh in Scotland, at the Royal Naval Base married quarters. Her husband, David, had been caught playing away so that was that; she was soon divorced. Sometime later another husband, Robert, and another two daughters, Nicola and Stacey. It was soon after the birth of their second daughter that Robert started having blinding headaches, which he would anaesthetise with alcohol, and when he couldn't sleep, he would get angry and sometimes violent with Merry and the older two kids. He would eventually fall asleep in the early hours and sleep till after lunch. It was then that the family planned to get Merry away from him. Dave and Stu, my Curly brothers in arms, came to my aid. I took my car, and they would drive our empty group van to Middlesbrough, where Merry was living with the children. While Robert slept off the drink he had consumed, the night before, we crept into the house and removed all the children's toys, clothes and some of the furniture. The boys then drove the van back to Hemel Hempstead and I took a very battered Merry and the children back to Goring near Pangbourne where my mum's house was. All their belongings arrived the next day. It wasn't long after Robert had promised to stop drinking and get medical help that he was killed instantly in a car accident outside Redcar.

My brother Mike had been sent by the Navy to learn Mandarin Chinese in Hong Kong. Along with another British officer, one Paddy Ashdown, he was there from 1967 to 1970 at the same time I was at Teacher Training College. He was fluent when he came home. His mastery of the language was to serve him well and the Western European industries based in China during the troublesome years there. Now he was home, the Navy was planning on giving him his first nuclear submarine, HMS Revenge, next year. First he had to complete his nuclear training at the United States Naval War College at Newport, Rhode Island. He'd had the same girlfriend for ages, and they suddenly decided to get married and go to America together. The wedding was set, and Anne and the girls looked forward to our first wedding as a family. Trying to find the small church in Richmond was proving to be a mammoth task and we arrived late, halfway through the ceremony. Jan and Mum didn't approve of the racket we made as we entered the church at a quiet part in the proceedings, but all that was forgotten later at the reception.

Fourteen

HERE COME THE DOGS

Anne and the girls were meeting members of my family whom they had never seen before.

At home in Boxmoor, Hemel Hempstead, the Farr family were getting used to being four. Anne and I had previously had the conversation about me being away at night and gigs and we planned to get a dog at the earliest opportunity. It wasn't long before our doggy prayers were answered. Anne's mum's boss, the gynaecologist, had parted from his wife and she was now living in North Wales at their comfy home with some large dogs. They were a Great Dane, an Irish Otterhound and a French Briard. Trying to find homes for these large creatures wasn't easy, so she asked the doctor to ask Marge if she could take one. Marge then asked us. My history with Great Danes wasn't great, an Irish Otterhound would also stand taller than me, so we opted for the Briard because we had no idea what one was like, being told she was big, but not as big.

So the day came when the old kennel name pedigree Lullingstone Meribel was put on a train in North Wales and travelled with the guard to Paddington Station. Marge collected her and the first time Anne and I saw her she was sitting bolt upright in an easy chair at the house in Chalfont St. Giles. Anne immediately fell in love with her, and I knew that this dog would soon not only become part of our family but also certainly do the protective job I wanted her to do. Whilst Lullingstone Meribel was her pedigree name, we would call her Loff. We put Loff in the car to go home.

She immediately sat in the front seat next to me, no arguments. Anne had to sit in the back. Almost home, the battery died on our car and while we were at some traffic lights I quickly jumped out and asked a group of young lads in the car behind to give me a push start. Three lads got behind my car and just before we started one of the boys shouted to me, "Perhaps your mate could get out and help?"

Anne and I started to laugh, and when he came up to the car and looked in the window, he saw Loff's great big hairy face looking back at him. It wasn't long before Jo slept with Loff in her enormous basket and Loff slept with Jo on her bed; she was a gentle giant and would sit still, get dressed up by Jo, crawled over by Zoe and ridden on by an injured pigeon called Willy (Willy live or Willy die?) that I had found on the kerb in Fulham with a broken wing and was nursing back to health. The lady who had given us the dog dearly wanted a puppy from Loff, so we made arrangements through the Briard Society to find a stud of good standing in the Briard world. This done, I took Loff some months later to meet the stud dog they had picked out for her, named Frodo. Soon after Loff had mated the puppies started to grow. It didn't end there though, we were left losing those puppies inside her, and for a week or so after the birth she wasn't well at all.

Weeks after this episode the Briard club contacted us again about a young Briard dog whose owner couldn't handle him and their small children at the same time. So, I went to Oxford to meet Bert. Briards are either black or blond. Bert was blond with a small black beard and this time it was I who fell in love with him and he with me. Much smaller than Loff at this time, I could see by the size of his paws that he was going to be bigger, much bigger. From the outset Loff accepted Bert but stood for no nonsense; she was and always would be the boss. We would take them into the park, and it was great to see them run free and then upon a command come bounding back to us. These dogs were very intelligent, being used by the French to identify live soldiers amongst the corpses during the First World War. One disadvantage of owning two enormous dogs: a poo bag just doesn't cut it, a carrier bag does though. Anne hated carrying the dog bag home just in case she met one of her mates.

Within the year Bert was fully grown, even more handsome now, and we refrained from having him neutered so that he could earn his keep by being a good stud for other bitches in the Briard Society. Loff wouldn't have any more pups since her disaster the last time, but it didn't stop Bert trying and all he got was his head bitten off or growled at as he approached. He didn't seem bothered; he did have his second love – me. If he sat beside me on the floor and I was on the sofa watching TV, he could still lean over and kiss and nuzzle my ear. I knew what he was after and pushed him away, saying I had a headache. On one occasion Bert, Loff and I were sitting in the lounge watching TV; the phone rang, and I sprawled myself across the sofa to answer the phone. It was a friend and I got into conversation, forgetting where I was and what position I was in – too late. Bert jumped and mounted me from behind, his grip on me was tremendous and face down I just couldn't get him off me. I called to Anne to come quickly as I was getting shagged to death. She ran in and, after collapsing in laughter, turned the vacuum cleaner on – he didn't like that and ran off. For a few days I was right off him, no apologies, chocolates, nothing!

Over the next months I did a few silly things. I accepted a bet that I wouldn't streak around the new complicated five-way roundabout at Hemel Hempstead. Streaking or running around completely naked at any time of day or night in any place was the new thing at that time. Again, Dave and Stu were with me; the plan was for me to jump out of the van with no clothes on, run around the five roundabouts, run back to the van, zoom home just in case any police were in pursuit, open the door and run into the front room, where Ann would have clothes waiting. The door opened and I was off, and it wasn't long before cars were stopping, hooting, lights flashing and as I got to the last roundabout traffic was moving slowly forward and I couldn't get across the busy road for waiting for a gap in the traffic. That done, back to the van, two minutes to the house, through the front door and into the lounge, straight to where Anne's parents were seated. They had arrived unexpectedly and she had no way to warn me – I did see the funny side when I had some clothes on later.

It was a long while since my last tour and it looked as though I was back on the tools for a while. I met a builder from Watford called Michael

Rance, who did a lot of work in North London. He had need of a plumber, he would show me the job and let me get on with it, he paid well and on time too. I was busy at a large house owned by a Jewish couple when the electrician sat next to me when we were having a cup of tea.

"Can you fit in an extra job that needs doing quickly?"

I wasn't that keen, as in just over a week Anne and I and our daughters were going on our first holiday to Majorca, and I didn't want to start something I couldn't finish. I agreed to go and see the job at a restaurant down in Sloane Square. He took me to the Liberian Food Centre, and I met a very smartly dressed owner who took me down to his kitchen, a long narrow room with heavy ovens, cookers and kebab heaters all around the three walls.

"I need a new bigger gas main supply pipe to go all around the three sides of the kitchen. Can you do it?"

"Yes," I said, still not feeling very keen.

"How much?" he asked.

I loaded the price hoping that he would say it was far too expensive and get someone else.

"Six hundred pounds," I said. I waited for a moment.

"OK," he said. "But I have one small request. You have to do it in one night. We turn the ovens off every night at 11pm and on again at 8am. Can you still do it?"

I thought for a moment, there's an opportunity here to earn a great deal of money in one night – too good to miss.

"OK," I said, and I would do it in a couple of nights, time enough for me to buy the fittings and the pipes I needed.

I asked a mate of mine (an out of work musician) to come and help pull out all those heavy cookers, etc. I would get behind them and fit the new pipe and he would push 'em back when I was done. Both of us worked hard all night and by 8am the next morning the ovens were re-lit. The owner came down, thrilled that we had been on time, and he paid me in £50 notes – great for the holiday.

I managed to finish at the Jewish house the day before our holiday and I was very happy, and they paid me up to date. The next morning the electrician called me.

"Hello Steve, can you come down to the Liberian Food Centre early this morning? The owner and the fire chief want to see you. The kitchen burned down last night."

Anne said I went white as I was holding the telephone, and before I left, I checked my liability insurances were up to date. I thought I would take little Zoe so it wouldn't get violent if I was to blame. I arrived at the restaurant in the morning and prayed they wouldn't keep me too long. Our flight to Majorca wasn't until the evening but we had to drive some two and a half hours to Gatwick Airport first. The electrician saw me and took me down into the kitchen. The ladies of the restaurant took Zoe for fizzy drinks and chocolate, saying it was too dangerous for her to go down there. So then we went to meet the fire chief.

"Are you the guy who put the new gas mains in?" he said.

"Yes," I said.

"Well, you can see the place is a real mess. The fire started in the air ducting running around the ceiling taking all the cooking fumes away, and it hadn't been cleaned for a while and when a fan motor broke down it sparked and the fat in the metal ducting ignited. What I have called you for is to ask you to check every gas joint you welded to make sure the gas supply is safe to use, as the owner wants to be open for business again tomorrow."

"I can do that," I said with a smile – I could have kissed him! All the time travelling into London that morning I was convinced it was going to be my fault. It took me an hour to check every joint, the firemen acting as my strongmen, pulling and pushing the heavy ovens as I moved in behind them again.

"All done, all OK," I told the fire chief, and at that moment the owner appeared, very grateful that I had turned out on the morning of my holiday and pressed another two hundred quid into my hand – this was going to be a good holiday!

Zoe and I stopped on the way home at the Edgware Road market to buy some fruit for our journey to the airport. As we stood in the queue waiting to be served Zoe kept tugging at my trousers.

"Look, Daddy, look, a kangaroo."

The people that were with us in the queue looked to where Zoe was pointing, and they smiled and laughed. Behind the market stall was a fenced area and gardens with a large Alsatian dog who was having a long crap, sitting for a long time in the dog crapping position. Poor old Zoe, I've dined out on that story for many years.

Fifteen

MEETING JOHNNY WAKELIN AND OFF WE GO AGAIN

Stu and Brian were writing songs and secured a publishing deal with Keith Rossiter. Keith had a publishing company called ERM International with his partner, Steve Elson. They had previously signed a guy from Brighton, who was having success singing songs about Muhammad Ali. "In Zaire" was the big hit of the day and it was Johnny Wakelin who was the writer and singer. Kinshasa was the name of the capital city in which Muhammad Ali had regained his world heavyweight championship title from George Foreman, Zaire was the country in Africa where the fight had been fought. There was an awful lot of interest from Germany as the song was an even bigger hit there than in the UK, and the offers for Johnny Wakelin and the Kinshasa Band to do German TV shows came flooding in. At that point there was no Kinshasa Band, so Keith asked Stu to quickly form a band to do it. Session musicians had previously been with John on Top of the Pops in the UK. Stu managed to get the two drummers John had used, Trevor Waters and Mark Pinder. Kelly would be playing bass and Stu would play guitar. Most of the TV slots would be miming anyway but Stu wasn't sure, so they rehearsed the number anyway.

They all flew to Hamburg to do the gig. The next two followed soon after and John wanted a tour manager to sort out the hotel reservations, together with the air tickets, so Stu asked me if I was interested – how hard could it be? A trip to Germany with all expenses: I jumped at it. After one TV show in Baden Baden we sat talking to John in the hotel bar. He was very eager to tour Germany and Europe and I sat and gave him a complete CV of Curly/Flirtations band and when he knew that Stu and I played saxophone he was sold. He was only going to use one drummer and Mark would be chosen to do the first tour. I would be wearing two hats, saxophone and tour manager. We booked the old Curly rehearsal hall and John would come up from Brighton in the week, rehearse and stay with Anne and me.

It was soon time for me to sort out the transport. Van and minibus companies were not keen on hiring vans to groups; they knew that the members of the band would want to travel with their equipment to keep costs down. So I went to Kennings Van Hire and explained I needed a huge van for six men to travel with huge organ parts as we were rebuilding a cathedral organ in Dusseldorf. It worked and they even put in extra seats for us. This van, however, did 50mph max – it was going to be a long tour! Up to the tour start date we rehearsed John's show. He had written several successful songs about Muhammad Ali, Black Superman, "Floats like a butterfly, stings like a bee" and together with his own rock 'n' roll songs this show was going to be fast-moving, just right for the young German audiences.

Years before, John had had a serious motorbike accident and lost his leg just under the knee. You couldn't tell when he walked but dancing on stage was a no-no; but the band would do that. Big companies like Coca Cola and the Sparkassa Bank financed these pop tours, and as well as the bands being paid nightly they paid for travelling, hotels with breakfasts and meals at the gigs every night. Halls with a capacity of two thousand were chosen so there were a lot of halls to play. We had beers backstage, but I don't think alcohol was served to the audience so that the younger fans could see their favourite acts live.

The whole show was fronted by the same guy every night we did. He was an American DJ who had settled in Dusseldorf and had a very successful radio show. Mal Zondoc was a household name; not only did he play exactly what the kids wanted, but on his live shows he had three enormous film screens across the stage behind him showing films of the Germans' favourite acts, a great live show for him and the bands as they appeared; there were usually three per night. His crew provided the large PA system so we only had to take our back line with us. As per German efficiency his stage crew changed the equipment as Mal played some records or films. The kids loved him; on his first tour at the first venue the place was packed. The first act was a young German act which all the young girls screamed at; we hadn't heard of them. Next up was Johnny Wakelin and the Kinshasa Band, his first live show ever, lots of screaming. "In Zaire" was up there in the Top Ten. Smokey was the headlining band, very professional and polished. This was going to be a good tour. Mal was very pleased as he had not seen John's act, and John and us Kinshasas were relieved it had gone so well. By his own admission John had said he was crapping himself to be up there in front of so many people.

We'd only been going for a week when one of the Smokey band fell ill, and the band couldn't continue. They returned to the UK, to be replaced by Kenny, the young band I was so fond of from the Russ Ballard football days. There was an extra rung to the band; they had brought in a musical director, Ian Kewley, who we were going to know so much better in a few years' time.

Ian said he had been asked to teach the band how to start and how to stop. He must have done a good job, as their act was good, and the kids went wild for them. Their song "The Bump" was soaring up the German charts. After the show they preferred to be in the back of our Bedford van with partition seats than be in their limo and then we would drive out into the snow to find a bar; trouble was finding our own way back! Ian remembered that we stopped on a quiet autobahn after Stu had been sick in the van; everybody, bar Stu, was standing on the seats now. Stu was sitting up on the floor next to his spew, laughing, we all jumped out wanting to piss in a long line. Stu again having done his job, lay in the snow and was making a snow angel when Ian had to drag him out of the way, narrowly missing a juggernaut that was fast ploughing towards us.

Still, after three weeks we were ready for home and some fish and chips. I even bought a new multi-children's garden entertainment unit only available in Germany at that time; it was a swing, slide, and seesaw in bright colours and the girls loved it. Packing it in the van with us had been a bit of a problem, though.

We still hadn't given Curly up, even though the next Johnny Wakelin and the Kinshasa Band tour was being planned again with Mal Zondoc in a few months' time. We had found a great guitarist to replace Bill Roberts. His name was Brian Marshall and he fitted into Curly like a dream. When Ken had booked us to record his material some years before, he befriended the studio owner, Barry Morgan. Barry, as I said earlier, was the drummer with Blue Mink, a regular British Top Ten band, and we heard he was looking out for new acts, so we contacted him. He had seen Curly working on several occasions and he was a fan and a friendly face. He heard the new material and liked it very much. He called us in to talk about a possible deal and recording time at his Morgan Studios – at last it was time to get back into it under our own steam. The day before we were to go into Morgan Studios Stu phoned with disastrous news; Brian had been struck down overnight with complete paralysis and was rushed to hospital. We were all stunned – whatever could have caused it? We later learned it was Still's Disease. All of his joints had seized, and it was going to be months or even longer before he could even walk, let alone play a guitar again. The recording slot was lost, and we did not know when we could do it again.

I had to look out for another guitarist and drummer for John. Mark Pinder, the drummer who had done the first tour, didn't want to do it again, so Stu asked a mate of his, Malcolm Green, to do the job. Bob Morledge from the Flirtations band stepped in on guitar. John's management had put together a small UK tour before we went back to Germany and the Mal Zondoc supershows. Stu and I bought a Bedford van, put some seats in the back and a wooden partition to keep the gear separate. The show was going well, and John said that after this tour I could find a keyboard player to add to the band. The last but one gig was in Portsmouth, at an enormous naval base. We had played a small one in Plymouth the night before and after the show Bob had pulled out a small bag of marijuana and rolled up a joint. I didn't smoke it and neither did the others, apart from Malcolm, the new drummer. They smoked the joint and I thought that was that. However, apparently the dockyard police had smelled it after we left and forwarded the warning to Portsmouth, a much larger force. There was a large crowd forming when I wandered into our dressing room with Kelly. We'd been talking for a few moments when three men walked in. I thought they were the promoters of the show and we made polite conversation. Then one of the guys said to me, "Do you mind emptying your pockets?"

"What's that for?" I asked, still smiling.

"We're the police and we think that you are carrying drugs on a Royal Naval Base. Now if you don't want to be put in the dockyard cells, empty your pockets."

Oh, how the mood had changed! Kelly and I followed orders. They had nothing and they started asking who had the drugs and we said we had no idea. Next in was Stu; they were all friendly to start with then Stu said, "Well, it's nearly time for us to get ready now, so would you go, please."

They explained who they were.

"Yeah, right," said Stu. "Why don't you fuck off now and enjoy the show."

They had him up against the wall.

"Right now, you, empty your pockets!"

Again, finding nothing, the policemen told him to drop his trousers as they were going to look up his arse and Stu was shouting obscenities as they lay him face down on the table there, with me and Kelly looking on. Was that legal? It was certainly funny to watch. By the time they had done the search Stu had unloaded every swear word that he knew. Kelly and I sat there, tears streaming down our faces – this story would last forever! John and his brother Bob came into the dressing room. Of course he had no idea, there had been more cops grilling him next door and he was pissed off that we were being accused – he made sure from the head cop that the show was going ahead.

He said it would but we all had to go to the dockyard police station for further questioning afterwards.

"Right now, we want to search your van."

I had the keys and went outside to unlock it. The van was parked in a covered area at the back of the gig, so all the lights were on, and it was quite bright. Next a small van drew up and out jumped another cop and his trusty drug dog. They cautiously put the dog in the van, shutting the door; one guy looking through the windscreen was giving a running commentary.

"The dog's sniffing, the dog's sniffing, the dog's seen a bag, the dog's seen a bag, the dog's got the bag, the dog's got the bag!"

The cop then opened the door and dropped the bag away from the van as if it was a bomb.

"The dog's in the bag, the dog's in the bag," the commentary continued. Oh, for Christ's sake we could all see that! I started to laugh as I thought of how this was going to finish. There was no way that there were any drugs in Stu's bag. Sure enough, the dog got his head in the bag and brought out a pair of Stu's dirty socks.

"Will you be needing to take them away for analysing?" I asked.

"Certainly," they answered.

"We'll need you to sign for 'em," I said. I could hardly get the words out as I was bursting inside with laughter.

With the dog back in his small van we returned to the dressing room and there was awkward shaking of heads. We had better get a move on because it was nearly showtime. Just then Bob and Malcolm walked in, laughing.

"Aye, aye," Bob greeted us, "ten minutes to go, just in time for Malcolm and me to have a small spliff."

The game was up; they were allowed to do the gig but would be arrested when they came off stage. They were kept in Portsmouth overnight, they still hadn't found any drugs, and were cautioned and told they would not be allowed to enter another naval, military or air base for the foreseeable future. The reason there weren't any drugs was that Bob had thrown his small stash into my saxophone as we walked onto the stage. John wasn't happy and told them he was changing them before the next German tour. Christ, you could not drive with any alcohol in your blood in Germany, God knows what they'd do to you if they found you were on drugs! So I contacted Pat McInerney, from the Sugar Band Jimmy James days, to ask him if he would tour with us. He'd just finished his university course in Manchester and was keen to start drumming again.

John introduced us to a guitarist called Tom Toomey, a good player, keen to impress. A little odd, I thought, but he seemed friendly enough. God knows how we found Bill Scott, the ex-keyboard player from the popular Edinburgh band called Hole in The Wall. He loomed over us as if he was Rob Roy, strawberry-blond head of hair with matching beard, great sense of humour. He also played a great piano accordion which was going to serve us very well. He was married to Grace, and we were all in love with her, but the trouble was all our wives were in love with him! We couldn't upset him if we tried – we were going to get along, we just loved him.

With the new band ready, John happy, we were now making plans and reservations to go back for another Mal Zondoc special. A couple of days before we left Bill phoned to say he had found us a great roadie. His name was Jake and he had been the bass player with the Hole in The Wall band in Edinburgh. He was down on his luck, homeless and jobless, and he would come for his board, food and beers. Bill stressed that it wouldn't be a good idea to let him have too many beers, though. It seemed a good idea at the time, so Jake was taken on. On our departure date we all met at my house to clamber into the van. We all met Jake and I threw him the keys to drive us to the ferry.

"I cannae drive!" he said in his broad Edinburgh accent. "I'm still banned."

Silence from us, then another Edinburgh accent bawled out, "Jesus, Jake, you didn't tell me that before!"

Too late. Jake was coming but we were driving, just hope he knew how to put the gear up!

This time the headlining act was the Bellamy Brothers from the USA, and they had a pair of English roadies with a large beaten-up truck much bigger than ours and it was to come in handy a bit later. To open the show was a young Manchester band called Taxi, on their first tour. We immediately got on well. A few nights into the tour the bass player with the Bellamy Brothers fell sick and Kelly was asked to step in and play. After a quick run-through Kelly busked the show and we were all watching him, and he did a really great job. He only did it once though; the Bellamy Brothers didn't want to pay him anything for his trouble, so Kelly refused to do it again. They made do with a stagehand playing bass until their own man felt better. As the tour went on, the Brothers continually complained at the roadies, who didn't really seem to give a shit; they laughed at them and got on with something else they were doing. One of them, though, thought he was a sound engineer and sat on the controls out front. The sound wasn't great with microphones feeding back. They called to see him after the show; he ran up the stairs to the dressing room, only to come tumbling down after one of the Brothers punched him – he didn't do the sound again.

It was big news, especially in the smaller towns we played, when Mal Zondoc's pop show rolled into town. Often a local disco club would advertise that Johnny Wakelin and the Kinshasa Band would be making a public appearance at his club after the Mal Zondoc show. "Come and meet Johnny Wakelin and the Kinshasa Band, or the Bellamys or Taxi tonight at the blah, blah Club." Of course, we didn't know anything about it until the disco manager managed to get in backstage. After the show he asked us to come: 'free drinks all night', that normally did it. On one occasion we all walked into one club that was not that well attended. Up to now the places we had guested had been packed, and John was happy to sit and sign autographs for all those who wanted, while the rest of us were happy to talk to the German crumpet and drink plenty of drink.

"Oh noo," that was the broad accent again from 'Rob Roy' Bill getting concerned. This place was no good for Jake, he said – too much drink.

Jake had his full share too early and was now dancing with a girl who looked as awful as him, matted dreadlock hair, perhaps one white tooth in her mouth. Jake was jumping and gesticulating around her playing air guitar. When the guitar solo on the record blared out, Jake went towards a large German bloke, dressed in full-length black leather coat sitting alone at a table with a large beer in front of him. It was Jake's intention to play the guitar solo on his air guitar for the guy in the coat, and when Jake raised his leg to put his foot up on the guy's table, thus getting into the lead guitarist solo pose, he kicked the full glass of beer into the German's lap. We saw it. Somebody said this is going to kick off now, but nothing happened. The guy just got up and left the club. Bill had a few choice words for Jake, and he left the club with the girl he had been dancing with. In the morning it was clear that Jake had stayed out all night, but he was back in time. Just before I drove off Bill got stuck into Jake again.

"What was that horror you were with last night, Jake? You do that again and you'll give us all a bad name."

Jake answered, "Bill, dinnae talk about my bird that way!"

We left that town crying with laughter.

Seeing as John and brother Bob were travelling in John's car, quite often Tom Toomey would go with them but quietly he was driving John slowly mad. One, he wouldn't stop talking, two, he was always on about how the show could be better. John had told him to shut up for long distances. Once in the show town our first job for John and us was to find the hotel and today the hotel was playing hard to get. After driving up and down for a bit, getting nowhere, Tom suddenly said, "John, I speak fluent German. Let me ask someone for directions to the hotel." (The Regent Hotel).

John stopped the car. "OK Tom," he said.

Tom wound the window down. "Entschuldigen, meine Dame," he said.

She came to his window. Good start, thought John.

"Can yous tells me ze way to zer Regent Hotel?"

The woman walked away.

We met them as they walked into the hotel reception. John, still laughing, said, "You're never gonna believe what he said."

It was 1977 and Germany was still divided in two, the Eastern half supported by Russia and the Western half supported by the Americans and English, as it had been directly after World War II. Berlin was right on the borderline and the Russians had built a high wall right along the border and through the city. The wall was policed by armoured soldiers who would shoot defectors from the East trying to get to the lights of Western Germany. We had a show in Berlin and were given strict instructions. There was one road that Westerners were allowed to drive into Berlin. The road itself had soldiers with guns on lookouts and the sides of the road were heavily fenced with barbed wire. We were told not to stop once they had let us through the checkpoint. We planned to go as early as we could and so we still had 90 kilometres to drive into the city. We approached the checkpoint and there were a number of East German border guards, all heavily tooled up with automatic rifles and pistols. Once they saw that this wasn't an ordinary van and that we had six people in it we were ordered out at gunpoint and told to stand in a line against the wall. They collected our passports.

"Vot's zis?" a guard shouted, holding up a white holiday passport only valid for one year.

"That's mine," shouted Mac the drummer.

"Zis passport's no good! Mickey Mouse passport!"

They went inside with Mac. The rest of us stood quite still against the wall, it seemed for ages. A hearse drew up and was stopped by the guards. The two funeral directors got out holding the paperwork for the coffin that they were transporting back to the East. This didn't satisfy the guards who promptly took the coffin out of the hearse, laid it on the ground in front of us and told the two guys to open it up. I couldn't believe this was happening. We stood in silence as the coffin lid was unscrewed, the body checked, and then screwed back. These two funeral guys didn't seem to bat an eye, as if it was an everyday occurrence – perhaps it was.

We did the show and were happy to get back to the West the next day. I never wanted to go back there again. I did, however, years later, twice!

There were only a few days left on this tour and our Bedford van eventually gave up the ghost. It had been playing up and Stu and Bill had nursed it before it died in the end. What now? Up popped the Bellamy Brothers roadie duo.

"Don't worry, boys, stick your gear in our truck. We'll getcha there." Laughing.

We were grateful as we cross-loaded the equipment into the Bellamys' larger truck. While John squeezed in as many as he could into his car, they voted that Stu and I should ride in the back of the truck with the gear, as we were the owners of the old van. Bill volunteered to come with us so he could play his accordion as we were going along – I loved that accordion.

A couple of weeks previously we had done another German TV show and afterwards we had been invited into the green room where all the acts and the television crews would be having a drink. The drinking had barely started when all the Germans sat down at a long table and started singing the local folk songs, lots of beer swilling about. Not to be outdone, Bill raced away, returning with his piano accordion and we started singing English folk songs at the top of our voices. Bill knew hundreds of songs. The Germans applauded so Bill played for them while they sang – how he knew the songs heaven knows. They loved the accordion and they loved him too. And very soon trays and trays of beers, gin and vodka were being passed to our table – another great night. Also, during that tour we played at a beer festival near Munich. The Germans dressed in lederhosen and sat at long tables, just like they did at the TV party, and drank excessively from 2 litre glasses. Enormous tents were erected, big enough for a stage for the bands and tables for up to two thousand people. Our dressing room was a canvas room with curtains instead of doors and next door to us was the security men's tent. These men, not policemen, were security men chosen for their size. When drunken trouble started it was dealt with very quickly; the troublemakers were dragged into the room and beaten with leather straps. They left with sore arses and arms, some in tears. On one occasion a guy was being escorted to the room but broke free just outside our curtain, we could see everything. Once free he took up a karate-type kung fu pose as if he was going to take them all out – this is going to be interesting I thought. The security men stood for a moment and then three of them attacked him with a leather strap, and kung fu Fritz fell on the floor and left with more than the average bruises a few moments later. While this brutality was going on the crowds still sang, swayed and swilled the beer while the oompah bands played on.

Sixteen

GERMANY AND MORE GERMANY

When the sun was shining, we would open up the two rear upper doors of the Bellamys' truck. It was like a small removal van and the bottom half of the door was a large ramp, easy for loading the equipment, so we could see what was going on during our journey. Perhaps we shouldn't have bothered. When the autobahn had ground to a halt and everything was at a standstill our roadie boys would drive at speed down the hard shoulder, blazing their horn, and on the same journey they went wrong in a small town doing a three or four-point U-turn. As we looked, they reversed straight through a wooden fence into somebody's garden. The elderly woman came out shouting and waving her arms but the boys didn't stop, all she saw was the truck driving away and three small faces staring at her.

That tour had been long and hard, and I was now looking forward to seeing Anne and the kids. I'd bought presents again this time but nothing as big as the garden swings like before. John had paid the half of the van hire to me, and Stu and he paid the other half at the end of the tour. Stu and I knew that we had to get the van repaired to get us back to the UK. So, the morning of the final gig I went by train to the small town our van had died in and collected her ready for the long journey home. It made it. Stu didn't trust it for further tours, so it was sold. Once home I started looking for another van.

Anne had wanted to drive for ages. She had been having lessons from Reggie Hall, our neighbour, and passed her test a few days after I got home. Her first car was a present from an old friend, Randall Grundy. A Mini Countryman with no second gear, awkward at first but we soon had the hang of it. A few months later we were able to get rid of the Mini and bought an Austin 1100 in very nice condition with one fault, the driver's door didn't lock. I promised to get it fixed. In the meantime, we bought a crook lock, a locking bar hooked from the steering wheel to the accelerator pedal, so if the car was started it couldn't move anyway.

On one Friday night I got a call from Chris Redburn, the Kennys' band bass player. They were all based around Enfield, North London, and they were keen for Stu and me to come to a party they were having to play our saxophones, as they were playing with added guests. I asked Anne if I could take her car. She wasn't at all keen, but I promised faithfully to put the crook lock on and drive very carefully. I arrived at the tennis club where the party was being held and carefully reversed into a parking space. After meeting the Kenny boys and Ian Kewley again I took out my saxophone ready to play. Stu was already there. We had a great time playing lots of Soul music and Ian was playing great on his Hammond organ. It was time to say goodnight and we all moved into the car park as the boys' party had run out of time. I threw the sax into the back seat and jumped into my shiny newish car; I would impress them as I swept out of the car park. I started the car and putting it into gear, swept forward at speed. I suddenly remembered that the crook lock was still on. I had inadvertently hooked the lock from the steering wheel to the footbrake pedal, steering and stopping became immediately impossible! Anne's car and I swept through the small car park wall of the tennis club – that stopped me. I quickly released the lock, reversed out and drove away as the Kenny boys waved goodbye, laughing.

Half a mile up the road I stopped again away from eyes that had witnessed me being a complete idiot and inspected any damage. The front of the car was slightly dented and scratched but it was the wheels that concerned me more. The driver's side front wheel was pointing slightly one way while the passenger wheel was pointing slightly one way too – the other way. I had twenty miles to go and I slowly kangarooed the car home to Hemel Hempstead. God knows what I was going to say to Anne in the morning! Luckily, she was fast asleep as I cautiously climbed into bed next to her – please don't wake up. It was 8am on the Saturday morning when we were woken by a ringing on our doorbell. I threw on my dressing gown and opened the door to two police officers.

"Morning sir, sorry to get you up early on a Saturday morning. Are you the owner of 1100 Austin reg number blah, blah, blah?"

"Yes," I said. "My wife's car."

I suddenly realised the car was not where I had parked it last night and I'd forgotten the crook lock!

"Well, it seems that your car was stolen last night, but they didn't drive far, just a couple of miles and they left it across somebody's drive. Most probably youngsters a little too lazy to walk home. Can you come with us to identify the car and take it home?"

"Certainly, officer."

Anne was up by now and had heard most of the conversation. I arrived with the police in their car and there was our 1100 still looking not too bad in the daylight.

"Yes, officer, that's our car."

"Well, sir, just before we go, could you check if everything inside and outside is OK?"

I looked inside – OK.

"Oh no! Christ, officer, look at the front of my car and these wheels are going in opposite directions!"

"OK, sir, we'll put it in the report that the car was stolen and damaged. Your insurance should take care of it immediately."

A couple of weeks later the car was back to its pretty self and they had changed the door lock too. It was some years before I confessed to Anne.

It was soon time to get serious about another van for the Kinshasas, and this time Stu and I bought a long wheelbase Transit minibus, very posh-looking in blue and white. Instead of putting seats in we were taking seats out. We were starting to collect bloody bus seats! Although the wooden partition from the old Bedford came in handy. Now those sitting in the back could see out.

Another change of drummer. Mac had joined another band called Bulldog and had teamed up with Ian Kewley from Kenny. Stu contacted Trevor Waters again and he jumped in and after a couple of rehearsals with John we had the new show ready.

Leaving day again, our house was like a mad place. The gear was loaded already, suitcases were stuffed in the minibus, and we were off. I had chosen another route this time and another ferry line. Olau Ferries went from Sheerness to Vlissingen in Holland. The cabins were better, the bar bigger and they gave me a very reasonable deal when I explained who we were (still high in the charts in Europe). It took a couple of hours to reach the Isle of Sheppey and I checked us all in and then on to the waiting area. We'd only been there a few moments when the tannoy system blurted out, "Would Steve Farr come to the ticket office urgently." I ran to the office. It could only be a problem at home – phone home immediately was the message. I called my house, and it was Lily Hall, our neighbour, who answered.

"Steve, is that you?"

"Yes, Lily, is something wrong? Are the kids OK?"

"Yes, they're fine," she said. "When you left this morning, you left your saxophone lying in the road!"

It was lucky I lived in a small cul-de-sac. She continued, "I'm looking after the girls. Anne is driving to Sheerness now with Reg (Lily's husband) with it, I hope you can wait for it."

I put the phone down. Christ, what a twat! I explained the problem to the Port Authority.

"We can only wait for just so long; if you want to wait on the quay, we'll load the minibus and the rest of the band."

When they were called the band and the bus drove onto the ship and I gave the paperwork to Stu. See ya later – I hoped. Anne and Reg came round the corner at the last minute. We had time to kiss each other, I said a grateful thanks to Reg. He had known that Anne could never drive that sort of distance alone and he immediately jumped in to ride shotgun. I had to run up the gangplank onto the ferry as they were slipping the lines to leave. Me and my saxophone found the band in the bar talking to some nuns. Stu had sorted out the cabins: they were all sharing and there was one berth ticket left for me. I would be sharing with a complete stranger, the band laughed.

"You've gotta take the rough with the smooth, Steve, it could be a nymphomaniac or it could be a homicidal maniac!"

I stayed in the bar for as long as I could then me and the sax went to the cabin. I crept in very quietly. My roommate was already in bed, snoring slightly, and he had his curtain across his bed for extra privacy. It was then that

I noticed a black crash helmet, black leather jeans, black biker's jacket – oh Christ, I'm with a Hell's Angel! I silently put myself to bed and slept badly until about 6am. We had an early breakfast planned and we were getting kicked off the ship around 7:45am. I slid out of bed and put my clothes on. Just then the lights went on and there was a message that went through the ship that breakfast was being served. A head poked out of the Hell's Angel bunk. He was bald, with a shiny suntanned head and I noticed two gold earrings.

"Oooh hello," he said, "that's a bright shirt! My name's Julian, what's yours?"

If he had said that last night I wouldn't have slept a wink.

"Hi," I said, "I'm Steve and I'm off to meet my mates for breakfast. Bye." I was out of there, pronto. I wouldn't have gone back if I had even forgotten my sax; thank God I hadn't.

It was summertime and now we could see Germany and the countryside properly. The shows were going really well, and at one gig an older woman came in with a younger girl and said she would like to take us for a drink. Four of us accompanied her and her young friend to a bar and then later to her flat. We were joking and laughing and drinking and then she said, without laughing, "Right, listen to me. Tonight, I will be with Kelly. Stuart, you will be with Anna (the friend). Steve and Trevor, you will go home now."

So much for sweet talk! Trevor and I walked home, moaning can't wait to see what happened to the boys, we'll find out tomorrow in the van. We got luckier when a group of girls said they wanted to come back to the hotel for a drink a few days later. We piled everybody into the minibus and had gone only a few hundred yards when a police car stopped us.

"Have you been drinking?" one cop said to Bill, who was in the driving seat.

"Not yet, laddie," answered 'Rob Roy'. "We plan to."

"You must not drink and drive even with one beer. Do you have your licence and papers?"

Bill's licence was back at the hotel.

"Right, you will come with us to ze hotel, ze bus will follow us." He pointed to Trevor. "You will drive ze bus, there are too many people in zis bus, four must get out and walk."

Mum comes to see me for the first time at the Royal Hospital School. The new uniform was the business!

Dad's evening job fighting the fire during the Blitz of London 1939. He's leaning on the big fire engine. His own one was a London taxi.

Rescued and pulled out of the water by the Australians. Rather than risk the perilous vougue back to Britain Dad and his mates accept positions in the Royal Australian Navy, at four times the wage of a British seaman.

The Volskys in full concert mode.

Ashley Ward Delegation. L to R Stewart Blanmdamer,I an Gabriel, Paul Green Jeff Stow, Mick Attwood and Stevie Farr.

Curly

Management:	Ken Hollway
	Mauldens Cottage, Venus Hill, Bovingdon, Herts.
	Telephone: Hemel Hempstead (04421 833215
Bookings:	01 643 0115

1973 NME and Melody MAKER outright winners CURLY, L to R Stewart blandamer, Alan Wicket, Kelly Cantlon, Stevie Farr and Bill Roberts.

The Dogs... Loff (black), Bert (Blonde).

Johnny Wakelin.

The Q-Tips.
L to R Stewart Blandamer, Barry Watts, Garth Wattroy, Tony Hughes, Paul Young,
Mickey Pearl, Ian Kewley, Stevie Farr.

The Q-tips Christmas Card.

The Adam Ant Band.

Adam Ant Toga party (somewhere in America!).

Over 100,000 miles on this bus! with Adam.

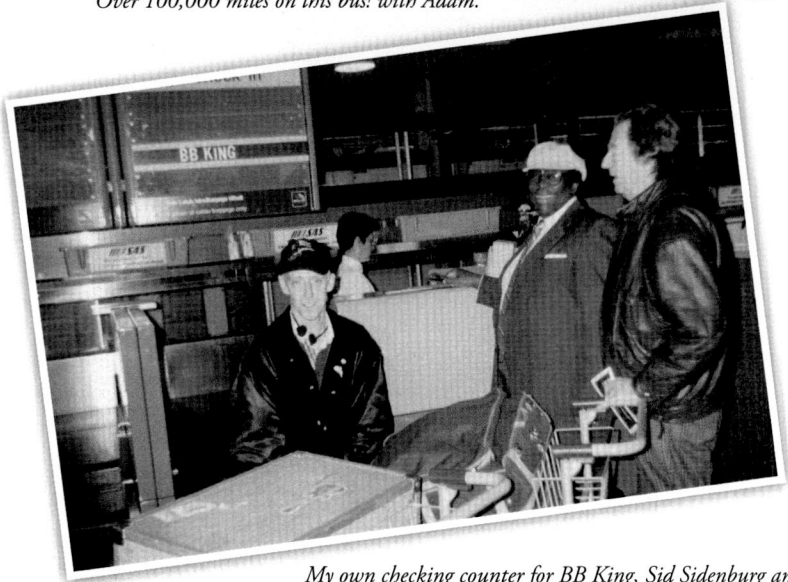

My own checking counter for BB King, Sid Sidenburg and me.

BB and his girlfreind with his man Joe on board our private yacht (for the day).

*Me with Chuck Berry and his bass
Player Jim Marsala.*

*Me introducing Chuck Barry to a
Swedish audience.*

*Stevie with Flo Foster (security)
and Jim Davidson.*

*Jim, Doing his bit with the British
Army in Macedonia.*

The Sovereign Sixties Orchestra.

The Paul MacCartney brass section Wacking it out for the Blues Brothers Other Brothers!

Brothers of Jake and Elwood Blues, Paul Cox and Al McClean.

My daughters Joanna and Zoe on our first Skiing trip!

My Lovely Sue.

Burns Night... Dave Lee, Stevie Farr amd Half Scottish Jim Davidson.

Guess who? Me, Stu, Jake and Tom were selected to get out of the van. It was several miles to the hotel in town. The police car moved off slowly ahead. Immediately Stu had a wonderful idea.

"Quick, we can stand on the back of the bumper, hang on to the roof ledge and get down so the police can't see us."

So we jumped on. It was a bit crowded, but it was better than walking. It was a wonder that none of us fell off as we were laughing so much. Just before we reached the hotel, the four of us, now Cinderella's rear coachmen, jumped off the van and walked into the hotel.

"How did you get here so quickly?" asked Bill.

"Oh, we got a lift," answered Stu.

The headlining act on this tour was Slick, a young Scottish teenie band that was very fast coming up behind the Bay City Rollers. The leader of the band was a young guy, Midge Ure, who had a full head of thick hair and the German girls screamed as he made a thing of combing it between songs. They had a pair of roadies who were both tall as they were wide. The opening act was a German folk artist, a household name in his country, Frank Zander. He was followed by Boney M, another German act, then it was us, then Slick, on stage. We got on well with these two Glaswegians, whereas they had no time for the Germans. Frank Zander insisted they sweep the stage before he went on; Boney M said nothing but looked daggers at the boys if they had forgotten anything.

One morning Stu and I were having breakfast. Sitting at the next table were the two Scots, with Frank Zander seated across the other side of the restaurant. One of the Glaswegians, in a low voice, said, "There's that Zander bastard."

"Oh, aye," replied the other, "let's get him."

Frank was sitting, reading his newspaper, smoking a dreadful-smelling pipe, quite oblivious to anyone else in the breakfast room. One of the boys loaded the end of his knife with a great big splodge of red jam, aimed carefully and catapulted it across the room. For the roadies it was the perfect shot, for Frank it was disastrous – the jam landed on his forehead just above his eyes. The Scots didn't even look up. Frank Zander stormed out of the restaurant shouting German swear words at the top of his voice.

If he'd looked at Stu and me, he would have seen us choking on our food; laughing and eating didn't mix well.

Another tour finished. We had another small UK tour to look forward to. It was on that tour that it just wasn't the same; the shocking part for John was that hardly anybody came to see us. "In Zaire" was a song in the past, somebody said. Disappointed, John pulled the plug on the tour, and we all went our separate ways.

With nothing else in the pipeline, I sometimes helped Stu with his recordings. I even tried to write songs myself. Stu recorded them in his small studio, but I was no songwriter, not complete songs anyway. On the home front, my eldest sister Jan and her husband John were returning to the UK from Mexico, having been there a few years. They brought the stray dog they had found in the grounds of their large house and now Suki was spending six months in quarantine at Heathrow. They had another large house to move into in Pangbourne, near Reading. Mum had been very busy redecorating the cottage she lived in, and she and Mike sold it, making a handsome profit. Mum decided to move nearer to Jan and Merry in the Reading area. Mike, my brother, was well into submarines now and was soon to take command of his first nuclear sub. At the time Britain only had four and he was going to be skipper of one of them. He was promoted to Commander, full title: Commander Michael Farr RN.

Johnny Wakelin Tour.

148

Seventeen

A GREAT NEW SURPRISE, THE Q-TIPS ARE BORN

It was back on the tools for me with Steve Turner, my new plumbing partner, busy as ever and always keen to do a good job. I hadn't been in long from working on this night in October when Stu called me and asked if I would like to play on a session tonight. Of course, I was up for it, so after a hurried dinner I grabbed the baritone sax and waited for Stu to collect me as we were going in his car. On the way into London, he explained that it wasn't a paid session, as I had thought. We had been invited to play with a view of forming a new soul band. A band from Luton called the Street Band had been formed two years earlier playing jazz rock, and their singer was a guy called Paul Young. They had a recording deal with Logo Records and had released a single called "Hold on Five Years". When it came to recording the B side they had nothing prepared, so ended up making something up on the studio floor, a throwaway song called "Toast", which Paul didn't sing at all but just spoke the lyrics about making a piece of toast. When Kenny Everett put the record on the turntable at the BBC during his show the B side was played by mistake; he laughed about it, and then the phones started ringing, requesting that the song be played again, and again. During this the band were on a short tour of the West Country. It was the manager who called them back to London to do Top of The Pops. It was then they found out, to their dismay, that "Toast" was moving up the charts. After that they were booked as a funny band, a bit like the Barron Knights, and the audience didn't like the jazz rock they were getting. This led to the band splitting up and Paul getting nodes on his vocal cords, under medical orders to rest his voice for six months if he wanted to keep any singing voice at all. Well now the six months were up and Paul was ready to go again and wanted to sing some soul.

We turned up at this house in Southgate, the house Paul shared with some friends, and I immediately recognised Tony Hughes, my trumpet player from Steve Farr and the Sobs – he was the reason Stu and I were there. Tony was best mates with Paul. Micky Pearl was on bass and John Gifford was on guitar from The Street Band. Baz Watts was the new drummer and he'd come with Dave Lathwell, another guitarist; I was on baritone sax, Stu was on alto, and Tony was on trumpet. On tenor sax was Richard Blanchard, a face I knew. He had gone to America with Bill Roberts to play with Russ Ballard. He didn't stay long though, as he had a very successful photography business. Rehearsals followed quickly and I could tell that this band was going to be something special. The soul tunes Paul was picking to sing were kicking and he was singing like his life depended on it – God he was hungry!

Within just a few weeks we were ready to play our first gig. It was November 18th,1979, my birthday, and we played at a pub in Harrow. From the moment we started, we had the entire audience, and we couldn't have done better. When I got home late that night, I couldn't help waking Anne and telling her what a great band this was going to be.

A week later Micky took a call. Could we support The Knack – remember "My Sharona" – at the Dominion Theatre? Again, we had them on their feet, The Knack boys watching us from the wings, grinning. Then something bizarre happened. John Gifford, who did much of the chatting to the crowd, sat on the front of the stage and talked to the audience. What was he doing? Let's get up, let's get kicking. He shouted, "What time is it?"

"Quarter to nine," someone shouted back.

"No. What time is it?"

Another answer from the audience. This was going on for too long. Just then John said, "No, it's time for "The Midnight Hour"."

Oh Jesus, we couldn't be subjected to that every night from now on! John was on borrowed time.

One of our favourite pubs was The Horn of Plenty in St. Albans and it was run by Vinnie Jones' mum. Previously, I had a job rebuilding a boiler on site at a house in Abbots Langley; the house was owned by John and Wendy Moore, and they had a very successful metal engineering business. John also ran the local football team and brought on young talent. One such kid staying at John's house was Vinnie Jones, a promising player who hated getting up in the mornings, especially when I had to turf him out of his bed as his room had the loft ladder in it and I had to get in there with my ladders. He, of course, became a great professional and an actor, too. I remember seeing him years later; he didn't recognise me, and I said nothing.

After one night at The Horn a familiar face came up onto the stage to speak to me and Stu. It was Ian Kewley, the keyboard player with Kenny on those Mal Zondoc tours in Germany. It was good to see him again. He thought the band was fabulous and asked Stu to put in a word to Paul, as he was desperate to play some good soul. He had a C3 Hammond organ and electric piano. We tried him out at a rehearsal and Paul loved it. So, Ian joined the band and Dave Lathwell left, although had we put it to the vote then it would have been John Gifford who went; he was trying to be too controlling and it wasn't long before he and Ian were clashing over musical arrangements. The name of the band had quickly been decided just before the first gig in November. There was a packet of Q-Tips lying on the table – everybody laughed at the suggestion, but everybody fell in love with the name. We also had a manager, Jed, a young guy from Manchester who was head booker and social sec at Sheffield University. He offered his services after booking us and it seemed he had only been in the job a few minutes when we had our first record deal, singles followed by an album.

News was travelling fast; the Q-Tips were fast becoming the hot band to see, not only in London but all over the UK. The work was flooding in. After a small, crowded gig at Ronnie Scott's in London, the two sound technicians who operated the hired sound system wanted to become our sound crew. They wanted to join us. Welcome Alan Lynch and Jimmy Madden. Two mates of Paul's, Keith Mcrombie and Big Youth (a big fella) came in as our backline roadies, and we loved them all. We were becoming more than just a band – we were a family. A song called "S.Y.S.L.J.F.M", which was Save Your Sweet Love Just For Me, was our first single on Chrysalis Records. DJs on Radio 1 loved it and our audiences loved it but it didn't make the Top Ten, reaching the higher end of the song charts. We were filling halls to capacity, constantly touring.

The album was planned for spring 1980 and booked into Island Studios. We just got started and it was decided that John Gifford had to go. He was replaced by Garth Watt-Roy, a great guitarist and a great character with a great sense of humour. He came from a string of well-known bands and his brother, Norman, was the bass player in The Blockheads. Later that year we were to borrow Norman for a few gigs to cover for Micky after his mysterious accident. It was important that we looked good on stage, so we were taken to Johnsons, a trendy shop on the King's Road, Chelsea, to buy new stage suits, dark blue mohair – we looked the business! Later on, we bought red suits; why we did that I'll never know. As the gigs were getting larger, we needed a tour manager, a guy who told us what time to get out of bed and what time the minibus was leaving and all bits and pieces like that. So Alan J Morris from Newcastle came, AJ for short. He seemed to fit in quickly and did his job well.

On one occasion at the Marquee in London for some reason there was a snake dancer on stage before us and AJ was watching with us from the side of the stage. When she'd had enough of this 12-foot python she'd hooked around her neck she beckoned to us to carry the huge snake back to its box. Bugger that! We were back-pedalling, so as AJ was nearest to her, she wrapped the snake around his neck and a petrified tour manager stood quite still while she finished her act and then put the python in the box. With the lid shut I lifted the handles of the box to see how heavy a python was – you wouldn't want them dropping on your head in the jungle – that's all I've got to say about that!

Word was getting around that the Q-Tips were always up for a laugh, and we would get challenges from other bands. Micky Pearl was our star act, doing anything for a bet. I've never seen anybody drink a pint of beer quicker than him, not even to this day. If the bet called for him to be stripped to the waist, he had shaved his chest hair so now he had a huge flesh-coloured 'M' under his shirt; there wasn't much mighty Micky wouldn't do to uphold the Q-Tips name. Our lighting guy was an old friend, Yan Styles, the very good-looking guitarist from Kenny who had a very nasty motorbike accident and lost the use of his arm; when the hospital doctors wanted to amputate, he refused, believing that one day there would be the technology to rebuild it. It certainly didn't stop him from working and he bought a lighting rig system for our gigs which he helped erect, wire up and operate – we loved him too.

On a gig in Middlesbrough some arseholes saw Yan's lazy arm and started taking the piss. Garth saw it happening and confronted the gang. What did they want to do? Fight? Yeah! All of a sudden Garth kicked it off and we came running to help for a few minutes. The club was like a bar in cowboy land, fists and bodies flying, even Paul was in there. Without too much damage, we still did a good show. The gang was evicted, only to trash our truck and minibus outside. We loved a joke, a prank and now it seemed a fight or two, and I couldn't get enough of any of it. I sat in the last row of the seats in the minibus next to Stu and they were known as the ferret seats; my nickname was Fixit, nothing to do this time with blond hair and Jimmy Savile. If things in the hotel got a little boisterous and a room was semi-trashed or furniture broken, I was always good at fixing it with tape just so long as everything looked normal at our leaving. Jed had said that complaints had come in sometimes weeks after we had been there; at least we could deny it for a while.

We toured constantly, the music, the stage act and the band, and the bond between us getting stronger every month. Garth had fallen for Tony's sister, Melanie, and there might be a wedding on the horizon. Barry Watts, or Baz, was our drummer and also the band's photographer; he had a small Olympus Trip on a strap around his wrist almost all of the time, only taking it off when he had to sit behind the drum kit to work. He also documented everything to do with the band and ran a tape player recording almost every rehearsal. Stu, Tony and I were too busy having fun and playing pranks on the others; no wonder they painted Stu's face when he slept on the bus. I always slept with my mouth open, often waking up to old cigarette ends, pencils, and any other old crap that was in the van at the time – happy days!

We were invited to play at the BBC Studios in Maida Vale to record several songs so that the Radio 1 DJ, in this case, Dave Lee Travis, could guest us on his daytime show. We showed up and met the studio technicians, two Welsh guys who would be engineering the session. Top Radio 1 producer and the producer of Dave Lee Travis' daily two-hour show, was the very well-known Rob Belshaw. As we were setting up, Rob Belshaw walked in, collar, tie, blazer and flannels and spoke to us all. He would be leaving us in the more than capable hands of the two techs who seemed to be nice guys, and he would return later in the evening. We got to work, the rhythm tracks went down well, and the tuning and timing direction came from Paul in the control room. It was late when Mr Belshaw came in, a different Belshaw. We all knew, including the Taffy techs, where he had spent the last few hours; in the BBC bar. He sat down by the techs; it was time for the brass lines to go down on the track. We took a note from the piano to tune up. Paul talked to us through the glass via a microphone.

"Tony, you're a little sharp, Fix, you're a little flat."

"Stop, stop!" yelled Belshaw. "Just who the hell do you think you are?" gazing at Paul Young.

"I'm the singer and I'm helping them get in tune, Rob."

"What do you know about music? They most probably know twice as much as you, and if they need any direction, it will be given out and it will come from me – right?"

"OK," said Paul.

We stood for a moment in silence. I for one was thinking, and it must have been for the whole band, how we could get back at this arsehole. Brass done, Paul went in and put his vocals down. Belshaw didn't seem to be interested in that, talking to Stu about famous jazz sax players he'd worked with – thank God the session was finished. Baz popped up with the answer.

"Rob, would it be OK if you sit at the control desk while the band have a couple of photos for a memento of tonight?"

"Of course, be delighted," answered the very pissed Mr Belshaw.

He sat smiling already at Baz, as the band stood side by side behind him. Baz said, "Great, good, OK just one more."

This time the whole band dropped their trousers and pants, and the picture was taken, Rob Belshaw and the Bare Bum Band. The Welsh techs saw what was happening and ran out of the studio, so as not to be implicated, and Rob Belshaw never knew that it had been taken, well, not for a good few months anyway! The picture, somehow, did get back to the BBC. Rob Belshaw, in a rage, said that we would never be working at the BBC again.

A couple of weeks later we were invited to be the live act at the Cannes Music Festival in France. We flew into Nice the day before and settled into our hotel. What was the plan for tonight, a day off! Stu and I were rooming together; we always roomed together to keep the tour costs down. It was always Paul and Tony, Garth and Ian, Baz and Micky. The boys wanted to go clubbing, Stu and I wanted a good dinner and a quiet drink then bed. The dinner was great, and we found a quiet bar off the main street. There was the bar with a few tables and a foosball table took centre stage. Four guys were playing, the commentary and complaints about each other could be heard above the music playing. Foosball machines were in nearly every club, bar and in every university bar in the UK; we as a band were always playing the game before we played the music and we considered ourselves to be pretty good. I walked up to the table and put my money, that goes into the foosball table slot, on the side of the table; indicating that Stu and I would like to play. After a short time one of the French guys who had been playing came over to us,

"Are you English guys? Do you want to play us French?"

"Yes," I said.

"OK," he said. "Loser pays for the drinks, OK?"

"OK," I said confidently.

I'd watched him earlier, good but not that good. We played ten times; the ball was launched onto the pitch. The score, one to us, nine to the

French; we bought the drinks. Cognac was the choice. We played again, eight to them, two to us, Cognac again. Played again, seven-three to them. After seven or eight large Cognacs I was getting hot under the collar and swearing at the French. Stu, not being known to hold his drink, was even more pissed than me and kept shouting about being British. By now, the French were playing with us, and they could even make their guys head the ball into the goal – we'd had enough and left the bar.

"Ay, Steve, these must be their cars, let's dance on their roofs for a bit."

We jumped on and did a little dance and got down and I wandered up the street and then there was a call from Stu. The guys from the bar had obviously seen us roof dancing, had come out and had hold of Stu and were punching him. I raced back into the melee and immediately ran into some punches and fell on the floor; they were kicking me – I was so drunk it didn't even hurt. Just then, by luck, the boys came round the corner and calmed everything down. Stu and I were laughing as we told the story of the quiet night. Stu flopped onto his bed fully clothed and shouted he was going to be sick. I quickly grabbed the wastepaper bin and got his head off the side of the bed facing the bin. I hate being sick and the sight of him puking into the bin immediately made my stomach turn. I was standing directly over Stu, and I was sick in the bin not realising that Stu's head was in the way! In the morning when he was showering, Stu couldn't understand how he had sick on the back of his head and behind his ears – I confessed a few hours later. Neither of us could remember the night before and we thought at one point we had been fighting each other. We went down to breakfast only to meet Jed, who wanted to see both of us in his room. He told us what we had done.

"Have you got any idea of the damage you did to that guy's Porsche roof? This is going to cost us dear. To calm the fight down last night I said I would bring you two both down to the bar this morning to apologise and work out a way of paying for the damage."

We felt like two scolded schoolboys.

"Sorry," we said. "We'll go now."

We entered the empty bar, and the bartender was grinning at us. Did we want a drink? Oh for Christ's sake, no thank you! We waited an hour and the owner of the Porsche never showed. In the end the barman called him on the phone to see where he was; the conversation was light, and they were laughing. He came over to us.

"My friend is not coming, don't worry about the car, you know he has four of these Porsches."

We were very relieved.

Jed said, "You're not out of the woods yet, there'll be trouble if you can't play tonight."

Until then we hadn't thought of our black eyes and swollen lips; at least our fingers were good.

"We'll be fine tonight," I said.

A girl's make-up covered the black eyes and we managed to play OK, another good gig.

Eighteen

HERE, HAVE OUR WAGES!

On another one-off European gig we went to East Germany to do a television show. Only Stu and I had been to East Berlin before, and the boys immediately noticed the lack of streetlights and shops, and quiet city deserted roads. After the show, for which we wore the red suits for the first time, we were taken back to the hotel. The night was still young, so we asked the hotel reception if there were any clubs nearby. He looked quite puzzled.

"We don't have clubs," he said.

He left us standing in reception, only to return a moment later.

"Please come this way."

We followed him into a party, or rather, a wedding reception. The wedding party greeted us warmly when he told them we were television stars from England. There was no turning back now, so we were soon dancing with aunties, and grannies, singing their songs and drinking their drinks – all in all a great night.

Jed wasn't with us so in this instance it would be Micky who collected any money; AJ was missing for some reason, so Micky did the tour manager bit as well. At the airport we had passed through security and were sitting about drinking coffee when a young lady walked up to us and asked if we were English.

"Yes," we said.

"Would you mind if I stick with you guys? I'm alone here and I've only been here once before."

"Of course!" we said.

She was being watched by an elderly couple through the glass wall; she explained that they were her mother and father-in-law, both East Germans. Her husband had been arrested for some political protesting and was facing a big fine or jail. She had been allowed to see him; his trial was up in a few days. Pearly asked for a band meeting right there and then. We had been paid in East German Deutschmarks, a currency not worth anything in the UK; had we been staying in the country for more than a day we could have spent it on nothing, there were no real tax items for sale – toy train sets were the only good buy, I thought. We immediately decided to give the girl our wages for last night so she could pay his fine and get him home. When we explained what we had done to earn the money and handed it over to her, she ran to the gate and was allowed to have a quick conversation with her in-laws. She handed the money to them, they all burst into tears and hugged each other. Apparently, we had just given them two years' wages, enough to pay the court and fly him back; we all felt good. Pearly then stated he had held onto some of it so we could go into the bar and celebrate – another good day's work.

We were gigging almost every day and the days we weren't we tried to rehearse new material. Several of the band were now writing original songs, Stu being the most prolific, having had success earlier with "Darlin". In the rehearsal room we would start a song from scratch. Mickey and Baz would start a rhythm, Hammond organ and guitar would follow, and when we had a chord sequence, I would try to come up with a catchy brass line or two. Paul would then hum along until we had the basis of a song and he could think of a lyric. The further this exercise progressed the keener the playing got until within a few hours the song was born. We all had a share in the writing stakes. No one could fault our sold-out live act but record sales, especially the singles, were a problem – we just weren't selling enough. In 1980 after "S.Y.S.L.J.F.M." was released, we did Smokey Robinson's "Tracks of My Tears", Marvin Gaye's "Some Kinda Wonderful" and even a song Stu wrote, "A Man Can't Lose What He Don't Have", didn't ring the bell even a little bit. The album went to No. 11 and then fell away a couple of weeks after its release.

Major festival promoters were now seeing how we could get the crowd going and soon wanted us to get their audiences in the dancing mood. We opened for Bob Marley, the Average White Band, and Joe Jackson at the Crystal Palace on a beautiful day. We were to open the proceedings. The stage was erected on the side of a large pond, the pond acting as a security barrier along the front of the stage. Once again, we did wonderfully well, opening the festival, and the crowd cheered and applauded at the end of our set. We lined up along the stage to take our bow.

Tony had a very old trumpet as an emergency instrument, and he threw it high into the air so it would land into the water. People were in the pond and stayed there throughout the afternoon, somebody even found a dead duck somewhere and threw it back onto the stage; Joe Jackson was playing and was seated at the piano when it hit him on the head. He wasn't very pleased with Tony who had started it all off.

Often, when the brass wasn't playing, we would dance around the stage, and I used to launch my large baritone sax into the air and catch it in time to play the next part. We were at Hatfield University doing a Rock Goes to College TV programme and I had thrown the sax into the air during the cameraman's rehearsal and sound check. The producer said that it looked great and to keep it in. The camera would follow it up and down and you catching it.

"OK," I said. All went to plan, and I threw the saxophone high into the air, spun round, and missed the catch. I quickly picked it up. There were no bits hanging off it and tried to play it – nothing! For the last two songs I mimed playing and it was only when we had finished the show Stu and I assessed the damage; it was badly bent, no good, had to get another one and thankfully Jed helped me pay for it. A second choker for me was what the producer said when I asked him.

"Yep, I got it coming up and I got it coming down." Oh Christ!

We opened for Thin Lizzy at Milton Keynes Bowl and Squeeze in Dublin. On that occasion we weren't the first on the bill, another new young act was going to open the afternoon. They were U2, and Bono, their singer, soon had the crowd going, waving his huge Irish flag on a pole. In Belfast we supported The Undertones. We arrived at the festival site early, before the main entrances were opened for the thousands expected, as The Undertones were a Belfast band. AJ, our tour manager, was driving the bus and he was directed to drive across the field towards the backstage area where we would park. As we moved slowly over the grass Paul suddenly recognised Chris Welch, a New Musical Express journalist who had not liked our album very much.

"Let's get him," said Pearly and Garth.

AJ stopped the minibus.

"Boys, I don't think this is such a good idea."

I thought for a moment. We weren't a violent band unless provoked or losers at foosball; I didn't want to see him get hurt.

"Hang on," I said. "I've got an idea."

In my wash bag I had a small bottle of stuff that was good for toe rot or athlete's foot. When you put it on your feet it was deep purple in colour and then faded a few days later to a horrible brown.

"What if we held him down and got his pants down and I dab his cock and bollocks with the stuff? It'll come off in a week."

"OK," they said. That was the plan. "We'll hold him down, Fix, you do the dabbing."

He was fifty yards ahead of us and we slowly caught him up. AJ still wasn't happy.

"This is going to backfire, boys."

Thirty yards. "Right, I think we should take a vote on this. Jed is going to go nuts if anything goes wrong."

Twenty yards. We voted, nine in the bus and it was five to four against dabbing. We were ten yards behind him as AJ swung the bus around him. I still have that bottle of purple gunge somewhere.

By the time we got back on the ferry Garth and Stu had had a skinful at the backstage hospitality and were out for the count. We couldn't leave them in the minibus when we were crossing the Irish Sea, so we managed to get them out and back onto the seats where the passengers sat. Tony carefully shaved Garth's eyebrows off completely and he and Stu had their faces painted with swear words while they slept. The pair of them woke up an hour later but the rest of us said nothing as they joined us in the food queue in the ship's restaurant. They cursed us when they looked in the mirror and Garth was only mad at Tony for a few hours.

Next it was down to Montreux to play the Montreux Jazz Festival. Out came the red suits and the golden cardboard saxophones; the French loved them and copied the brass section's moves and sways. The highlight of that couple of days was that I met BB King in a local record shop. He was appearing the night after us and was such a great guy to talk to. I would be seeing a lot more of him a few years later. While we were jumping on and off planes on these trips, Alan and Jimmy would be driving in the seven and a half tonne truck with the backline, never complaining, so we tried to include them in all the good hotels and everything we did and were invited to.

We had just played a great gig at a college in Bath and the plan was to drive home that night to keep the cost down. It was a filthy night, and the rain was coming down in buckets. AJ was having trouble finding the M4; we had to turn around on two occasions. "Bloody Hell, AJ, get it together!" we chanted, sitting behind him. We stopped for a third time to look at the map again.

"Oh, Christ, I'm bored!" shouted one of the lads. "Anybody fancy taking me on in a wanking competition? Everybody's got to bet with money. The first to get up steam wins the lot. Anybody?"

There was always some sort of wager going on in the minibus to alleviate boredom. Most of us might prefer to sleep but finding things stuck up my nose and in my mouth when I woke up, nowadays I preferred to keep my eyes open. The challenge was met by another, and the rules were laid down. No touching of the knob until the go command was given, no lubricants or gloves to be used as props, no visual aids, normally lying around the floor of the bus. Next the betting was sorted out. We sat in a layby with the rain hammering down. Alan and Jimmy passed us; they must have recognised the minibus as they were hanging out of the window and Alan was blowing the truck horn. Their 7.5 tonne truck was painted bright orange. Betting and rules sorted, the command, "Ready, steady, go," was given. There was a lot of vocal encouragement from the rest of the band and AJ as each shouted for his champion. AJ kept looking round as he drove to see how his favourite was doing. Meanwhile, Alan and Jimmy had laughed as they passed us, blaring their horns and arses – great. A mile up the road they suddenly thought that we might well have broken down, they decided to do a three-point turn in the middle of the road and come back to see if we were OK. By now the noise in the minibus was deafening for the competition was at full pump, AJ was driving, still looking over his shoulder, seeing how his bet was doing. How he didn't see the huge orange truck in the middle of the road, I'll never know. Stu and I were sitting in the ferret seats furthest away from AJ.

Stu said to me, "We're going to hit that truck," and he called to AJ. Alan saw what might be happening and tried to steer his truck out of the way.

We hit the side of the orange truck on our driver's side and the van veered off the road and settled half turned over in a ditch. All the vocal accompaniment had now turned to an ensuing, "You bastard, AJ," and me and Stu were laughing.

"They'll never believe this police report!" Stu said.

AJ shouted, "Is everybody OK? Everybody out."

We all stood on the pavement, nobody hurt, but there was one man short. We found him round the back of the bus.

"It's not over yet!" he said as he desperately tried to finish the bet and take the kitty. We laughed so much he almost deserved it, but he didn't get it. Both vehicles could still be driven and the bus, minus front lights, was ready after we had been pulled out of the ditch. Alan and Jimmy couldn't believe the pre-crash story and the hire company boss, by now a friend of ours, was told a couple of years later. I hope he laughed.

Nineteen

THE WHO AND PAUL MCCARTNEY. IT DOESN'T GET BETTER!

My favourite tour was the 1981 English tour with The Who. They welcomed us when we met for the first time, and we played well. When they first formed, The Who liked to play soul and Tamla tunes. I first fell in love with the band in 1964 when "I Can't Explain" went into the charts and I waited for weeks for the first album, My Generation, to be released. I really looked forward to the tour and it didn't disappoint. On the last night we joined The Who during their last encore on stage and we hoped to have a good drink with them when we got back to the hotel. At the bar there was only John Entwistle, the bass player, and the tour manager. We all knew about the wild parties The Who had after their tours, and we all went down into the bar hoping for a lively night.

"I'll get things started," said Stu and he climbed up and swung on a chandelier.

"No, you won't," said the tour manager. "No one's coming. So, I suggest you go to bed now."

So much for the lively night. We sat having a drink and somebody called us all to come quickly. We ran to the hotel entrance, where Micky Pearl was crawling in. Somebody said he was hit by a car that didn't stop, others said it could have been a bus. An ambulance was called, and we waited for the verdict. Broken jaw, lost six teeth, broken right wrist, right leg and hip crunched and extensively damaged, black and blue ribs right and left side – he was going to be out of playing for some time.

Garth's brother played with us for a while as Ian Dury and The Blockheads weren't very busy. Micky insisted on coming to the gigs in plaster cast, and bandages and crutches – a true Q-Tipper.

The year was up on the recording contract, and we hadn't managed to have that all-important hit single. Chrysalis Records were reluctant to pay us another huge amount of money for the second year. We were all disappointed and the boat was rocking very slightly. However, still gigging like crazy there was another occasion to look forward to, Garth's wedding to Melanie, Tony's sister. Just prior to that Jed and Micky had been looking around trying to get us another deal. Harry Barter of Rewind Records offered a single and album deal without much money upfront. They accepted the deal and Micky, knowing that we would all be together at the wedding, brought the contract to be signed by each of us. With the service over he called a band meeting at the reception hall. We sat in an anteroom while Micky explained the deal. Before he could finish, the door burst open and Melanie, in full bridal kit, and June, Tony's mother, steamed in and gave everybody a bollocking for having a meeting at her reception. Garth should have been outside welcoming guests, and Tony got it right in the neck from his mum. She loved us really, though. We signed throughout the evening and got back to the job of partying at the reception.

Our last single with Chrysalis was "Stay the Way You Are" and Paul hated it. I think from that time on it wasn't long before we parted company. Paul and Jed were looking for a solo deal for Paul; there had been some interest when the word went out that we were out of contract. From the start there was no contract between us and Jed. He had become our manager on a handshake, so secretly trying to get Paul away on a solo deal was, to us, unethical but there was nothing we could do about it. When we formed the Q-Tips we were a partnership which didn't, again, include Jed. It was at this time that Stu left the band to follow his own writing career, but when we got the news that we had a VAT bill for £30,000, he offered to come back and play in the VAT Attack tour. We saw a couple of tenor sax players to replace Stu and settled on Nicky Payne, tall, blond, with a cracking sense of humour. He was going to be ideal for this forthcoming album and his playing gave the band a lift when we needed it most. The new album was going to be called Live at Last and it was recorded at the Rock City, Nottingham, over a couple of nights. Overdubs were taken care of at Don Larkin's studio in Luton.

Within a few months it was clear that Paul was going, and Ian, on keyboards, said he was going with him and that meant the end was clearly in sight. Plans were made that a couple of nights at The Venue in London would be our last together and we all wondered what to do next.

We didn't have to wait long. Micky called me.

"You lucky bastards!" he yelled down the phone "Paul McCartney wants the Q-Tips horns for a few weeks to play on his short film video to accompany his new single "Take It Away". Be at Elstree Studios next Monday."

He had wanted the four of us, so Stu hurriedly came back into it and got on famously with Nicky. Nick had a basement flat in Camden Town and part of it was a music rehearsal room. We'd learnt the brass parts to the song just by listening and picking out each part on the piano. We turned up at the studios, were given breakfast rolls and coffee and as soon as Paul and Linda McCartney arrived, we were introduced to them and the other members of the band. They were Ringo Starr and Steve Gadd, from Paul Simon's band on drums. Linda was playing keyboards alongside George Martin, and Eric Stewart from 10CC was on guitar. Paul, of course, was on bass, and the Q-Tips horns made up the band of nine. We were told the storyline of the film. Paul is a young writer and he is playing in his bedroom; his mum and dad don't like the noise much. He sends his music to a manager, in this case John Hurt, who likes what he hears. In the recording studio we make our first appearance, playing the tune, and finally the song, that is a hit, and we are all together playing a concert something like the Hollywood Bowl. The film fades with us all having fun, chatting up girls at an after-show party (no acting skills needed there then!). The floor manager showed us to our dressing room.

"You'll not be needed today, lads. But we will be collecting you for lunch. If you need anything before that just ask and walk into catering."

We were being paid by the hour for nothing, we couldn't believe it. Later that morning we were called to lunch; the band were sitting at one huge table and Tony, Stu, Nick and I were placed directly opposite Paul, Linda, Ringo and his wife, Barbara. I ran to the toilets only to find Tony in there. I had been plumbing at the weekend and Tony had been racing his go-kart, both of us had grubby, stained hands. Luckily, we had run into the crew toilets and there was a proper hand cleaner there on the wall, so the embarrassment was averted. Paul and Linda were vegetarians and ordered eggs and chips. We had the chef come to us in his big white hat and offer us all sorts of meats and lovely veg, followed by desserts no one could even dream about. The conversation was a little stunted so I thought I would throw in a clean joke or a story. That seemed to do the trick and from there on everything was fine. Then back to the dressing room to be measured for the clothes that the powers that be wanted us to look like. The test cricket was on the television. Nick was a big fan and wondered how much he'd earned that afternoon watching the cricket. We had a few days of this so sometimes I crept down to get a cup of tea and watch the filming being rehearsed and filmed over and over again, changing angles, lightings, until they were satisfied.

At the end of the first week, we were allowed to get our instruments out and go down onto the set. The scene was an old recording studio, and we were put in our places and lit. Paul said that the music would come through the monitors, and we could look as though we were playing. Nick said we knew the parts and would play along.

"Oh yeah, let's see then," said Ringo, thinking we were some extras brought in just to hold the instruments.

The drummers were tapping lightly to the tracks, Paul and Eric were playing along, we hit the track perfectly in time and real tight.

At the end of it, Ringo said, "Sorry," thinking we were just extras, and Paul said what a great sound we had. Later that day we put on the sixties clothes and filmed the scene for real.

A couple of years before I had had the idea to write a book called Tales from the Transit. From the early seventies, up-and-coming bands always bought a double wheeled Ford Transit van for their equipment; there was almost always room for the band members sitting in old aircraft seats or bus seats behind the driver. Tales from the Transit was to be a collection of stories of the humorous things that happened on the way to and from gigs. One afternoon, I sat with Paul, and we had a chat over a cup of tea. He tried to remember any early Beatles tales from the Transit. When they first started before the Transit time they travelled in an old van with no real seats, just boxes and small amps. John had sat on a battery. Across the back of his jeans was a long zip and the zip had shorted out the battery and started to fill the van with smoke. I had collected stories from The Who, Argent, Chas 'n' Dave, The Barron Knights, Colin Blunstone, and many more, but the book was never finished – who knows, perhaps one day.

During the time of the filming, it was Paul's 40th birthday and we had a small gathering in his artist's caravan parked next to the studio. He and Linda handed out cakes and drinks and explained to us, the band, that the last scene of the song is the hit, and we are going to be playing a concert. For the previous two weeks carpenters and plasterers had been constructing a stage like the Hollywood Bowl. What was going to happen was that eight hundred people from the fan club were coming down and because the floor was going to be chromed they would only be let in at the last minute. They would have been waiting hours for the chance to be in the video in the studio next door so would it be OK if we played some live stuff for them before we film Take It Away. I thought it was a great idea.

Nick asked, "What do you want to play?"

"Just some good old rock 'n' roll," answered Paul.

We made a note of the songs Paul wanted to do and the keys were given to us by George Martin. Upstairs in our room we worked out several changing rock 'n' roll riffs, and just to be that little bit cocky, some brass section moves. The Q-Tips had been known for some slick dance steps. For the concert we were dressed in naval dress uniforms, and the songs Paul had chosen went down great with the fans. Paul thanked everybody for taking the time to come and would sign autographs and have pictures taken for those who wanted them. We slipped away upstairs to wait for the after-show party rehearsals and the filming. When we were all done, we said our goodbyes and thank-yous for the opportunity to make our music CVs that much stronger. I wished it could have gone on for longer. Paul was the sort who would have made a great mate and a few years later I was to run into George Martin backstage at the Royal Albert Hall on an enormous tribute to Johnny Dankworth and Cleo Laine. Just before George was introduced to play a few tunes with the jazz couple, waiting in the wings, he looked at me with that 'where do I know you from' look.

"Hello, George," I said. "You remember me? You played in one of my bands a few years back."

"Did I?" he replied. "How did I do?"

"Just OK," I said and then burst into laughter and explained who I was.

"Oh, I remember now," laughed George. "You brass boys did more than OK that day."

"Thank you, George," I said gratefully.

Twenty

THE THRILL OF A LIFETIME, JOINING ADAM ANT!

The gig gods were looking down on us again; thankfully, it was just a couple of weeks after Paul's filming that the phone rang again. This time it was Adam Ant who wanted us to join his band, and he was very keen to crack America. He and his Ants were already huge in the UK and now Adam was forming a new band. I was over the moon that he had chosen us. This time it was the three of us, Stu, Tony and me. Nick already had loads of work, eventually teaming up with Bill Wyman of The Rolling Stones fame to form Bill Wyman and the Rhythm Kings. Tony had had a short gig with Nick with Boy George and Culture Club. The three of us went to meet Adam for lunch at a restaurant just off the Bayswater Road in London. He walked in with another, a coloured bloke who was going to be playing bass. After some polite conversation the jokes started flowing, Adam having nearly as many in his joke arsenal as me. Somehow the conversation got onto drugs.

"Yeah, man," the bass player said, "they have some great drugs available in the US. If you're into that kind of thing, you can have a great tour."

Adam said calmly, "I don't drink, I don't smoke and there will be no drugs around my band or crew." We never saw that bass player bloke again.

At the first rehearsal we met Don Murfitt, Adam's manager, and the rest of the band. On drums was Bogdan Wiczling from Poland, and Chris

Constantinou was the new bass player, whose parents had come from Greece and had a large restaurant in Plymouth. Adam's guitarist from the Ants would be playing but first Adam said he had to lose some weight. He was Marco Pirroni, with Italian parents who had a restaurant in central London. Jake Burns was the guitarist from Scotland. Our backline techs were Stuart Monks and David Fee. Stuart would be taking care primarily of Adam's guitars and Davey Fee was a drum tech. He didn't like us boys much, saying our instruments were like bits of brass pipe with holes in. He was a broad Scot so he took the piss; we didn't care, we couldn't understand a word he was saying, his accent was that strong.

We would rehearse in the mornings and then travel half a mile to a nice little café that Adam knew for lunch. One day, during that first week, we bundled into Tony's car, a souped-up Ford Capri, and he offered Davey a ride with us.

"Aww, I'm going with the stars," he said. Approaching the café, the road was quiet. Tony accelerated to great speed then braked hard, doing a 180 controlled spin, and came to a stop expertly outside the café. Davey Fee got out of the car a shaking mess and we didn't hear from him much again.

Adam also wanted a second drummer, so we suggested Baz, who came down the next day. He and Bogdan became good friends and drummed perfectly together. Adam was over the moon.

Before we started the small UK tour later that year, Adam gave us a few ground rules.

"I don't mind if you want to smoke on the band bus but please don't do it next to me. No booze on the bus, and no booze before the show. I want you stone cold sober on stage when we play, there'll be a lot to think about." Fair enough. "Oh, and absolutely no drugs! If I think you are doing drugs, I think I will just give you your plane ticket home. OK?" It was fine for us because we didn't take drugs anyway. To me marijuana smelled like shit; no wonder it's called that, never again. Tony and Stu weren't even cigarette smokers, neither was Baz.

"Only, on the drink thing," Adam went on, "seeing as there will be no booze in the dressing room I will put on the rider anything you'd like to drink, and it will be delivered to the hotel for you after the show, our tour manager will see to that."

We would be meeting Stan Tippins later. Stan had a great tour manager CV; early on he'd been with Mott the Hoople and not only was he the tour manager but offstage singer and helped the band with their harmonies. His other act besides Adam was The Pretenders with Chrissie Hynde. During the rehearsal week we often went down to Primrose Hill to meet Rowena Luke-King, great at making Adam's off-the-wall fashion ideas come to life, and Adam also presented us with a pair of boxing boots each in red. He also gave us a recording Sony Walkman for those long periods on planes and in the bus. All of us would be in the bus together, Adam only taking flights with Stan when they had personal appearances and TV interviews. The bus would go on to the next city, sometimes hundreds of miles away, and we, the band, would be left alone.

The first gig for us was at the London Astoria Theatre at Tottenham Court Road, the world-famous music venue right in the heart of London. When the tour dates were announced the gigs sold out in hours. Stan had made arrangements that we would all meet at a hotel in Wembley and then be taken to the venue stage door in the afternoon in large black limos. "There's no space to park the bus there, the roads are too narrow. All wives and girlfriends will be at the hotel, of course, and would have tickets but would have to make their own way there and their own way back after the show."

We sound-checked at the venue and just before we were to go on stage Adam came down to the dressing room in his stage costume and fabulous make-up. Earlier that day he had given us all US-style military dog tags which had our names and S.F.C.T punched into them (Spit Fire, Crap Thunder). Another gift that day were pale blue lightweight cagoules which folded down to the size of a Smartie box; the Ant logo was printed on the breast.

Nothing could have prepared me for that first show in London. Through the thick black stage curtains, we could hear the sell-out crowd yelling, and when the auditorium lights went down the screaming and yelling got louder and louder. The drummers started perfectly in unison as the curtain peeled away, the noise was indescribable. We brass boys moved forward to play and at that point I could not hear a note I was playing, not even inside my head. We signalled for more monitors, but it didn't help much. The stage set was a raised stage across the back on which the two drummers were side by side with a walkway between them with steps down to the actual stage. Adam made his entrance walking between Bogdan and Baz to deafening applause. Two hours of the greatest fun I have ever had in my life, I thought, and it was all over too soon. We had a full tour crew on stage with us. There was a guy who took our saxophones from us as we sped past, as per Stan's instructions, to the waiting vehicles. Adam was out of the door in a flash and was gone and a few moments later we were ready to go, the limousines lining up outside.

By now, though, Adam's adoring fans were round the stage door and round the cars; security held them away as we ran to get inside. Once we were in, moving off was a problem with so many kids around the limos in the narrow street backstage. They were shouting through the glass and beating on the roof, the noise almost as loud as if they were still in the theatre. Out on the main street, Tottenham Court Road, we were able to get away properly to Wembley, where we had family, friends and clothes waiting. It was only then that we could talk excitedly about the show, all of us being completely knocked back by the volume of the fans. Once changed into civvies we had a word with Adam, who was pleased that the show had gone so well. Did we need another rehearsal before the next show in Brighton? I hoped we would.

It was important that the brass section over to Adam's far right could hear his voice and each other, so I asked for a side speaker to be put just off stage, pointing directly at us, that would solve the screaming fan problem – it did.

The next gig was at the Brighton Centre. We met in London to board the bus, saying goodbye to families for the small UK tour, a warm-up for the American shows at the end of the year. I was excited about everything and first it was the tour bus – so this is what they look like! Fabulous, TV, coffee and tea machines, fridge for cold drinks, bunks. I loved them, not knowing at that stage of my career just how much time I was going to be spending with them, they always gave me a great night's sleep too. The daily routine was quite simple: travel after breakfast, arrive in the city early afternoon and check in to our hotel rooms. Then down to the venue where Adam would like a full sound check with the band, and afterwards he would discuss lighting with Peter Clarke, our lighting director. Peter was an Irishman and owner of his enormous rock 'n' roll lighting company, Supermick Lights. A tall, handsome man, he always came to the show in a suit and a tie, ready to charm the pants off the ladies with his smooth Irish accent and humour. Another person of note on the tour was Dave Whiting, Adam's personal dresser. They were great friends, and it was easy to see why. Dave was a short guy with especially short hair, and a thin pencil, spiv-like moustache; great dancer, great company, great sense of humour. When he wasn't touring, he was a professional costumier specialising in military uniforms, he was in great demand on film sets. There weren't many people who could dress an actor in a German Corporal Second Class Uniform with the right head gear; Dave could do that, or so he said, so he became Corporal Whiting to us, and the name stuck after all the years we spent with Adam. On the road, with his luggage he brought several props which he would wear occasionally: a large black SS-type German leather greatcoat with matching eye patch, and a large wooden box that had a whole host of miniature military medals. He said he would explain the purpose of them later.

After the sound check we ate. Fifteen or twenty minutes before showtime we would all arrive stage-side, suited and booted, we brass boys tuning up and taking any extra notes from Adam. We would then huddle and do a war chant before we walked to the stage. Brighton, another cracking show, and we raced back to the Grand Hotel, where Stu and I were thankfully sharing a room. Talking and laughing about the show I had a small disaster; as I pulled up my jeans zip, I zipped my manhood up to my jeans, my bellend and half a bollock looking very forlorn. The pain was excruciating. There was only one thing for it, Stu had to get me out of it. It took a good twenty minutes, but my best mate stepped up and did a great job. However, my little winkle wasn't all that happy, looking like it had just been run over by an even smaller motorbike. I was rather hoping that when the pain had gone the swelling might have stayed, it didn't.

That same night Cha Burns, Adam's guitarist, broke his wrist. He was being stupid, most probably having had too much to drink after the show, when he wanted to read the plaque under a large picture at the hotel. It was high up so he pulled a small table to the picture and put a chair on it so he could reach the height of the plaque. Got up there OK, read the plaque, turned to dismount and fell. Adam was not amused, and Marco hadn't planned on returning so soon. After treatment Cha was fitted with a wrist brace which enabled him to play (albeit painfully) and he managed to continue. Had he not, Adam would have replaced him for the up-and-coming US tour, and we certainly didn't want that. Marco did come down to help out, if but briefly.

We finished the small UK warm-up tour and with Christmas now looming we met at Heathrow to fly to New York. This was my first time, and I couldn't wait. We arrived in the evening and met Adam; he was not pleased as there weren't enough cars to take us to the hotel, what hotel? We had been double-booked and Stan made very rushed arrangements to get a roof over our heads. It didn't matter to us where we stayed for the first night, but it was important that Adam had somewhere decent to stay. Though Stan, like the professional he was, got it sorted for the band.

Leaving us and going off with Adam, that was his job; we were all grown-ups, and we could take care of ourselves. It was late when we got into our small shabby hotel rooms and I went straight to sleep, eager to get up early in the morning to witness New York waking up. Breakfast was at The Star and was a must and we went there every time we were in New York. Around lunchtime we were moved to our Holiday Inn hotel in downtown Manhattan, a hotel a lot bigger and better than the Holiday Inn hotels in the UK.

As our first gig was in New Jersey we met the bus earlier than usual. The band bus was even bigger and grander than the English equivalent. Our driver was a black giant called Mack, who we warmed to straightaway; he was going to be with us for the whole tour. Again, in New Jersey, we had a hearing problem. The gig was a large dance club, packed out, and the kids were very close to us on a small stage. We stormed it and got back on the bus happy but tired. Adam was pleased it had gone so well. Cha was mended now and gave it everything on guitar. It was a small tour and by the end of it we were all happy that the boss was happy, getting larger crowds and larger venues. So, it was home for Christmas and soon after New Year we were back on the Pan Am flight to Orlando, the first gig of the '83 tour. About a week or so after, another disaster.

Adam would dance around the stage and every now and then do a high hop jump on the spot which the girls loved and screamed every time he did it. In Cleveland the gig was storming along as Adam did the high jump; next thing he was on the floor crawling to the drum riser. Stan was at his side in an instant, cradled him up and got him off the stage, as we, as a band, played to the end of the number and then left the stage too. Adam was hurt, the crowd cheering at first, then chanting, wanting the rest of the show. The backstage doctor told Adam he had shattered his knee, then Adam told the doctor to give him a painkiller and strap the joint up, he was going back on stage. Fifteen to twenty minutes later we all took to the stage again to great applause and Adam, this time, standing quite still, finished the show. In the morning, Adam, having spent a lot of time at the local hospital, was told that the knee could be repaired with surgery and a lot of convalescing.

The tour was cancelled and after a few days hanging around Cleveland, it was decided that Adam would have the surgery in Los Angeles, and we would go home to await further instructions. Adam was determined to finish this tour, whether it be in one, two, or three months', time. He was on Cleveland television channels telling the fans it was just a small hiccup and he was definitely coming back as soon as his doctor said so. Having done the Cleveland gig, we stayed for a few days where we were in the same hotel. At the after-show party (these parties that Stan had arranged were now a huge success) we made some friends who told us where the good music bars were.

One lunchtime, I, Tony, Baz and Stuart went to a college bar for lunch, a beer and a band. There was a young kid with an equally young band playing some great rocking stuff and during the break, when we could talk to each other, Tony said this kid was soon going to be great. I agreed, Stuart didn't. So as in a Q-Tips fashion a bet was made, a magnum of champagne to the winner if he wasn't heard on the radio within the year. The band finished their set, we finished our food, and I went to the stage and said to the kid how much we had enjoyed his show. He was quite shy but opened up when I told him that we were Adam's band. He'd heard about the accident and asked if he was OK.

"By the way, mate, what's your name?"

"Bryan Adams," came the answer.

Stu was made to pay heavily to me, Tone and, of course, Baz. We still jibe him about it even when we meet up today.

Twenty-one

EATING UP THE AMERICAN MILES WITH MACK AND JERRY THE COWBOY

During those few weeks we were back in the UK the lucky gig phone rang again. It was Paul McCartney's people on the phone, asking if we could play and be in his next feature film, Give My Regards to Broad Street. We explained we would love to do it but were waiting for the call from Adam to return to America to finish the tour as soon as he was fit. As we couldn't give them dates when we would be available it was thought best that they find some other brass section – shame.

We didn't have to wait too long kicking our heels. Adam's surgery was a great success, he was having physiotherapy with a major American football club, and he was healing well. It was spring and America was warming up. We flew into Los Angeles and met Stan and Mack with the bus. We were raring to go; Adam, too, was feeling great and ready. During his time in Los Angeles, he had met Jamie Lee Curtis and they had been seeing a lot of each other. We were looking forward to the parties and Stan had planned it well; he would wander round the gig before the show with forty or so invites to a small soiree to be held at our hotel starting at 11pm. Adam and the band would love their company. Adam didn't always come down to the shindig, preferring to stay in his room getting a massage from the pretty masseuse. We took it in turns to have a party in our rooms, usually large double rooms with two double beds; one bed was put on the other, leaving room for dancing and the booze was delivered and put into the bath covered with ice. We had all chipped in at the beginning of the tour to buy a good second-hand ghetto blaster and that took care of the music. Should one get lucky at the end of the night around 2am, pairs would drift away. Some enthusiastic hotel managers would offer their pool area instead of the room and even provide snacks, enjoying the party just as much as us. On the bus the next morning we had to give an account of ourselves; anything caught on tape with our recording Walkmans carried extra points. Dave Corporal Whiting and the other band members would judge the person claiming the points. For every ten points awarded Dave would pin one of his miniature military medals on the person's chest at a ceremony that day, after sound check but before food. He who had the most medals at the end of the tour was deemed the champion bird puller; it was always Tony Hughes.

There were times when the parties didn't go quite to plan. Stan's wife had just had a baby and we were celebrating hard. There was a knock at the door, and it was the police.

"Keep the noise down."

"OK, officer," says Stan.

An hour later they were back. "Last warning! Keep the noise down. If we have to come back, we will arrest you."

"OK," said a very unsteady Stan.

An hour later somebody was leaving the party only to see the two cops thundering down the corridor. A quick warning to Stan, who jumped over the balcony straight into a rubbish skip. They ran in, demanding to know where Stan was because he was going downtown with them when they caught up with him. They demanded the party finish there and then; it was almost over anyway. They walked round for ages. Stan by this time had made himself comfortable in the skip and was snoring away. We left him there and woke him at breakfast time. He stank like he'd just spent the night in a dumpster and there wasn't time to clean him up before we left so we put him in the back of the bus and let him sleep it off until the next town.

Stan would hand out the party invitations to those girls who looked as though they were well into their twenties so there was no chance of mistaking an underage girl. In America the drinking age laws were different in almost every state and Stan had given us a sheet of state laws at the beginning of each tour. The party in Portland, Oregon was in full swing when the phone rang in the room. Stan answered it.

"Hello, is anybody here in the room called Alison Smith?"

"Yes," came the answer.

Stan's face went white just then when he put the phone down.

"Alison, you and your mates get out, now! The party's over, everybody. Thank you and goodnight."

We were puzzled. Stan said it was Alison's dad. She was fifteen years old, and he was coming with the police to get her and arrest all of us for giving a minor booze. He said he was coming in from out of town and would be about forty-five minutes. Adam was alerted and in twenty-five minutes we were all on the bus, hoping that we would be able to be out of the state before the police caught up with us. We made it. Stan certainly wasn't to blame as the girl looked well past her teens. Had we been caught the press would have had a field day.

There were parties going wrong and then there were parties that were going really wrong. Stu had left the party room to be naughty somewhere and he'd called the party room to speak to me.

"Can you come and help me? There's three of them in my room."

I was having a great time dancing in the party room, so I didn't plan on staying. Sure enough, when I got to Stu, there were three women, and they were all over him. I put my head out of the door to see if there was anyone about. Peter Clarke was right down the end of the corridor. Our lighting director was dressed in a suit and a tie and when I quickly told him of Stu's plight, he ran at full speed, ripping off his tie and jacket before he got there. I left them to it.

A week or two later Stu asked to see Baz, Tony and me. Did I remember the night of the three girls and Peter Clarke? Of course. Well one these women had taken Stu's UK address from his suitcase label and written a letter to him, not knowing it would be weeks before he would get back to the UK. Diane, Stu's wife, had seen the letter, thinking it might be important, opened it and read how much she had enjoyed the night and could they do it again, perhaps on the next tour. She told him this on the next phone call; she also told him to stay in America as she didn't want anything more to do with him. Stu was very upset and told Adam. Adam called a meeting to see if there was anything we could do to make it better; he even volunteered to speak to Diane to say it was a prank that had got out of hand, but I don't think that ever happened. Stu would just have to go home when the tour ended and face the music.

We loved going to New Orleans, as it was so different out there on the streets, different from anywhere else in the United States. It was so colourful, jazz and Orleans music everywhere; the bars always had bands playing in them when they were open. When they were closed the musicians played on the street corners. The people were really friendly, always pleased and tickled when they heard an English accent. We arrived as usual around 3pm in the city and we had gone straight to the venue for the sound check, any last rehearsal moves and, of course, dinner. Then it was back to the hotel for a couple of hours before we changed into our stage clothes and left on the bus to do the show.

I was sitting having a cup of tea in the café by the hotel reception desk when a middle-aged woman sitting by me asked if I was British. I explained what I was doing in New Orleans and she and her friend were very interested and chuckled when I pronounced words in that English way. Their accent intrigued me; when they spoke, it was just like a scene from Gone with the Wind, two such lovely southern belles. Josephine was making most of the conversation and told me she was the assistant police commissioner for Baton Rouge and she was in town in New Orleans to attend an important conference on crime. We talked about Adam's music, and she had certainly heard of it; he was big news on the Louisiana radio stations. So, I asked if she would like to come to the show with her friend, as my guest; she politely declined but said it would be nice if I could meet her in the bar afterwards, perhaps.

After the show it was the usual race to get away from the screaming audience and back to the hotel. I showered and changed into my civvies and went to meet the others, ready to get the party started. Stan had done another good job inviting mostly young ladies plus a few couples to our small soiree and we were all getting along nicely. Then I remembered the assistant police chief downstairs and hurried down to reception to see if I had missed her. I hadn't. She had changed into her civvies also and looked a million dollars. I was quite content to sit talking all evening, not wanting to go back upstairs. It was getting late, and we had certainly had a few drinks. She said in that southern accent, "Would you like to continue talking and drinking upstairs in my rather fine hotel suite?"

"Certainly," I said. A suite, eh? It was only fitting that the Louisiana Police Force treat their senior officers correctly and she was very matter of fact. Her suite didn't disappoint, and we laughed and drank for a couple more hours. I told her stories of being on the road and the games we sometimes played. I also told her of the Sony recording Walkmans we each had and how we could get our adventures to be recorded for extra points and perhaps medals from Dave Whiting. She became very interested and snuggled up to me.

"Where's your recording machine now?" she asked.

"In my room," I said.

"Go get it," she ordered softly.

By the time I returned with the Walkman in my hand she had changed again out of her civilian civvies and into silk lingerie. She snuggled up close again and told me to turn the machine on.

"Hi there, my name is Josephine and I'm from Baton Rouge, Louisiana, and I'm here with Steve from the Adam Ant Band. I'm recording this so he gets a medal on the bus in the morning. So come on, Steve, bang me sugar, bang me honey, give this southern belle some sex, baby!"

It was just about bus leaving time when I staggered out of there. As for the points, I was awarded extra for not faltering in the line of duty. I will always remember Josephine; was she really the assistant police chief of Baton Rouge? Who cares!

During that tour we did a few TV appearances. On The Dick Clark Show we appeared with Prince. He and Adam got on very well, and Tony got on very well with Prince's ex-girlfriend; her name was Vanity. Around the time of the '83 tour, Mack, our beloved bus driver, got sick and had to leave us for some time in hospital. What's worse, he had to leave his beloved bus to another driver. Jerry walked in, another big man, this time white, wearing a huge Stetson hat. Nice guy, great driver and he kept the Adam Ant tour bus looking and smelling like new.

We arrived in Des Moines for a gig and a day off. The bus was going to be parked up outside the hotel for two days. Jerry would be, as always, sleeping in his comfortable bus bunk. After the show, he had delivered us back to the hotel, and while we were getting ready for another nightly gig party, Jerry settled down in the back lounge of the bus to watch a movie before bed. The kid had put a small charge underneath the windscreen wiper, and it went off, shattering the windscreen; a few seconds later he was in the bus, picking up what he could see – a few recording Walkmans, acoustic guitar. He looked up and he was looking down the barrel of a Colt 45 pistol held by a very large Texan. He put handcuffs on the boy and tied his legs so that he couldn't move, then he got his address and jumped in a cab to the boy's house. The conversation must have gone something like this.

"I have your boy," he said. He stood facing the parents, his jacket open so they could see his pistol in the top of his jeans.

"He tried to rob my band bus. Normally I would have just slapped him around, but he broke my windscreen. In the morning I expect you to bring $600 to pay for it if you want to see the boy again."

His cowboy hat and southern drawl told them he was from the deep south, not known to be that tolerant of young black robbers. We knew nothing of this until we boarded the bus for the next town, and he'd had the new windscreen fitted. He told us what had happened two days ago.

"The parents showed up, then," I said.

"Oh yeah," said Texan Jerry.

The tour had had a break with Adam's accident, so we were now into the twelfth week, although it certainly didn't seem like it. I tried to call home every other day to speak to the kids. Towards the end of the tour, we were in California for several dates and we were invited to go into Disneyland. The people there were great to us, giving us loads of freebies which I knew Jo and Zoe would love. So the '83 tour came to an end. Adam was taking time out with Marco, his song-writing partner, to complete and record their next album but we weren't to be part of that.

When I arrived home, there was a new car on the drive, new carpets and curtains and all the girls had new wardrobes. I planned a really good holiday at the end of the summer. Just now I worried that Anne had spent all the tax money I thought I'd saved; who cares, we had an even longer tour planned with Adam next year. I'd just have to be skint then.

Towards the end of 1983 we were called into the office. Adam had earned enough money and was now a tax exile living in Los Angeles, close to and seeing more and more of Jamie Lee Curtis. Don had called us in to speak about the forthcoming tour, which would start early in January. His secretary dropped a sack of mail in front of us. "Here's your fan mail, boys." While Don was talking, she sorted all the letters into piles for us.

"Adam is away, so we will be rehearsing without him. Marco will go through the new material with you. Then two weeks before we open in Atlanta, we are sending you to Nassau in the Bahamas to rehearse with Adam at Compass Point Studios. It's Robert Plant's studio and they are re-wiring the control room. We are using the studio floor with our own monitoring system. Two of our sound crew will be there to meet us."

Oh God bless Adam; he had chosen Nassau over Dublin.

"Oh, by the way, he wants to give you guys a raise to £500 a week plus $230 a week PDs. What do you think?" Most of us were smiling. Stu wasn't.

"It's not enough, Don," he said. "I want £700 a week."

Me and the rest of the band couldn't believe what we were hearing.

"Come on, Stu, don't be stupid," said Don. "We're not paying you £700."

"Well, OK then," said Stu, "that's me out," and he left the room.

I still couldn't believe he'd never complained before or said that the £400 per week we had earnt for the last two tours wasn't enough. I was stunned. We'd been together since 1966; there must be more to this decision than just the money. We talked about it with Don.

"You don't think his missus has banned him from touring with us after the suitcase incident?" he asked. When Adam heard, he said he was disappointed, but life must go on. Instead of hiring another brass section member, Adam asked me to play tenor and alto and baritone with Tony. So I went out and bought two new saxophones. The section would be augmented with the addition of a keyboard player. Within a few days Steve King joined us, a shy but great keyboard player. We started work and rehearsals were going well. The album was called Strip and Adam asked us to be in his new video. I loved this part of being in a successful band. It was our second time; we had done another one with Adam called "Desperate but Not Serious".

One evening, rehearsals were pumping away when Adam walked in. I didn't know he was even in the country, but he was with Jamie Lee Curtis and a tall, slim balding guy. He introduced Jamie to us and when she shook my hand it was like shaking hands with a bricklayer; any tighter and she would have crushed my fingers. The tall guy was Barry Mead, Adam's new tour manager. Stan Tippins had been called away, as The Pretenders, his main account, were going on the road at the same time as us. Adam stayed with us for an hour or so and heard how Marco had shaped us into the new songs. He was pleased and said he would be waiting for us in Nassau in the New Year. We would be staying just down the road in a house on the beach. He and Barry, and this time, Marco, would be staying in the studio house. Rehearsals would be at night, so we were free up until 5pm to get some sun on our white bodies – perfect. Adam left the room with Jamie, leaving Barry to talk to us.

After talking tickets, business with tickets, passports, and the general tour stuff that we must know, he said, "I've heard you like a prank and a laugh. Well, leave me out of all that. I will be looking after Adam and just Adam, so if you get yourselves into trouble, you will be by yourself. Adam has told me about your parties. I will do the ticket thing but that's as far as it goes. OK?"

He turned to leave the room and follow Adam and Jamie. We'll soon see about that, was the group decision of the 1984 Adam Ant Band.

We were by ourselves, slightly missing Stan at Heathrow, so we decided to all be tour managers so we could shout orders to each other. We arrived in Miami and took the short flight to Nassau in the Bahamas.

Barry was there with cabs to take us to the house on the beach. It was dark when we arrived, but we could still hear the sea. In the morning I got up early. I wanted to see the beach, and the turquoise waters of the Caribbean and I wasn't disappointed. From the house we could walk down through the grass lawns with tall coconut trees to the fabulous sandy beach. There wasn't then nor would there be any other person in sight. After breakfast we worked out who was going to be doing the cooking and who was going to be doing the washing up. A stout but very jolly Bahamian woman arrived and said she was going to be the cleaner and she would also be taking care of the bed making – we loved her for that. All that day we lay around sunbathing and talking. I wished Stu was there and so did they all, secretly.

Twenty-two

GETTING A BIT OLD TO BE A POPSTAR!

We ate early. Tony was going to be the chef and he and Baz had gone into town to get some supplies for the week, paid for out of our PDs. Adam had offered a full catering service with the chef, but he would have had to take all our PDs to pay for it. It was better for us this way as at least we had some money left in our pockets.

Rehearsals took on a new high when Adam was involved. During that week he told us of his new stage show. At the end of the show a huge glass tank 8ft x 10ft x 8ft would be unveiled, full of water and during the last song Adam would do a strip down to a very tiny pair of shorts then climb a ladder and get into the water. He would swim around submerged, looking out on his now screaming, soon to go bananas, girl fans pressed up against the security barriers. Some even started to strip themselves. One girl standing in front of Tony and me pulled up her T-shirt showing a very ample pair of breasts with a felt message written across the top of them. "Want these?" You know, it's hard playing a saxophone and a trumpet while trying to nod your head.

That fortnight in paradise was over too soon and we packed up to get ready for the short flight to Atlanta, where we would be for four days for full production rehearsals. These were with the full American sound crew, a British backline crew and, of course, Fay and Peter Clarke from

Supermick Lights. Baz, as always, had his little Olympus Trip round his wrist ready to catch the moment.

On the beach the previous week Chris Constantinou, our bass player, was sitting on a small beach jetty getting some sun on his large bollocks, hanging them out of his shorts – snap. Baz had him, full face and full bollocks. "I'll use that later," said Baz. So it was in Atlanta in the Atlanta hotel that printed pictures were displayed with the caption 'Beware of this man and his balls.' Chris was ready to make a move on the receptionist down in the hotel spa, pool and gym. He was busy trying to lay some sand down when she picked up a flyer that had been left and said, "Er, is this you? It is, isn't it?"

We could hear Chris thundering down the corridor, swearing, and shouting what he wanted to do with Baz. Once in the room we said, "Calm down. If you want to be in on the jokes you've got to be ready to have a joke on you, you gotta be able to handle it." Chris listened, smiling, but still not very happy.

And so, in 1984 the tour was under way. I was pleased I was playing tenor and alto sax with Tony; we played together well, and the sound was made fatter by the very able keyboard player, Steve King. Some months before, Rowena Luke-King had measured and made our smart new uniforms and I was very glad Tony and I were in blue; Chas, Chris and Marco were in black, but poor old Baz, Bogdan and Steve King were in bright pink. New boxing boots all round again – great. Our favourite bus driver, Mack, was back with his bus and back with us for the marathon tour. It was going to be four months of very hard slog, but the weather was warming up and we were looking forward to it. We would all be travelling by bus, including Adam and Barry from city to city. Adam and Barry would fly off when they had TV interviews and signing sessions at record stores. Marco preferred to be with us, playing cards and watching movies. There were a lot of after-gig parties coming up so Tony had the idea to put his case back on the bus early in the evening, and after the show, when the soiree with the Adam Ant Band finished, he would put himself to bed on the bus, hence he didn't have to get up early. We did have to stop at the nearest McDonalds though; Tony and Mack loved their McMuffin breakfasts.

With the bags loaded at Atlanta airport we boarded the bus for our short journey to our Atlanta hotel. There was a large comfy captain's chair next to Mack facing forwards, and behind that there was a small wall and we sat on long couches going down the sides of the vehicle. There was a door going through to the toilet and the bunks which were three high; there were twelve of them. Doing a poo on the band bus was strictly forbidden; Mack was happy to stop when somebody asked him, but what he didn't like was cleaning poop out of his toilet pipes. As the band entered the bus a few steps Barry was barking orders – everybody to move well inside and well down the bus.

"The big captain's chair is mine and will be for all the tour, now get on board and hurry up."

We pulled out of the airport onto the freeway taking us to Atlanta. I just hoped that these awkward silences and these loud orders weren't going to be for the rest of the tour. Tony, who was sitting directly behind Barry, stood up, dropped his trousers and his pants, stood on his seat, his bare arse in line and about six inches away from Barry's left ear. No one said a word as he called, "Barry!" Barry turned his head ninety degrees and caught Tony's loud fart full force against his left cheek. There were unanimous shrieks of laughter, I thought I was going to piss my pants and ran to the toilet. Barry swore at Tony; what else could he do?

That afternoon we went down to the gig to see the main stage and our new stage set. The tank was there, empty of course. The crew were finishing off their work, as we did a sound check before we ate and rehearsed and returned to the hotel. Work on the show would start in the morning. Already there were girls hanging around outside. This was going to be a great few days. Rehearsals went quickly and soon it was the opening day and we were all dressed up in our new stage clothes and boots looking very dandy. Adam had a new costume too. Dave Whiting, wardrobe man Shuggy and his new assistant, Lesley Morrell, were busy doing their jobs. We had a new start to the show, too. The curtain would open as the introductory music started and the first thing the fans would see were the two drummers and Steve King, in their positions but silhouetted; the rest of us would be on one knee huddled together in a line at the front of the stage. I was on the far left and the first to stand with Chris (at the other end of the line); as the tape music grew Chris and I would stand up together under spotlights and side-step to our new stage positions, next up Tony and Cha, then Marco, who everybody recognised. Adam would then appear between the two drummers to great applause and screaming. The not hearing problem for Tony and me had been well taken care of. At the end of the show, which came round after a very quick two hours, it was time to see if the swimming in the tank thing worked – it did. The fans went wild almost as much as Adam did. When he came off stage, he cursed everybody; nobody had thought about heating the water! It was freezing, when his legs went in he couldn't back out and didn't now. Still, a great first gig, everybody happy.

The dates had been planned to have some time off mid-tour and we played the Austin, Texas show and stuck around there. The girls we met at the Austin party were really great, saying that they would plan our activities so our free time would not be wasted. The weather was great, so it was a picnic in the park with the USA versus UK in a softball match. The girls brought their brothers, again, great lads, who brought plenty of ice-cold beers. One of the men had a water-skiing boat which he kept on the Colorado River, so skiing was next on the agenda. Adam had gone back to LA to be with Jamie Lee Curtis, so Barry was with us and soon got into the fun. After skiing, another brother took us to a part of the river that had very steep sides, where they had strung a thick rope from a tree bough, and the idea was to swing out high over the water and then let go to drop twenty or thirty feet. We were all over it and then Barry said he wanted a go. Barry couldn't swim so we all got into the water in a circle, and when Barry dropped, we would make sure that he came to the surface and got back to the shore safely. Baz could swim a bit and it had worked for him. I thought at the time that it was really brave of Barry to do this; I wouldn't have gone anywhere near it if I'd been a non-swimmer.

It was early in the evening, and I was in the hotel foyer. Adam walked in. Surprised to see him, we had a cup of tea and he told us about his time off. He had met and stayed with Jamie and things were going really great. She told him she was going to hold a small party for him and invite a few of her friends. Everything was in full swing when he noticed that some of these guests were taking and cutting out drugs; he asked Jamie to ask these people to leave, as he couldn't be around drugs, not like this, besides he hated any form of drugs. She said they were her friends, and she didn't want them turfed out, so Adam put his coat on and left.

"That's that then," he said. "Shame, life must go on. Oh, by the way, who's leading the medal stakes at the moment? Tony?" It was always Tony. "Right," said Adam with a grin. "Let's see if I can catch him up." A valiant effort. Adam deserved a separate medal for catching Tony's score, I think by the end of the tour he did it too.

Just a few weeks before the end of the tour Tony asked to see me and Baz. For once Tony looked serious and worried.

"My Uncle Cliff has just died suddenly."

I knew Cliff well and he was Tony's dad's business partner. Tony worked with them whenever he was at home. June, Tony's mother, had been on the phone asking him to come home straight away as his dad wasn't handling his brother's death at all well. Not much was getting done and Tony was badly needed now.

"You can't just walk out," said Baz. We agreed that he must talk to Adam now. He went off and we met with him an hour or so later. How did it go? "Not so well, I'm in danger of being sued if I go," he said. Then he went off to talk to his mum to let her know the position.

"It's only a few weeks before the end and we will all be home," I said, and I would help if he needed me, although there wasn't much I knew about making UPVC window frames. Besides Garth was now working with Tony and Jack, he could keep the ship running. I felt sorry for Tony, but I was glad that he was staying.

It was now a week before the end of the tour. Adam called to see me, Tony and Baz. He explained that he was trying to move on from the Dandy Highwayman image and his new project was called his Apollo Project. The new single, "Apollo 9", didn't include brass and only needed one drummer, so this was to be our last week with Adam. Half of me was disappointed; I'd made some really good friends, and I loved being on stage, but I was now thirty-seven and I thought I was getting too old to have young girls waiting at my gate. I dearly wanted to stay in the music profession and had my sights set on becoming a top tour manager just like Stan or Barry.

A few weeks before, Mack had lost his old dog at home. He had an old trusty Rottweiler that protected his wife and kids while he was away. Don Murfitt, Adam's manager, was with us for the last part of the tour. His son Bradley had joined the crew and was having the time of his life. When Don heard that Paula, Tony's new girlfriend, was coming out to join Tony when the tour finished, he made a plan. Tony and Paula were going to drive down to the Grand Canyon before coming home. Garth and June were getting the company going again and Jack Hughes was fast becoming Jack again. Paula arrived with her case and a large cage at the hotel, and inside was an adorable Rottweiler puppy for Mack. Don had made all the arrangements and he had asked Paula to be the dog-sitter from the UK. Mack was thrilled and it made a great ending to the tour and our time with a great bunch of guys; the last party was for all of them.

Months later it was announced that Bob Geldof and Midge Ure were hurriedly organising Live Aid at Wembley Stadium. Adam was in there helping, too. All the top acts were invited to play for free for the charity that would help the starving kids in Ethiopia. Status Quo, The Who, Queen were all being given twenty minutes each to play their hits. The whole concert was a ten-hour spectacular being shown all around the world. I called Adam. If he needed us back to play a medley of his hits we would be pleased to be there. He thanked me but said he wanted to push his Apollo Project and would play stuff from his new album. On the day it was a mistake. The crowds, seeing Adam not dressed as a highwayman but in black leather, soon lost interest in music they hadn't heard him play before and went to the toilets and went to get more beers; by all accounts it was a disaster. I watched on TV, I could see it wasn't good and felt for Cha, Chris and Bogdan. It could have been so different, but it was brave of Adam to take that next big step in front of 100,000 people.

Twenty-three

JUMPING OVER THE FENCE INTO TOUR MANAGEMENT

The first thing I needed to do after leaving Adam was to have a rest. I'd been working almost non-stop and couldn't remember the last holiday I'd had with the girls. So I hung around the house, walking the dog, and I got the feeling I was in the way. Was it me? I didn't think so. Anne was going to see work colleagues and friends in the evenings and after some heated questions she told me she had been seeing a work colleague for evenings out. Had she slept with him? Yes, she had. So now what? I took myself off to talk about it with Stu. He confessed he had known about the affair and had confronted Anne about it, telling her that she had to tell me about it as soon as I got home. We'd stopped shouting by now; I knew I hadn't been an angel with the Q-Tips or Adam, and in a way, I understood Anne welcoming a drink in a pub, and being lonely for month after month. She told me it had finished, and I told her of my tour manager plans and stepping back out of the limelight. We agreed to keep it going, as the girls were only ten and thirteen and didn't deserve this.

Since Stu had left Adam, he had formed another band, playing pretty much the same material as the Q-Tips, including his own material. I also looked up Dave South, our old Curly soundman, and a good mate; he was doing well and was now the soundman for Gary Glitter, a very popular act in the UK. I wanted to see the act, and when I did, he offered me a little job to help him out. I jumped at it. I would be travelling with him and Tony Slee, the lighting director for Glitter. My job was to help with the backline (ie amps, keyboards and drums) and I felt I would be learning every gig I was with Dave. It was a great pleasure to meet the Glitter Band when they walked in, I knew most of them. The leader, John Springate, had offered me a job as sax player in the Glitter Band very soon after Curly had won the national Melody Maker Band Competition and I was very flattered but said "No thanks," as the Curly Band, Dave and manager Ken, thought Curly was going to be the next big thing.

Gary Glitter arrived with his tour manager, Alan, and dresser just before the soundcheck. Gary, who was a larger-than-life character, shook my hand warmly, welcomed me and we talked about Adam. His hairstyle was the largest Teddy Boy look I'd seen for ages. I already knew it was a wig, Tony and Dave affectionately called it 'The Rug'. Soundcheck done, Dave, Tony and I took a break for food. There was no band catering; perhaps the Glitter office couldn't afford it at this stage. They were to play medium-sized halls and after a couple of Glitter Band numbers Gary made a dramatic entrance to the stage to howling applause. What happened next really surprised me. The Band and Gary wore lots of glitter, of course; his audiences, on the other hand, were punk rockers dressed in black with studs. They jumped up and down, bashing into each other, spitting large amounts of phlegm out onto the stage and over the musicians.

"Is it like this every night?" I asked.

"Oh yeah," said Dave, "we have to be careful when we wipe down the leads and wires that cross the stage that we don't get phlegm on any of us. It's dangerous stuff."

A couple of gigs in, Tony and Dave explained 'The Rug' operation should it happen. "If a Punk jumps up onto the stage and gets to Gary someone might just pull off 'The Rug'. If that happens, Steve, I will kill the lights to complete blackout, then you run on with a towel, throw it over Gary's head and get him off stage immediately. You might have to fight off any clingers-on, push 'em off the stage any way you can. Oh, and don't forget to pick 'The Rug' up – it's worth a bloody fortune!"

Indeed, 'The Rug' was treated with great respect. Alan, the tour manager, would spray it down with water every time Gary would get to the side of the stage; after all, everything else under it was sweating profusely. So every night after that I was ready with a towel and only had to run on stage a few times with Alan to free Gary from some pissed-up Punks or some girl fans who managed to jump up on stage.

Hammersmith Town Hall was a sell-out show and the tension grew in the auditorium when the lights went down. We had recently acquired a dry ice machine which would flood out the entire stage floor to a depth of about 18 inches in eerie-looking graveyard smoke. The last thing that Dave would ask me to do through my earphones off stage before the band came on was to check the amps were all on and ready to go.

The crowd were now singing at the top of their voices, "Gary Glitter, Gary Glitter, woo oo oo, Gary Glitter."

I quickly went on stage to check on a very dimly lit stage with the dry ice.

The crowd changed its song to "Jimmy Savile, Jimmy Savile, woo oo oo Jimmy Savile."

I had a tracksuit top on and, oh yeah, of course, my blond hair. Right you bastards, I thought, and as I left the stage I mooned 'em with my bare arse, only to be attacked with sea of phlegm coming towards me. I never did that again, though Dave and Tony thought it was hilarious.

On another gig, Gary left the stage and fell into the arms of Alan, totally exhausted, and insisted that as soon as the Glitter Band followed him, he wanted to talk to them. They gathered round and we all stood and listened. "Boys, I've just had an out of body experience!" said Gary. "My spirit left me and rose above us on the stage, I could see everything from twenty feet up. I floated over the crowd and when I got to the back of the hall I was above Dave and Tony at the control desks, and I looked back and could see us on stage. Man, it was incredible!"

No one said anything for a moment, then Brian Jones, Gary's sax player, said, "Hang on, Gary, let's get this straight. You looked at us all from the back of the hall, could you see us all quite plainly?"

"Yeah, yeah," said Gary, still wiping his sweat from his face.

"Well, in that case, how did my new suit look?"

I'd only been working with Dave and Tony and the Glitter show for a couple of weeks when I was asked if I could go with them to Abu Dhabi. They had been booked to do a show for all the expats, it was going to be on an open stage and there were going to be a lot of people there. Just how many punks are there in the Middle East? I thought. The gig itself was in the gardens of a very large Holiday Inn hotel and we all had rooms there.

On a day off Alan asked me if I would like to go with him and Gary on a boat ride offered by one of the local promoters. So that afternoon the three of us met this guy and his wife and went aboard his very large and very powerful speed boat with cabins. We left the jetty and went out into the green waters of the Gulf of Oman. Gary was sitting next to the pilot and was talking and laughing and drinking with the company. The boat owner and captain turned to Alan and said, "Now let's get going." He opened both throttles fully, the boat lifted her skirts, and she started to fly. The sudden rush of wind caught Gary full face and he only just had an instant of time to put both hands on 'The Rug' and fall to the floor on his knees. I had to turn away choking with laughter. What if 'The Rug' had left Gary's head? What would be the order of events? First a shout, "Rug overboard!" Next, towel on Gary's head, next, over the side to find Rug hopefully floating – do Rugs float? I don't know.

When I told Dave and Tony we howled with laughter. During that short trip I managed to sit quietly with Alan and tell him about my plans to become a tour manager. He told me I would be great at it as I was always a friendly face and he would have a word with a company he worked for; they were a well-established London firm of promoters that went under the name of its CEO, Derek Block Concert Promotions.

So in a couple of weeks' time, I had a call from Alan asking me to meet him at Derek Block's plush offices on Dean Street in the Soho district of central London. There I met Derek, a middle-aged promoter, who still had his full dark hair and good looks. He had a partner, Jeff Hanlon, a shorter, younger man. Jeff was Gary's manager and Alan answered to him. I went and sat with Derek, and we talked all about the bands I'd worked with and, of course, he knew them all, he'd even come out to see Curly when we were riding high with our win; he'd liked us.

"Shame it didn't continue," he said.

At the end of the conversation he said, "I've got The Crusaders coming from America in a couple of weeks, do you think you can handle it? Alan reckons you could."

"Yes," I said without hesitation.

The next week I was back at the Dean Street office to get info about my first tour managing gig. I was to meet a bus driver and bus at Waterloo Station. The two of us would drive to Frankfurt in Germany to meet the band flying in. There would be a few dates in Germany and then we would all come back together in the bus to the UK to do the national dates, which included Northern Ireland.

Twenty-four

DEREK BLOCK, MY MENTOR AND FRIEND

I met Derek's tour accountant, a middle-aged lady called Gloria, who spoke directly to me looking straight into my eyes. Alan said later, "Christ, you don't want to be a penny short with your accounts with that woman!"

I'm glad I had the warning. So, on the day I thought I was early at Waterloo station but the bus was there, looking freshly washed and smelling like a tour bus, like it should. Even the American buses had that smell and I loved it. Peter, the driver and I talked a lot on the way to the coast and the ferry and I made tea from the fully stocked drinks bar. He was from the West Country and had an accent to match. We crossed the Channel in a trucks and buses-only ship and we ate with the other drivers and the crew in a very plain room, hardly a restaurant. By that evening we were at the hotel and it was there that I met the crew that were doing the tour in a large estate car; there were three of them. I didn't want to sit all night in the bar so I suggested that we go to my room where I would pay them their travelling money and their PDs. We sat for ages talking about different bands and tours and drinking most of my mini bar. The hotel was going to be our home for three nights.

In the morning I met the band. Of course, I had heard of the band. Joe Sample was the brilliant keyboard player, together with Wilton Felder, the sax player that every other sax player looked up to. The new young bass player was playing with the group for the first time, as was the girl singer who replaced Randy Crawford. The drummer was Ndugu Chancler, and he had been playing with Michael Jackson. "Street Life" had been their monster hit of 1980 and they were now still in great demand, filling medium-sized venues. The bus journeys were not like the Q-Tips' or Adam's – laughing, loud music and game playing – the band were almost silent as we ate up the miles. Joe Sample had a wooden keyboard with no strings; he played in silence, just the gentle thud of the keys going down. He would occasionally tighten a tension string to make the keys harder to press, thus strengthening his fingers. Together the band played really well, and the German crowd certainly liked it, but after the fourth gig it was time to pack up and go back to the UK.

A couple of the band had changed rooms during our stay so there was some confusion when I sat down with the front of house staff to pay the bill. Some had had room service assigned to rooms that were now not theirs. After an hour I could see the receptionist was getting more and more confused. She called the manager, and I explained the whole thing again. Another half an hour with him; I was glad I'd done this in plenty of time for our leaving. In the end he threw his arms up in the air, wrote a figure on a piece of paper, and said, "Will you pay that?" I looked. It was well down on what I had worked out that we owed.

"Certainly," I said, and paid immediately so that he couldn't change his mind.

When we were well on the way Joe asked if the band owed anything, that is, room service, as room service wasn't included on their hotel deal. But it had all been taken care of including my massive mini bar bill. Not only did I get brownie points from the band, who thought I was a genius, but also from Gloria when I presented my tour figures at the end of the short tour.

The last date was a show in Northern Ireland, and on the way, Joe told me that he had put his wooden warm-up keyboard on the truck; the crew had now a small truck as the band and their equipment were leaving for the States from Belfast the next morning.

"I wondered because I have some drugs in that keyboard case. What if the boys get stopped and searched? Do they do that sort of thing crossing into Ireland?"

I wasn't taking any chances and called the crew immediately. They swore like fuck. They were now in the police queue going onto the ferry; they found the drugs and put them in the bin. They also told me that it wasn't just a small amount of drugs. It must have cost Joe Sample dearly but that was his fault, and it would have been a lot worse had he had them on him in person. The last show went well, and it was with a little relief that I waved them goodbye at the airport. The bus driver, Peter and I were together again, making tea, listening to loud music all the way to London. Derek and Gloria were very pleased everything had gone so well according to me and immediately offered me the Country singer Charley Pride, who was coming in a couple of weeks. With the same preparation and homework, I was ready to greet Charley Pride at Heathrow Airport, where I met Ian, the limo driver for Mr and Mrs Pride, and Rodney, the bus driver from Bristol. They seemed nice enough and were eager to help with their luggage. Charlie was very smiley and polite, his wife a huge woman, who was very friendly; but it was she who wore the trousers in that band. There was one singer/percussionist, pretty girl called Mary, and from the outset Rodney wasn't far away from her and making her laugh. The tour was only going to be for a couple of weeks and we'd been going for just about a week when it was late and I was doing my books, accounting for the daily expenditure, when there was a heavy knock on my hotel door and I opened it to find Charley's wife, not smiling, more like looking for blood.

"I'm so cross," she began and started to tell me the tale which the pretty girl had told her just earlier on. It was usual for the bus driver to come into the hotel, perhaps to have a drink with the band after a show; his bus and his sleeping accommodation would be parked up all night just outside. He was laughing and joking with Mary, bringing drinks and sitting close. As she left, he followed her up to her hotel floor and when she opened her door he was suddenly by her side. Startled, she asked what he wanted. He said he wanted to be with her, and that she'd been giving him signals at the bar. Now frightened, Mary ran to Charley's wife.

"What are you going to do? You're in charge of this tour," she said.

"Easy," I said, "he's gone and he's going right now!"

It wasn't hard to get rid of Rodney, I just told him to fuck off now or face the band in the morning; I was doing him a favour. Luckily the messages I left with the Bristol Bus Company were heard the next day very early and there was another bus waiting outside the hotel after breakfast. That was the first time I had ever had to sack somebody and through my career it sure wasn't going to be the last. I never thought I would do some of the things I was asked to do by my acts, but they did make good stories.

I was really excited when Derek called with my next tour; the original Temptations were coming for a UK tour. I was a great fan and loved their music. We played their songs in the Sugar Band in the sixties and seventies, Q-Tips played their material in the eighties, Paul Young doing a great job of "My Girl". On the day I took a train to Gatwick Airport and met the bus driver. We walked over to Arrivals at the time they were supposed to appear but there was no sign. I called the office and they had just got a message from the USA to say that they had missed the flight, why? God knows! They would now be arriving tomorrow on their first show day. Derek told me to find a local hotel for the night, but I preferred to stay with the bus and David the driver, who would make up a bed for me. So, after getting permission from the airport for the bus to remain at the bus picking-up point for the next twelve to fifteen hours, we left the airport to find some food. Back to the bus for dinner and a movie with beer.

They arrived the next morning just before lunchtime. There were five Temptations, their pianist, bass player, guitarist and drummer. Their equipment was hired, so getting to the gig early wasn't that necessary; a full soundcheck was, though, because there was a sixteen-piece horn section of British players joining the act. The first show was in Ipswich at the old Gaumont Theatre. We arrived late and went straight into the rehearsal. The British sound crew had a stage plan and had carried it out to perfection. A couple of the band had brought their wives along for the ride and they were put to work immediately, going out to find a takeaway food that they liked. They came back with a bunch of menus and when I offered to pay, they wouldn't hear of it – it was their fault we were late so they would pay. On the journey up to Ipswich I talked to the band, saying how much I enjoyed their music.

"Do you play, Steve?"

"Yes," I said. I gave them a very quick CV. They knew about Adam Ant, of course, but never heard of Garnet Clarke Sugar Band or the Q-Tips; we'd never released records there. There were many questions, though, about Paul McCartney. After we'd eaten, they went to the dressing rooms, and I had a lot to do with the ticket office returns and the paperwork. I had to pay the security team which had been brought in from outside.

After a warm-up band, the sell-out crowd started to get impatient, the musicians took to the stage and blasted their way through a Temptations overture and the curtains opened. My heart was pounding with the music and then the band were behind me; they were immaculately dressed in dark blue suits with glitter bits in the material and identical black patent shoes. They stood next to me, then Otis shouted over to me, "Come on Steve, play with us!"

"Oh, no, no, no," I laughed, "I'm the tour manager I'm not up to that," and I pointed at the stage; he looked at me oddly and then they got into a huddle.

"Oh Lord," he shouted. He prayed on. Oh, Christ! He didn't say play with us, he'd said pray with us. I turned to apologise but by now they were in a line and started their entrance walk/dance onto their microphone positions with the whole Ipswich crowd going nuts. I could see the show could have had some better movement, but these guys were a top US Tamla soul act for years and the experience showed through, together with exquisite harmonies. Ninety minutes later they did the same walk/dance off stage, said nothing to anybody and went to the dressing room, closing the door; even the two wives stayed with me for a few minutes. I knew why; if there had been anything wrong with the harmonies or the act they would be sorting it out now and if someone was due for a bollocking it would be given and then forgotten.

It wasn't until we were on the bus the next morning that I apologised to Otis. He said, "Steve, the music was so loud I couldn't really hear what you were saying, I just thought you weren't a Christian."

Then we told the rest of the band what had gone down and everybody thought it was a real joke, although I wasn't asked again to pray with these

Tamla angels. Not angels all the time, though; two of the guys had their wives on tour but the rest were always on the lookout for some British crumpet and in Manchester it badly misfired. They had brought one of their own security guys, a very large white fella called Joey. He would give me names for the guestlist and if anyone in the band needed anything it would be Joey who would ask me. The gig had gone well in Manchester Apollo and the Temps had danced off the stage. One of the guys said something to Joey. Joey went off the front of the stage, had a word with two girls and then helped them onto the stage, leaving the stage and going towards the band's dressing room. Joey was tapped on the shoulder. He turned to face a bunch of lads asking where their girlfriends were going.

"None of your business," said Joey and picked up a mic stand, turned it sideways and pushed all the boys back. They weren't taking that and immediately attacked Joey, kicking and punching him. Our monitor man jumped over the desk and was straight into it, I ran to help and was beaten to the floor. Stage security were there within seconds and the gang of boys were thrown out the back door, still swearing and saying they wanted to leave with their girls. I found the girls and quickly explained what had happened. They weren't happy but left when I said. Back to the bus and back to the hotel pronto, we didn't want a vandalised bus. Joey and the monitor engineer had stayed to talk to the police, who had been called. Back at the hotel and somewhat safer from the gang of lads from Toxteth, a rough part of Liverpool, I was just settling down when Joey and the monitor engineer came in to the hotel. The sound man was holding a towel up to his ear and Joey's shirt was running with blood. I could see they had both been stabbed with a blade and called a cab, and in a few minutes we were at the hospital. The emergency room was full, and I managed to get the boys taken to a cubicle within minutes. I took a seat. It might be a long night. The reception desk was like a Post Office counter with bars from countertop to ceiling. They were obviously ready for any trouble that walked in; it was Saturday night in Manchester, and they didn't have to wait long. Two young blokes walked in. They had been in a pub when a fight broke out and broken glass had gashed one of them in the arm.

"My brother needs a doctor, get a doctor now!"

The reception lady told him it wasn't that dangerous a cut and to sit down and they would be seen soon. A few minutes passed.

"My brother is bleeding, get a doctor now!" Again, sit down and wait your turn. This must have been repeated another three or four times; after the fourth time the brother who didn't have a cut on his arm picked up a chair and put it through a glass partition window. He then picked up a large, pointed shard of glass and stuck it against his neck.

"Get the doctor now or I'll kill myself!"

By now the hospital security staff and the police were there. He stood with his glass shard against his neck while the police talked to him from a short distance. Each time they made a move towards him he shouted, "Get back, I'll kill myself. I will. I will."

There was an elderly gentleman sitting next to me with his wife, who had a towel wrapped around her wrist; she'd had a bad night too. The old boy said to the kid, "Yep, you keep saying you're gonna do it son, so do it. We'll be much happier when you do as there will be one less fucking idiot in this town, so get on with it!"

This incensed the boy, who started to come towards the old man. He moved forward and in that second the police pounced on him and knocked the glass out of his hand. They took the lads away, both of them swearing at the police with the occasional "ouch" or "please don't do that" as they were put into the police van. The mood in the waiting room changed immediately, everybody talking and laughing about what had happened. The old boy was hailed the hero and my two brave soldiers appeared, sewn up and ready for tomorrow.

In the morning the band were taking care of Joey and they were very thankful for the stage monitor, Anthony, for trying to help out. On the last night of the tour, when the governor of the sound company was ready in the wings when the Temps asked for volunteers to help sing "My Girl", he was first there and when it was his turn to sing, he started with a blood capsule in his mouth. The blood ran down his chin and onto his white T-shirt and, still singing, he started to stagger and fell to his knees. At first the Temps looked horrified but then got the joke – I'm not sure about the crowd though, one girl was screaming, this time not for the band.

Twenty-five

CHARIOTS OF FARR, THE COMMODORES AND ROD STEWART

Between tours I hung around the house, not doing too much. It was then that I had the idea to build a small tour bus. The buses that the bands were hiring were always full size and very expensive so I thought I could build a shorter one from a medium-sized panel van and I bought a German Markus Deutsch van from a luggage handling company at Heathrow. It took me several months to complete it. It had eight seats, a TV high up front, then behind the seats was a wall, behind that the toilet, opposite tea and coffee making facilities. Storage for bags and guitars was accessible from the doors at the back and from the inside, thus making the emergency exit that buses had to have. A generator to power the TV was slung underneath the chassis. Pleased with the finished vehicle I looked for an artist to paint my logo. I had had the van sprayed white and wanted a Roman Centurion head screaming at his chariot horses, heads only, and I came up with a great name for the van 'Chariots of Farr'. A young man, who said he could do it after seeing my sketches, set to work. He only worked half a day. In that time he had painted a donkey on the side of my lovely van bus. I told him to go home and cleaned his efforts off before it totally dried – I forgot that idea. I told Derek about it and showed him the photographs.

"Here's your first job," he said. "You and the sound man can drive to Hamburg. Engelbert Humperdinck is doing a corporate one-off gig there and you will be perfect for ferrying his crew and band back and forth to the hotel." The crew were made up of a couple of English guys and some Americans who had travelled with Engelbert from the USA. I'm so glad Steve Foxall, the sound man, was there with me as we had a nightmare journey to Hamburg, the van coughing and spluttering all the way. We stopped and both looked at the diesel injectors and cleaned them, but it didn't help much. As soon as we arrived at the hotel I called the garage and then they were soon put to work changing all the injectors for new ones.

The gig Engelbert was playing was a perfume convention and they had hired a proper music venue with the dancing and the dining in an adjoining room. The stage was huge and great rolls of lino-type flooring were put down for his dancers. At the sound check a grumpy Engelbert complained his way through it, saying the band were too loud and his monitors weren't high enough. I could hear his voice very loud and I was watching at the side of the stage. The dancers, too, were complaining, saying that the stage floor was too slippery, so I suggested to their tour manager that a couple of cans of Coke, sprayed on the floor and brushed in so it was all covered, would help. We quickly tried it with two brooms. It worked like a charm, they thanked me, and I said I would do it again just before the audience came in. I went to dinner with the English crew and told them I thought Engelbert's monitors were blaring. "Yeah," they said, "we know, he's a bit deaf but won't admit it." They went on, "When we go on tour we each of us turn up with long hair, glasses and beards. When he complains about his monitors, he often sacks his monitor engineer, so he cuts his hair or shaves his beard, the next day it's another engineer. When he gets the sack again, he shaves his head and takes his glasses off. There are two or three blokes in each of us," he laughed. "We just move around."

I went back to the stage. There was nobody there apart from the drum roadie who was changing some drum skins on the spares he was carrying. I didn't say much to him, and he watched me as I re-Coked the lino and brushed it in. I walked off, leaving him alone. I was only gone for a moment and then I remembered I had left my jacket by the side of the stage. I walked back and to my surprise saw this huge American hairy-arsed drum roadie prancing round the stage doing a ballet dance, jumping and pirouetting to no music, toes pointing, finishing with a grand jete. I stood there with my jacket in my mouth, the tears rolling down my face; the British crew just wouldn't believe me.

With the gig over I helped the PA load into the truck and Steve and the rest of the Brits came home with me, drinking beer and watching films. My Chariot of Farr was going to be a success.

Derek offered me another job with the Chariot a few days later. It was to meet and tour with the musicians who were Roger Whittaker's band. First, I had to take the bus around to Roger's manager's office so she could have a look at it for herself. No problems there. Roger's manager was a middle-aged German lady who, after seeing the vehicle, took me back inside her office. We agreed on the daily rate and the fuel costs.

"There is one thing," she said finally. "I have booked Roger and the band in five-star hotels; would it be all right if I paid you a nightly fee plus your per diems to find a cheaper hotel?"

"Absolutely no problem," I said. As she said it, I was thinking ahead. When I dropped the band after a show, I would take a power line from the hotel to say charging up my inverters was the excuse, and there I would be, parked up all night, heating and movies courtesy of the electricity from the hotel and I would sleep in the bus – it worked like a dream every night.

While I took care of the band, Roger had another Derek Block man driving him in a Range Rover. His name was Don Archel; his main account was to be the PA to Rod Stewart, but he went to work when Rod wasn't. He and I struck up a great friendship; he had great stories and with my great jokes many a good night was had in a hotel bar.

At one hotel it was crowded, and we could only sit at the bar and drink. We were laughing and joking when Don noticed three women in their thirties sitting next to him. He pulled me in and whispered, "I'm going to tell you something now, keep an eye on these women as I will have my back to them." I nodded.

Don started, "Well, we were going to my room as she was very keen to have slow, satisfying sex," he raised his voice towards the end of the last sentence, all the women stopped talking and looked at Don's back, "when she pulled my pants down, she said, oh my God, that's enormous, I'm not sure I can take all that! I'm sure you can," he said. "Let's go slow and see." By now all three women had moved closer and their jaws had dropped. With that Don finished his drink and said, "See ya in the morning, Steve," and calmly walked away. The eyes of all the women followed him to the lift and then they huddled together, giggling away. I smiled at them and went to bed.

The ten days of the Roger Whittaker tour went by fast enough. I slept very well on a bed I made up in the bus and each morning Don let me use his shower and I had made almost the same amount of money as I had with Adam. I hoped Don and my paths would cross again soon; they did.

Next tour from Derek was the Commodores touring the UK and Europe, as their hit "Nightshift" was riding high in the British and European charts. This time I wasn't travelling with the band. There were so many musicians and American crew that two buses were being used. I soon made friends with the additional musicians as the tour swept through the UK and into France. Don was travelling with the Commodores, and they liked him very much. One of the most prestigious gigs we were playing was going to be the Negresco Hotel in Nice. The hotel was owned by Madame Jean Rougier, a very famous name in Nice because of her flamboyant lifestyle and her support of French art and animals. She and her two dogs watched as the loading started; the show was going to be in the hotel ballroom. When she saw the size of the aluminium lighting trusses being carried in, together with huge speaker cabinets, she put her arms up and shouted, "No!"

I put my production manager's hat on and said, "Why not?"

"This is too big for my hotel, I will not allow it." That sentence was a huge pain in the arse for me; the trucks were reloaded and they sat on the fashionable Prom des Anglais while I got on the phone for new instructions. My orders were to find another gig – I did, at the Exhibition Centre, and the trucks were on the move again, much to the relief of the French police.

The Nice Exhibition Centre was enormous and could have easily garaged three or four jumbo jets. We were now hours behind and the crew of the centre and our own crew worked tirelessly until a stage was built, seats were put in and sound and lighting were ready. The hotel said they would call the radio station to tell people the venue had changed, and Madame Rougier said the band could still stay at her hotel. All went well and everybody was happy. I remember that night, the heavens opened as we had a big Mediterranean storm. I was in my room, not wanting another day like today, when the phone rang. It was Don. Could I come downstairs to a street bar, as he was having a drink with one of the band? Strange, I thought, the Negresco bar would have been much posher. After a drink, Don said, "Steve, we need your help. Neither Jim nor I speak French and Jim is desperate to get laid. You speak French, can you help?"

"You mean he needs a hooker?"

"Yeah, right," he replied.

"All you have to do is go out on the street and the girls will be there," I said.

"We've tried that," said Don, "but it was pissing down with rain; there weren't any women around."

The rain had stopped now, and it was warm and fresh-smelling so I stepped out into the street with Don and Jim. Sure enough it was almost midnight and there weren't many ladies of the night to be seen. Then a pretty girl came round the corner with a dog on a lead. I took a chance of getting a slapped face or at least a mouthful of French abuse from her if I'd made the wrong choice.

I asked, "Excuse me, Madame, are you working this evening?"

She stopped and looked at us. "I was, and now I am walking with my dog. I do it every night."

"Can you fit one more in?" I said; perhaps I could have put that better.

"Just one?" she said. We pointed at Jim.

"OK, I will go with him to my apartment, you will walk with my dog until I return." She passed me the lead and went off with Jim. Don was laughing.

"Oh no," I said, "you got me into this, the least you can do is walk with me and Fido here."

That summer I was working hard for Derek. He liked the stories that I came back with. On a weekend with Jack Jones to do a television spectacular for Welsh TV in Cardiff, he and his new bride had hired a car and had driven to Wales from the airport. We met at the hotel; he would be recording tomorrow. I took my car, a new Rover, and he followed. He flashed me to stop, I did. He got out of his car and they both got into mine. "Your car is newer and better-looking than mine, we must look good as we arrive."

"Fair enough," I said.

A night with the St Petersburg National Ballet at Sadler's Wells; well, this was going to be a new one for me. I was at the theatre to meet them. It seemed only their tour manager would be talking English to me. The Corps de Ballet or the group arrived in scruffy-looking coats, jackets, and jeans, and they wandered in, nearly all of them smoking, and they changed their footwear to do their warm-up routine. Holding onto empty lighting bars lowered from the gantry they started their practice moves. A very stern Madame banged her large stick on the stage floor and each ballerina knew what position to take. All this was done in silence, and they finished and wandered off to their dressing rooms. The orchestra arrived early, and the conductor ran through a few pieces. They wandered off to return at show time, looking the business in dark suits and ties. The dancers gathered in the wings both sides of the stage, nearly all of them still smoking. When they were due to go on and dance onto the stage to a sell-out crowd, they carefully handed their cigarettes, still alight, to Madame or the tour manager, then, after they had done their little piece, they came off stage to pick up where they left off with their fags. If it was a long dance a fresh cigarette would be lit. I was watching from the side of the stage and the proscenium arch of the stage was between me and the audience. When the ballerina was lifted into the air by the male dancer he would let out a huge gasp as he raised her off the floor and when she came down another huge gasp and a loud thump on the stage; the noise of the whole company doing it was deafening. It was the proscenium arch which absorbed all that noise and cigarette smoke from the audience. They went down very well, and I thought I would pass on another ballet gig or tour if it came along.

Another of those non-music tours Derek gave me was the hypnotist, Robert Halpern. He was very popular in the day, appearing at nightclubs and theatres. Robert used his Rolls Royce to travel to gigs and I had his props in my van. He was somewhat strange I thought; his act was fraught with danger and controversy. He would give the whole audience a single test, asking everybody to clasp their hands together and shut their eyes for a moment, then he said some words, then asked the crowd to open their hands. Many just couldn't do it and they were asked to the stage. He would release them and keep them sitting on their chairs. The interviews were amusing, and as he left them, he tapped them on the back of their heads and they were gone, ready to perform under hypnosis. Eating a raw onion or seeing the audience completely nude made it fantastic fun for the theatre audiences, loving every moment of it. Then at the end of the show he would send all his subjects back to their seats apart from one and, still under his spell, told the person they were going to hang him. That's what I was carrying in the van, a complete set of gallows with a large pull handle to the side; it released a trap door and there was a drop of about 4 feet to the stage floor. Robert would then give clear instructions to the person under hypnosis who was going to pull the lever. As the dramatic music built, Robert stood on the gallows and put his head in the noose, then he put a black hood over his face, and he held his hands tightly in front of himself. At the moment he wanted the trap door released, he would shout to his hypnotised executioner. As he went through the trapdoor, I electronically let off a very large bang. To the audience it looked very real; they were aghast and there were some screams. We would then close the curtains slowly, Robert hanging quite motionless. The person who had pulled the lever would just be standing there, so as soon as I got Robert out of the harness, he would wake up his executioner who had no idea what had just happened. Then without opening the curtains he would take the mic and tell everybody he was still with us, thanks for coming and a very good night.

On one occasion we had a message that concerned parents were waiting to see Robert immediately, as their son, having been part of the entertainment, had not come out of the hypnotism and was behaving strangely. He saw them and tried to reassure them that everything was OK but sometimes parents weren't happy when they left. I had always thought it was a complete act, these lads going under not being hypnotised at all, they just wanted to make fools of themselves in front of their mates.

A year later my old mate and trumpet player Tony Hughes had a party at the house and booked a hypnotist. Stu and I went along, Stu always saying it would be a load of bollocks. He planned to be a chosen subject and would then refuse to go under. The hypnotist spoke softly to Stu, just like Robert had done, and then tapped Stu on the shoulder; our undercover expert agent dropped like a stone. He followed the hypnotist's instructions and did performances and acts, making everybody howl with laughter. Job done, Stu was woken and wouldn't have it when people told him what he had done. So much for my disbelief, then.

Robert had a large mansion with a great deal of land in Ireland. He told me one day that a year before he had bought a tiger cub which was now almost fully grown, and he was bringing it up as a tamed pet; he now wanted to put it in the act.

"It's quite tame," he said, "it could travel with you in the back of the van."

"Are you mad?" I said. "Can you imagine the panic when I had to let it out of the van for a piss at the motorway station? I am not carrying a year-old, almost huge tiger and that's that."

Imagine if I was ever stopped by the police with a set of gallows and a fully grown tiger in the van! It might have been fun though if this had happened.

"Can we see inside your van, sir?"

"Yes, officer. The doors are unlocked, help yourself!"

I didn't work much for Robert Halpern after that.

Different again were the Chinese Magic Acrobats from Taiwan, a large group of men and women who I was advised to keep apart, if I could. The men did all the dragon dancing stuff and feats of balance and strength, while the women did the national costumes and the Taiwanese dancing. I was going to be with them for a week. All their equipment was not packed in flight cases but rickety bamboo trunks, which never seemed to fall apart although they all wanted to. What they did on stage was truly amazing. The trick cyclist and the sword balancer were the same man and he was also the chef. Once inside the theatre I would go off with him to a fish shop or butchers and he would buy lots of everything, leaving me to pay; no beer was allowed. He would set up his stove and the gas cylinder in an open area and start cooking when his part of the act was over. The food he produced was nothing short of brilliant and every day in the theatre when the show had finished anybody still left in the building, like ushers or box office staff, would be handed a bowl and a pair of chopsticks (no forks or spoons allowed); we all got into the Chinese crouch position to eat and smile at the cast of the show. I had to keep my eyes open, remembering faces, as if a male was missing there would be a female missing too. I caught two banging away in a cupboard under the stairs at one gig – not allowed. One guy asked me to buy some condoms for him and I said I would. Seeing an old cardboard television box waiting to be thrown out, I taped over the printing on the side and took it to him.

"You want condom? Have plenty condom." He soon got the joke, and everybody fell about laughing when he told the rest of the cast; after that I was 'number one condom man'.

At the Fairfield Halls in Croydon the chef was creating when the backstage smoke alarms went off. Luckily the show was over, and the auditorium was empty. The alarm had gone directly through to the fire station and a few moments later two flashing fire engines pulled into the rear parking area. The firemen came running up the stairs, their leader barking on about using a gas cooker in an open area. He soon forgot about that when I said it was a one-off and we were normally careful about activating alarms. The chef immediately invited both fire crews to squat and eat with us. I wish I'd had a camera that night.

Derek Block called me one day to see if I would help with the Rod Stewart tour. He had his own tour manager, I was going to be doing the promoter's rep job. Great, I would see my old mate again, Don Archel. First gig was at Wembley Arena and the first thing I had to do was organise an enormous mobile generator to be parked out the back of the gig; more power was needed, much more power. Another first for me in the tour knowledge and it was all going in. Next, fuel supply in huge diesel oil drums. Next, twenty or so footballs had to be bought; Rod kicked them out into the crowd through the show. Next, meet the caterers; there was already a place for them, so they were no problem. After that the guestlist was enormous, meeting security so that we all knew who was who and where the guest enclosures were; these guys did this every week so why was I worrying. Rod arrived with his band and staff, including Don, who looked very busy. After the sound check everybody ate in catering and an hour before the show started Rod and the band played in a room set up with a drum kit and amps, together with a monitoring system so they could all hear Rod's voice. They didn't play Rod's show set but old soul and Tamla tunes to warm up, the same tunes I had played with the Q-Tips and the Sugar Band. I sat in the corridor and lapped it all up. It was a great show. I didn't have to stay for the load out, the band were together in the hotel and I went home; it was Brighton tomorrow, so I had an early start.

For me the lighting and sound crews each morning were the same, perhaps with a few problems, but these guys were at the top of their profession just like their act. That afternoon, however, was very different. The band and Rod arrived and there was no sound check. Don found me and explained that Rod had a throat infection, and we would have to see if he could sing at all; a little food for him and certainly no soul singing before the show. I was a little nervous as the sell-out crowd were shown in; they and twenty footballs were ready to go. The doctor took a last look at Rod at showtime, the support act had played, and it was decided that tonight was going to be cancelled. The tour manager found me and said, "Stevie boy, it's your gig, you must tell 'em it's off," he pointed to two and a half thousand people waiting for the show, "do it now."

I walked out onto the stage. I wasn't nervous, perhaps a little wondering what the reaction would be. I explained that Rod had a throat infection and the doctor had advised that he didn't sing tonight; the date would be rescheduled so keep your tickets, any refunds would be taken care of in the morning. There was some moaning from some, but overall, I thought they handled it well. The band left; the equipment and twenty footballs were loaded into the trucks to fight another day. I went to the hotel bar alone and went home in the morning. The tour was rescheduled but I wasn't on it. Derek had other plans for me.

The "American Pie" man was next to be met at the airport. Don McLean arrived with his wife to do a short tour of the UK. He was going to be accompanied by another guitarist and the duo would be playing around fourteen concerts on their tour. Ralph McTell was the warm-up act. This fortnight was easy for me. Don and his wife were enjoying the UK, being driven around in a very large car, so all I had to do was to turn up with this other musician, no equipment to worry about. This tour did teach me one thing, though, that their personal instruments were part of them. Don's guitar had gone missing when he arrived with his wife at Gatwick Airport; when it was clear that the flight case wasn't on the belt, he had gone into one as if his own child was missing. He came through to meet me and told me what had happened. After explaining who I was to an airport official I was allowed to go to the luggage handling area. After a lengthy search we found the guitar on a trolley with another band's equipment and instruments. He was overjoyed to be reunited with his guitar and, of course, I was the hero.

In the dressing room on that tour, we laughed about weird lyrics and songs and poems, and I started quoting Chaucer The Canterbury Tales (I'd covered this poem in my GCE English Literature, which I passed) and we howled at the sex scenes. Later he wrote on a picture of himself, "Thanks Steve for the great tour, Chaucer was a tosser." I still have that picture somewhere.

Twenty-six

DEREK GIVES ME THE GREAT BB KING

Derek thought I'd done enough by now and knew that I could handle most performers, could I handle a monster act? Let's see. To my delight he gave me BB King's UK tour and I welcomed BB, his manager Sid Seidenberg, and his seven-piece band, together with two helpers, at the airport. Once the bags were loaded, and there were a lot of them (BB had five suitcases!), the musicians and their personal instruments went onto the bus. They all went to different positions; Sid told me that BB has his own touring bus in the States and each musician had his special seat. The band seemed really friendly. Joe was BB's personal aide, and the other guy was an older man they called Bebop. He sat there, picking his gold teeth with a stick. When I introduced myself, he just grunted, and when he did speak it was to give orders to the band in a Southern drawl accent that was beyond me; I could only decipher a two-syllable sound he made when he was saying 'Sh-it' and he said that a lot.

BB was a big heavy man. A nicer guy you couldn't wish to meet, his band loved him, and it was important, he told me, to take great care of them as they were his family. Through the years I was with him, I tried to do just that. Sid Seidenberg was BB's business manager and a New Yorker; to me he was the spitting image of Robert Mitchum, especially when he wore his fawn raincoat.

After a few days I asked Sid what Bebop did on the tour.

"Nothing over here," answered Sid, "back home he deals with the money and the box office. All he knows about money is the dollar. Put him here in Europe and he would be useless with all the different currencies." Years before he had been a cab driver and, after taking BB to an airport, he talked himself into a job and got out the cab when BB did and walked away from it, never to return.

"BB takes him everywhere he goes, 'cos he's got nowhere else to go," Sid said. I didn't care for this Bebop and neither did Sid, or come to that, the rest of the band, but he was a friend of BB's, so I had to make sure he was OK.

When we arrived at a hotel, as the rooming list had been done by me over the phone the day before so as not to overcrowd any lobby, BB was immediately taken by Joey to his room, and I would give everybody a rooming list. Then Bebop would give the orders out to the band of what suits they were to be wearing for that night's show. During the afternoons I would go down to the gig to see everything was OK with the crew. Many of these lads knew me well and I knew they would do a great job even though BB didn't soundcheck, neither did the band. BB would be chauffeured to the gig with Sid, arriving about twenty minutes before showtime. The bus would be outside the hotel, the band members would arrive early, already dressed in their show suits, ready to go. Then, to my annoyance, we would have to wait for Bebop. When my bus leaving time was well overdue, I went into the hotel to try and find him. He wasn't in his room when I rang; I found him coming out of the bar. Joey rode with us so he could set up BB's room, a different dressing room to the rest of the band. I didn't say anything to Bebop as I wouldn't have been able to understand his reasons for being late. The next night we were waiting for Bebop again, so I asked James, the trumpet player, if he did this every night.

"Most nights," was the answer.

I told the bus driver to go, leaving Bebop behind. This was my tour and if he was coming with us it would have to be when I said. He must have got into a taxi and got to the gig; we had words – I made sure he understood mine, I still didn't understand a word he said, only the word sh-it.

On the bus the next morning BB called me to his seat and said that he knew about Bebop last night. "It's good that he doesn't get his own way all the time, I don't think he'll be doing that to you again." He didn't.

One morning I was the last person to board the bus apart from Sid, Joey and BB.

"Morning boys," I shouted. I sat down and BB boarded the bus. "Good morning all," he shouted. The band stood and said good morning. Once we were well on the way James Bolden came and sat down beside me.

"Steve, can I have a word with you?"

"Sure," I said, "how can I help?"

"When you get on the bus, can you not call us boys? It's black thing, you know what I mean, we know you don't mean anything by it, but we have had enough of being called boys."

I couldn't apologise enough. I hadn't given it a thought, and yet I had upset them, and they had been so welcoming and so friendly to me. I never did that again.

BB and the band loved my jokes and I had to tell them one new one every morning going to the next town. Thank God the tour was only three weeks; I was starting to run out.

In a few weeks' time I had a call from two Dutchmen, Dick Jaarsma and Bauke Algera. They had a company installing fruit machines in clubs and pubs in a part of Holland. The Dutch government had cleverly allowed the company to put machines only within a certain area of the country; this stopped any warfare between different fruit machine companies. Dick and Bauke had kept to the rules and were doing very well. They wanted to do something different with their money and had made a new company called DIBA International Concerts. Now they wanted to put on shows in Holland and Germany with acts that they liked. Unbeknown to me they had seen BB on the UK tour and approached Sid about touring in Holland and Germany. Sid and BB were keen to play. Now Dick and Bauke were asking if I would tour manage BB on their tours and I immediately said yes.

Within a couple of weeks, I was on a flight from Luton to meet the Dutchmen. Their hometown was Sneek in the north of Holland, and they had invited me to Amsterdam to meet them at the airport hotel for lunch and a pre-tour briefing. I liked them immediately. They had driven down to the meeting but that didn't stop them drinking. I returned to

Luton that evening. The flight then was handled by Nether Lines, a very small turbo-prop plane carrying about twelve people. I sat next to Bob Monkhouse on his way home, and we made polite conversation. At the arrival hall we were taken into a small room and asked to sit down; our luggage was brought in, and we were asked then to place it in front of our seats. Bob got a little impatient, asking what this was all about; he did this trip regularly. This was a first for him as well. In came two policemen with their dogs and the animals soon got to work sniffing every bag, never stopping wagging their tails. Nothing found, the policemen apologised for the inconvenience and Bob was out the door like a shot.

When BB, the band, Sid, Joey and Bebop arrived at Schiphol Airport, Amsterdam Dick and Bauke and I were there to meet them and greet them. The Dutchmen had followed my advice to the letter; a huge Mercedes limo was to take BB and Sid to the first hotel. The band bus was brand new. It was a Vanhool and everybody loved it. The hotels were all five stars and above, all with elevators to BB's suite as he found climbing stairs very taxing. I had a small problem that I hadn't faced on the UK gigs which I hadn't managed to head off earlier with Dick and Bauke. The dressing room and catering couldn't have been better, the equipment on stage exactly what BB would have used in the USA; we were all impressed that DIBA Entertainments had gone to such great trouble to get everything right. The problem I had was that each night I had a guy or a woman, obviously well known in Holland or Germany, that would stand in the wings dressed up to the nines saying that they were going to introduce BB King and the band on stage – oh no they weren't! For a start the band took to the stage first and played an introductory piece, then Walter King, BB's cousin, would bring on BB; they weren't going to change it now. I politely told the introducer that I was the tour manager. BB started the show this way so thanks, but no thanks – some took it well, some didn't and complained to the Dutchmen. After a few days they had let all the other introducers know that they didn't have a gig and that was that. Everything else went like a dream, they even paid the band (through Bebop) in dollars! I even got paid in dollars which didn't bother me.

BB and Sid left the short tour having made some very good friends in Dick and Bauke; Sid gave all the European work to DIBA. BB was happy, so were the band, the Dutchmen were delighted. Up to now in Holland there had been only one main promotion company called Good News and they handled all the big acts. They called to congratulate Dick and Bauke after hearing their first tour had been such a success.

The next European tour came round very quickly. I thought the Q-Tips worked a lot, but BB liked to be working all the time, doing over three hundred shows a year, every year. The band had wives that understood, their children were being educated, they had nice cars and houses, even if their husbands and fathers weren't there most of the time.

We met again at Schiphol Airport, and the high standards that Dick and Bauke had set on the first tour were present again. Their friend and partner in crime in handling the German dates was Kirsten Jahnke, and later we were to play in France at the Nice Music Festival. BB loved this new Vanhool bus as it drove us around Europe and ordered one for himself and the band. Their American bus was getting a little old, he said. So while we travelled up and down freeways and the highways, BB had his two drivers come over and be at the Vanhool factory while they built BB's new vehicle. "This way," he said, "they would know everything there was to know about the new bus." Apparently, they studied hard with the Dutch engineers during the day and each night they went drinking together. They joined us for the last couple of nights of the tour. The new BB bus had been finished and shipped to the USA. Eagerly BB wanted to know all about it; luckily they had taken plenty of photos for all to see. Now Bebop had two new people he could order around but the drivers were having none of that. It soon transpired that they thought he was a waste of space too.

Just previously we had flown into Europe to do the Italian dates; Dick and Bauke had given the dates to an Italian promoter to cover. From the moment we met him I knew this guy was going to be wrong for us. He came straight up to us and said, "Sid and BB must hurry up, forget the band, he has people and press waiting. The car is there, come on, let's go!" For one, the car was nothing special, the bus was a regular 45-seater; I'm sure if Dick and Bauke had been with us this guy would have been fired immediately. The hotels were OK but he always gave orders for the next morning, always wanting Sid and BB to do this and that for him or meet other dignitaries that would help in some other business deal later on.

I sat at one gig with BB and Sid before a show, it was the only time I heard BB say something derogatory about another man. "I really don't care for this guy," he said. Sid was almost wanting to punch the guy, but BB wouldn't have had that. The Italian part of this tour was the worst; it hadn't started well. When waiting for our luggage some sniffer dogs had jumped up Bebop; that was enough for the police to take him away into an anteroom for a search. I quickly told Sid and BB what had happened. Sid didn't want to leave BB, just as well, as it was just before we were about to leave to meet Mussolini's brother. I went into the room – Bebop was sitting there looking defeated – had they found drugs? Yes, they had. I asked the Italian policeman if anybody spoke English, yes one did.

"What happens now?" I asked.

"We take him downtown," was the answer.

I said I would come when I had put the band into the hotel. BB was disappointed, Sid was furious with Bebop, hoping that Mussolini wouldn't hear about it and leak it to the press. Sid and I took a cab to collect Bebop. Sid asked to speak to the police chief and offered to pay any fine plus a donation to the police if it went no further. To my great surprise they seemed keen so as not to do all that paperwork. Bebop got his passport back and we returned to the hotel. We were so glad to be getting out of Italy when it came around.

I got the message from our Dutch travel agent that there were no flights leaving Italy into France that day; someone somewhere was on strike. The Italian promoter told us that we would have to travel back to Nice by that awful bus. I said nothing but goodbye to him. As we drove away, I told BB of my plan.

He said, "I just can't be sitting on this old bus for the next ten hours, Stevie boy, try your best." I immediately told the bus driver to take us to the airport, where I bought tickets to Switzerland, and from there we could catch a train to Nice and still be in time to play at the festival that evening. We made it in time and after the show BB called me in and said, "I don't know what you did, but you did it. Son, I'm so grateful to you." Thanks indeed.

We would be playing at the festival for three nights, such was the demand to see BB King and the Band. All the musicians were staying at the same hotel opposite the beach; the place was full of English, American and European blues greats. It was like one big club where the members hadn't seen each other for a while, everybody was laughing and hugging and many of them were asking me if they could meet and talk with BB. I pointed towards Sid; even David Gilmour of Pink Floyd asked me if he could have a moment with the great man. Even Chuck Berry was somewhere in the hotel. The band met an old friend, his tour manager, a guy called Quinny, who soon had them reeling with laughter telling them about his exploits. He said that Chuck would not be mixing with the others as he liked to keep himself to himself.

One day I was in my room and the phone rang. It was Ann Turner, a woman I had known in Hemel Hempstead. Some weeks before I had met her in a pub, and she knew that I was a tour manager. She asked if I could help get her son a job as he was finding it very hard to find work; he would love to do what I did, she said. Then out of the blue I heard from the Derek Block office that George Benson, the great American guitarist/ songwriter, was going on tour and his valet had walked out. I met Ann and her son, David, a softly spoken, shy boy but like his uncles he was well over six feet tall and built like a brick shithouse. He knew nothing about valeting but was very keen to do the job. So he came to my house, and I taught him how to press a shirt and fold it properly, how to press trousers, how to lay out clothes and toiletries. If he could do all that, I said, just be quiet, polite and look after your man, you'll be OK. Nervously he left Hemel Hempstead to meet up with George in London. They would be doing some dates in the UK and then go on to Europe.

After a week David called me to say it was going brilliantly. George had really taken to him, he felt safe when David was on his shoulder, especially in restaurants and when autograph hunters interrupted his dinner David would politely usher them away. He bought him new clothes and treated him well. George had even said that he could invite his mum for a few days when they reached Monaco. I would be in Nice at the same time and as Nice was the nearest airport I told him to tell his mum to call me and I would make sure she got to him safely. She arrived late in the evening after BB's show and the transport manager of the festival very kindly put a car and driver out to pick her up from the airport and drive her through to Monaco – another job well done.

With the hotel being downtown on the Promenade des Anglais, there was a regular private bus service taking the bands to the show site out of town. It was always in the same place every year, a huge area that everybody called The Orchard. It had several sound stages and large tents and thousands attending every day for a week. I rode up to The Orchard about two hours before our show time. The band had already changed and were milling about the green area backstage talking and watching other acts. I asked Calep, our drummer, if he knew if everybody was here and he said he had seen Eugene, our keyboard player, drinking with Johnnie Johnson, Chuck's keyboard player, earlier, but he hadn't come up yet to the site. I felt something wasn't right; Johnnie Johnson and Eugene Carrier were both big men and could drink bigtime. I took the bus back to the hotel and looked around for Eugene; not in the lobby waiting for transport, not in the bar. I had to find him as time was getting on. I knocked loudly on his door, no answer, nothing. I had to be sure he wasn't in there, so I went down to the concierge and asked him to accompany me to Eugene's room and get the door open. He was a little reluctant.

"What if he has a woman?" he asked.

"He hasn't," I answered. Eugene was about 300 pounds in weight; to me, a Brit, that's over 21 stone. He opened the door and Eugene was out cold face down on his bed with just his underpants on. "Oh Christ!" I swore. "We'll have to dress him." It was like dressing a tailor's dummy, a very heavy tailor's dummy. With his shirt on I picked up his suit pants and started to laugh; they were so big I could have camped in them if I'd had a couple of tent poles. That started the concierge off too, and we struggled to get them on him – what a laugh. That done, the concierge then called room service for coffee, now please! Eugene was awake by now but still very unsure on his feet. We had to help him to the lift and to the taxi that was waiting. At the show site the cab driver got right up to the band dressing room door, thank God for that – we stumbled into the room, the band saw him and got him more coffee. The cab turned around and had to stop to let BB come into the backstage area in his car. So far BB knew nothing about what was going on. The show started normally, and the crowd erupted when BB walked on stage, looking out to the crowd and waving. He still hadn't looked across at Eugene, who was on automatic pilot, head well down but playing. A few minutes later BB looked across and saw Eugene and dropped his head as if he wanted to see in his eyes, still playing; he looked into the wings of the stage at me, all I could do was shrug my shoulders. From that moment he gave a solo to Eugene in almost every song, and Eugene just about covered it. Sober, he would have done this with his eyes closed, he was drunk now, still doing it with his eyes closed. They finished the show. BB asked me into the dressing room. Walter King had just told him of Eugene's saga.

"Steve, I hear you got us out of trouble again, son." I smiled, saying it was my job and gave him a few details of the dressing of Eugene with the concierge, to whom I was very thankful.

"Oh, I'll take care of him," said BB. I started to tell BB about the camping idea I'd had with Eugene's trousers but suddenly thought better of it; he might not have thought that funny, seeing as his trousers were just the same size, if not bigger than Eugene's. Later Eugene was summoned to BB's room. BB didn't rant and yell at anybody, but you knew when you got a dressing down so the band said to me. The keyboard player got a very long dressing down and didn't drink again on those final days of the tour.

I was summoned again; BB gave me $2500 to find a boat for the day so he could treat the band. A very handsome middle-aged American woman had arrived that day to stay with BB and he wanted everybody to have a great day out. I went to the marina and after talking to several people in several offices I managed to hire a luxury motor yacht with a full crew, and they would be providing a sumptuous lunch with drinks. The next day I got the bus company boss who was ferrying all the artists to the show site to ferry us all to the quayside. Sid didn't want to be in the way of BB and his lady so made his excuses to stay behind, Eugene said he didn't like the sea, so he wasn't going either, so Sid offered to buy him lunch. We arrived alongside this beautiful yacht and the five-man crew and the captain were lined up in dress uniform; he came ashore and welcomed BB and his lady on board. The band were keen to get going and eat the long, long luscious lunch. We didn't sail far, just around the coast, and stopped by a lonely sandy beach. There was hardly anybody on the shore. For those who wanted to go for a dip, luxury towelling robes were waiting when they had had enough. After a swim with all the different toys the yacht had provided, I put my soft robe on and sat with everybody at the huge lunch spread.

"I wanna say something," BB said. "Some of you might know it but Stevie boy has organised all this for us today. In fact, if it hadn't been for him the other day, we might not have made it here, and I would have missed seeing my very dear friend here," he pointed to the lady.

"It seems, Steve, that every time we get a problem you get us out of it. We haven't known you too long but now you are part of the BB King family." Kind words indeed.

The night before we left France and the festival, for some rest in our own hometowns before the next one, Sid took me aside for an evening snack and some drinks. I liked Sid a lot. He was great company and told me a lot about his past. He was Jewish and had joined the US Army as a young GI towards the end of the war. He was part of the group that guarded Nazi war criminals and took them into the trials at Nuremberg; after being sentenced he led them away to be hanged. I asked him if that ever gave him nightmares. He was pretty cool about it and he said he just thought of what they had done, mostly to Jews, and felt no remorse. I'd have been the same.

We had some fun together, too. In Turin we sat at a restaurant and ordered a steak, each not realising that we were to cook them ourselves on a red-hot stone that was put in front of us. In Paris we had gone to the Folies Bergère and watched a fabulous variety show although no word was spoken throughout the whole show. Between acts glamorous women with plenty of feathers, but still showing their tits, paraded up and down the stage; that, while eating a great dinner with drinks, what more could you ask for? After tonight's meal Sid said that after Christmas they would be going to Australia and New Zealand for a month's tour. Would I like to go with them? I'm sure my face and smile gave him his answer. I perhaps would never get the chance to tour there again, I was thrilled. The next morning, I said goodbye to BB and all my friends in the band, I even got a goodbye from Bebop, who was behaving himself lately. With them away, I went back to the hotel to wait for Ann Turner as we had arranged to fly back to the UK together. She had had a great time being spoiled by George Benson and his crew. I hoped that David would keep his job, and he did for a year or so.

Twenty-seven

BB KING IN AUSTRALIA AND NEW ZEALAND THEN HELLO DIBA

I hadn't been home long when I got a call from Sid's office. After some small talk he offered me a full-time job to be with BB and the band; he did have several other acts which he needed to do more with, one being Gladys Knight and the Pips. He would find me temporary accommodation in New York State where he and his family lived. I was dead keen and said that I would talk to Anne about it. Anne was not keen at all. For one, she said that once in America, she would never see me if I was out with BB on tour all the time. Two, it was the wrong time for the girls to change countries let alone schools. Thirdly, there was no way she was going to move that far away from her mum, Marge. I sat for hours thinking about it and each time I came to the same conclusion that she was right. I would tell Sid when we got to Australia.

A few weeks before that Christmas, Sid's office sent me my ticket to Christchurch in New Zealand on a British Airways flight and, of course, I was coming from London and BB and his band were meeting Sid in Atlanta so they would take the flight from there. They were going around half the world to New Zealand whilst I was going the opposite way. My flight took 26 hours, stopping in Dubai and Singapore and then on to Sydney before arriving in Christchurch. I had arrived the evening before the Americans, so I thought I would be by myself for the night; not at all. The Australian promoter was there to meet me, and he introduced Toby to me. Toby was a huge Samoan, I mean really huge; he looked super fit, as if he was a rugby player. He had been with the Samoan Wrestling Team some years before but now he was going to be my helper and I was grateful that they had given me such a nice bloke. He didn't drink but sat talking to me in the hotel bar. He wanted to know so much about the Americans and London, I can't remember the last time I talked so much.

In the morning Toby and I went to the airport again with the promoter to meet BB, the band, and Sid. After greeting hugs all round I suddenly noticed there was no Bebop and no Eugene Carrier. James Bolden and Calep told me that they would tell me later. Having cracked Christchurch with a fabulous show we crossed islands to play Auckland, another great success. Christchurch was about twenty years behind with their cars – apparently cars did not decay so much here as in the northern hemisphere – so I was sure to see old Zodiacs and Austins in great condition. The people in Christchurch were warm and welcoming, in Auckland another story. I was taking a look round on a warm sunny morning and I saw a park that I could walk through; after a while I sat on a park bench and two schoolgirls sat on the bench opposite me. They were smartly dressed in their school uniform, white shirts, blazers check skirts, that sort of thing, most probably attending a small middle-class school for girls. Then one of them took out a bottle of clear glue or something and they both started sniffing it eagerly. They saw me watching them.

"Why the fuck are you doing that?" I said.

"What's it to you, you Limey bastard?" the one answered. "Now, why don't you fuck off!"

"Oh, I'm going," I said, "have a happy but very short life, girls. Bye." I was off. Well, you can't meet nice people all the time.

On the plane to Australia, Calep told me what had happened to Bebop and Eugene. The keyboard player had suddenly quit the band, saying that he wanted more time with his family, but Calep knew he'd had a heart scare, and that if he was in for a heart attack, he wanted to be in his home state. Eugene was very much overweight, waddling rather than walking, and not waddling very far without having to take a rest. BB had had serious words with Bebop, saying that he was becoming a liability to the band's name. He'd known him for some time, but Bebop would make false receipts and cheat the band regularly. When we were in Europe and played small squares, and sometimes castles, in the summer months, almost every time the band and BB were given gifts: beautiful, embroidered linen, china mugs, T-shirts, and they were all handed to Bebop while the band were playing. The band would never see them. I was given a box of T-shirts commemorating the day with BB's name all over it, together with the town in Andorra and the date on it. Bebop had flown into a rage, saying that they were his responsibility.

"Not now," I said, "the band have got theirs; Sid has the others." This was why he had been so unpopular with the band. BB had always let Bebop hire a car on the band's account when they were in their own hometowns. When Bebop thought he was for the chop he got in the car and drove away to where? Nobody knew. He was stopped and arrested for car theft later. Sid was relieved he was gone as Bebop and his drugs would have spoiled BB's name had it been brought to public knowledge sooner or later. I was certainly glad that he was gone. The new keyboard player was a guy called Tony, middle-aged, with a great sense of humour. I felt the band was steady again, but I was wrong; there's always something.

Late one night I was fast asleep in my Sydney hotel room when I was summoned to the foyer. It sounded urgent so I was there in a minute. A hotel manager was on his knees, giving mouth to mouth and artificial respiration to Calep. I ran to this side.

"He came into the hotel and collapsed, he's stopped breathing."

Oh Christ, thank God for this hotel manager. I'm not sure I'd have known exactly what to do, but this guy did. He was breathing again soon after the ambulance arrived. I explained who he was and who I was and that I would follow them to the city hospital where he would get a full check. I referred them to Sid who would take care of the insurance policy details. Later we learned that Calep had met some guys in a club, they had been drinking and taking something and it had backfired badly on Calep. I'm sure BB got to know of the incident from Sid and that he had spoken quietly to Calep, who was devastated that he might have damaged the tour. He never did anything like that ever again.

Passing through all the major cities playing great shows we ended up in the Gold Coast, a city south of Brisbane. There BB was playing an enormous casino, very like those casinos in Las Vegas that had hotel gaming rooms and huge entertainment theatres. This was right up BB's street as his home was in Las Vegas. The promoter had thought that as we had a couple of days' rest, he would find us somewhere along the beach to stay. He did, a large apartment block, and we all had our own apartments. The band immediately started planning some home cooking and came up with recipes from the southern states of America – fabulous.

It was there that I sat down with Sid and said that I couldn't take the permanent job with him and BB. He understood of course, it would have been a big step. However, he needed someone who understood the world so he would be looking for someone soon. He said that this would be, most likely, the last tour that I would be on, but I did run into BB and Sid again in Europe at a major festival years later.

Dick and Bauke were relieved that I was not going to be living in the States, as they had tours they wanted me to cover. First up was Fats Domino. He and his band of about ten came from New Orleans – understanding Bebop was hard enough, understanding Fats and his band was nigh on impossible. He had a couple of special New Orleans session musicians who had played on some very famous records; the rest of the band, when they weren't with Fats, would play on the streets or in funeral bands in New Orleans. It seemed to me that being chosen to play in Fats' band was like reaching the big time and sometimes it went to their heads. At that time each flight we took was managed by me and I could get the exact seats they wanted, a window or aisle, two seats together, smoking, not smoking. But sometimes it was not possible, and they didn't like it when I said the flights had been full. In a heated discussion with one of the drummers he threatened me with a knife; I threatened to call the police and he would be on the next plane home before teatime – that didn't happen again!

Herbert Hardesty, one of those famous names from New Orleans, was a tenor sax player and responsible for some stunning sax solos in the 1960s. He had more money than the rest of them and it showed. He had better clothes and was well travelled, but deep down he was just like the others.

I was called down to the hotel lobby in Vienna where a row was ensuing between Herbert and the hotel manager. Apparently, Herbert had gone into his room, settled in and lay down on his bed for a nap before it was time to go for the show. He said he was awakened by a bug or an insect that had just bitten him on his lower arm. He went to the manager, saying that the bug was part of the hotel, so they had to pay for the doctor to come and treat the bite. The manager refused, saying how did Herbert know the bug was on the hotel staff; he could have let it in or it might have come in on his luggage. I listened to this and rather than waste my time mediating the argument that was due to go on for ages, I said to the manager, please get the doctor. I'll pay. Dick and Bauke wouldn't have minded, they would be laughing for days.

Fats was a quiet guy who liked to keep himself to himself and stayed in the hotel suites, only coming out to be driven to the show. I had the band on the bus again.

Home for a couple of weeks and then it was back to Holland for the Everly Brothers European tour. For some time now the Everly Brothers hadn't spoken to each other or travelled together but DIBA International had miraculously talked them into coming to Europe, promising two limos, one for each, same hotel but separate suites on separate floors, separate dressing rooms. Their manager, Peter Brown, had handled them brilliantly and was soon a favourite of Dick and Bauke. The band was made up of famous faces; Albert Lee on guitar, Phil on bass and Ian McLagan, ex-Small Faces, on keyboards; on drums was a well-respected Larrie Londin, ex-Elvis Presley. He had also worked for Berry Gordy and played sessions on many Motown hits, that part of his life didn't end well. He was full of fun and enthusiasm and had arrived on tour with his wife. Peter Brown was the Everly's manager and he'd come along too. The tour itself was an outstanding success and on the final ride back to our hotel I had both Phil and Don on the bus with everybody, Dick and Bauke handed out the drinks and I told the jokes – what a party, albeit a short one.

During this time Peter and Larrie Londin came to me asking whether I could acquire two red English phone boxes. They each wanted one for their gardens back home. I fished around and found some for sale in an ex-military yard in Banbury near Oxford, so when I got home from the continent I drove over there to have a look at them. For £600 each they would knock the concrete off the bottom and crate them up and put any small glass panels in that were missing. It wasn't long before the money for each arrived, and I gave the go ahead to the yard. I got a phone call late one evening, it was Larrie Londin. "Hey, Steve, your phone box has just arrived, and the crane has put it just where I wanted it, thanks very much. Peter got his yesterday. How about that, we both have English phone boxes in our gardens, mine still smells of British piss!"

Everley Brothers.

Me and Dick Jaasma.

Twenty-eight

THE LEGEND OF ROCK AND ROLL, CHUCK BERRY

I was now working more and more with Dick and Bauke and I loved it. DIBA International Concerts was certainly making a name for itself in Europe. After BB King's Italian tour they chose their associate promoters more carefully. They had some really great ones for Denmark, Sweden and Finland.

"Steve, Chuck Berry is coming to Europe, and we want you to be the tour manager."

Sounded great at the time and I duly waited for him at the airport at Dusseldorf. Chuck had his own way of touring. He would bring his long-time girlfriend Cherie Camp and often, but not all the time, his bass player, Jim Marsala. There would be a large Mercedes saloon waiting at the airport. Bauke had the key, they would pack all their cases plus guitars and Chuck would drive himself to the hotel following Bauke and me. After day one Bauke wouldn't be there so I would be travelling with Chuck, too. His suite had to be just so, with a one-piece king-size single mattress bed. He would ask me what time we should be ready to leave and then he would disappear. I had coffee with Jim Marsala and Jim asked if we had the musicians he had asked for, a competent drummer who knew Chuck's material, together with a piano player who also knew Chuck's tunes. The DIBA management boys had done their homework, and everything seemed OK. The amps Chuck wanted were two Fender Dual Showman, speaker cabinets left and right of the drum stand and each amplifier stacked on top of the other – there would not be a soundcheck and no rehearsal with two new guys. James told me that Chuck had a reputation for being hard and he trusted no man. Bauke told me that they had paid him for these shows before Chuck had left his house in St. Louis. Jim's PDs were paid to him by Bauke in dollars and Chuck would always ask Jim if he had been paid before the show. At the hotel leaving time Chuck and Cherie would walk out of the hotel elevator to the rest of us waiting in the foyer. I had been to the show with Jim during the afternoon and he showed me how Chuck has his stage plan, and this should never change. I also had to know the door we would be arriving at and let the security know that Chuck didn't like to be kept waiting so be sure to look out for him and have the parking right outside for the car. Again, Dick and Bauke were well ahead of me, but it was good for me to know what was what.

The dressing room had to be the star dressing room with candy and fruit, no alcohol; tea and coffee would be accepted. When we arrived at the first show, a sell-out crowd was waiting. Everything went as expected and when a security man offered to park the car properly, he was waved away. Just before show time Chuck would meet the two new musicians, then somebody said, I think it was Cherie, "Who is going to be introducing Chuck?"

"He will," said Chuck, pointing at me, "he will be doing it every night, nobody else."

The auditorium lights went to half then Jim led the musicians onto the stage. I followed. I went to Chuck's mic.

"Ladies and gentlemen, welcome to (wherever we were) please welcome the absolute legend of rock 'n' roll, Chuck Berry."

The place erupted. Wearing his guitar that Jimmy had just tuned, a smiling, laughing Chuck Berry strode onto the stage, took my hand and raised it above my head. I left the stage, and they were off. Sounding surprisingly together I had orders to stay in the wings just in case he needed anything and to keep an eye on the time. Towards the end of the show, he would look across at me and I was told by Jim to hold up my fingers showing how many minutes he had left to play to complete the hour. When time was up, he would back towards me, still playing, taking off his guitar in the wings and he was gone; he handed me the guitar and the show was over, no encores. Jimmy would bring the band to an end, and they would all leave the stage. That was the Chuck Berry show on a good day. He never changed out of his show shirt that was quite colourful and would wait for Jimmy to pack the guitars away and then we would all be off to a pre-booked Chinese restaurant. Chinese food was his favourite, with Indian next. He would be in a better mood by now and that was the first time he and I had a conversation. He asked me about my touring history and seemed impressed with whom I had worked. He asked about Dick and Bauke, how well did I know them, were they true to their word, was I paid on time.

DIBA International Concerts had us jumping on and off planes every couple of days. I would get him sitting up front if the aircraft had no first or business class, which he didn't mind. Cherie sat with him while Jim and I went to the back so we could talk. What Chuck didn't like was small turbo-prop planes only holding a dozen or so people; he just didn't trust them, although to get to gigs in Sweden and small towns in the north there was nothing else. He told me that on his rider attached to the contract he had a fine system. If there was anything missing or wrong with the rider requests, ie the size of his bed, the mattress, the car, the dressing room, the piano (only a grand piano on stage would do) and his Dual Showman amps and Jim's amplifier he would fine the promoter immediately. This meant the promoter had to find and give Chuck $2000 in cash before he went any further. This again meant if the car was wrong at the airport on our arrival, he would just sit down in the terminal and wait until the money was given to him. All this, he said, was my job. I would impose the fine and hand the money to Chuck. I'm not sure I was going to like working for this guy. At one airport we had arrived early enough to take a seat near the departure gate to relax for a while and I went off looking for a toilet. Cherie had gone off the other way to a magazine stand and we both happened to return to the seats at the same time. He glared at me. "Where have you been with her?" he asked.

Surprised, I said, "Nowhere, I went to the toilet."

"And I've been to the magazine stand," Cherie said. "We've not been together."

"I think you have been off with her," he said. "You don't worry about her at all, I'm the one you're looking after, I'm the legend. You got that, Steve?"

He was starting to piss me off. "Sure," I said, "from now on, Chuck, I won't walk beside you or any of you, I'll walk five paces in front of you so you can see where I am going, follow me and I'll get you to where you must be, OK?"

"OK," he said.

Frankfurt Airport is one of the busiest airports in Europe and we were using it a lot on that tour. We would load all our luggage onto three trolleys, and each of us, Chuck, Jimmy and I would push one through any police or customs check. So it was on this day that my trolley had my case, the two guitars and a couple of Chuck's bags. I approached the police check.

"Two guitars," the officer said to me.

"Yes, I'm with Chuck Berry, he's just over there going through another check point."

"Oh, yeah," said the officer. "What's this?"

"My bag," I said.

"Then, what's this?" he pointed to Chuck's video camera. It was a large, old-style video camera that you mounted on your shoulder with a full-size video tape loaded in the camera itself.

"That's a video camera," I said.

"Open it," came the order. I did, he lifted out the camera from its large case.

"Then, what's this?" he said, putting the camera down and lifting out a 10 inch black rubber dildo and holding it high in the air. People started to laugh as I feebly said, "It's not mine." He placed it back in the case and put the camera back.

"You can go," he said, still laughing.

I joined the others who had taken some seats, waiting for me.

"Any trouble?" asked Chuck.

"Not really," I answered.

"Did they look at my guitar?"

"No," I said, "but they did look at the camera."

"Did they find anything in there?"

"Yep," I said.

"Did they confiscate it?"

"Nope," I answered.

He smiled. "Good," he said.

If we were travelling through Frankfurt Airport and had less than an hour and a half to make our connecting flight, the chances were that our luggage would not make it on until the next plane. We found that out when we arrived in Vienna for the show; we had what we stood up in. As soon as Chuck was in the hotel with Cherie, I rushed down to the gig to find the promoter; his aides had met us at the airport with a car. Jim wasn't on this particular tour so I was on my own looking for a solution.

The moment I explained everything to the promoter, he smiled and said, "That's OK, come with me." I jumped into his Porsche and he drove like lightning to his best mate's music shop.

"Choose whatever you need," said the owner, "I am privileged to be providing Chuck's guitar for tonight." I chose three Gibson Stereo 335 guitars, and he also gave me sets of strings and a guitar strap. He also sorted out the long stereo lead I needed so Chuck could move around the stage and, of course, do his famous duck walk. On the way back I bought a colourful shirt, so he looked the part. I asked Chuck if he could go down earlier to the show so he could choose his guitar for the evening. We arrived and I introduced the music shop owner to Chuck. Chuck shook his hand and said thanks for helping out; he chose the guitar, and the owner was pleased to get it in tune for him. The musicians on stage that night were fine, and the show went well. Standing in the wings watching the show, the shop owner asked me if Chuck would sign the back of the guitar when he came off so he could put it in the auction, for the town's orphanage, that was happening later that week.

"OK," I said, "I'll speak to Chuck and get it done for you."

At the end of the hour Chuck passed me the guitar and went with Cherie straight to the dressing room. I followed with the shop owner.

"I'll go in, you wait here," I said.

"OK," said the shop owner.

I knocked on the door and entered with the guitar.

"Chuck, the shop owner would like to ask you if you would sign the guitar, only he wants to put it in the auction for a children's charity later this week."

Chuck looked at me and said, "Why should I do that?"

"Well, perhaps because without this guy we wouldn't have been able to do the show tonight," I said, starting to get annoyed.

"The last time I signed a guitar I was paid $3000. Does he want to pay? No, well I won't do it then."

If only the guy hadn't been right outside the door, I would have signed the bloody thing myself, but I had to go out and say sorry, Chuck didn't want to do it. The owner took the guitar, obviously very disappointed, perhaps thinking you can be a legend but that doesn't make you a star.

In Oviedo, northern Spain, we played the Antonio Amilibia Stadium, a huge gig, and there was a roadway right into the venue that went right up to the back of the stage for trucks and even tour buses. We parked the car close to the dressing room area and Jim and I went to the stage to find that the amplifiers were not those specified on Chuck's rider.

"You know what to do then, Steve," came the order. The promoter wasn't happy.

"They're amplifiers and they work," he said. He obviously wasn't a guitarist.

"Can you read English?" I said.

"Sure," he answered.

"Well, did you read the bit on the bottom of Chuck's rider about the $2000 fine? I know you don't like giving money away, I don't, so I would have read the document carefully. You haven't done that, but you have signed it (as all the promoters had to). So now you have got to find $2000 in cash before the show. If you don't, Chuck will not play and then you have paid a lot more than $2000 for nothing, then you've got to give all the money back for the tickets that people have paid."

He left me, cursing, and later walked into Chuck's room with the cash. The musicians were good and did a good show, we packed up and loaded the car. The massive steel doors into the gig area remained closed and we waited for somebody to hit the switch; nothing. The promoter went to Chuck, saying he had paid enough and wanted his $2000 back. Chuck said no and said to us that we would most probably have to sit there for a while. Now he had the police standing by, together with a couple of his friends. After about forty-five minutes I thought they'd have to open the doors to let the trucks in for the load out, this was pissing me off. I got out of the car and went to find the promoter. One of the stage crew had spoken to me in perfect English earlier, so I found him and asked him if he would accompany me and be my interpreter. I called the police over as well.

We stood in a circle, and I said, "This has gone on long enough."

I explained to the police that the guy had signed the rider document without reading it, so what we had done with the fine was perfectly legal. He had not fulfilled his rider contract, he had signed the main contract and rider weeks before, and he'd had plenty of time to find the right amplifiers from any rock music hire company. Every other promoter could do it, why not him? Because he thought he was a bigtime promoter, but he'd messed up. If he didn't open the doors for us now to leave right away we would be suing him for holding us against our will and I would implicate the police for aiding and abetting; they wouldn't have their jobs next week, so what were they going to do?

They spoke, half shouting at each other. I didn't ask my interpreter what was going on. The promoter pushed me and pointed to the exit. "It's open!" He turned and walked away. I walked back to the car, we shook hands, and my interpreter went back to his load out.

I got in the car. "We're moving, I'll tell you about it tomorrow." I don't think Chuck ever asked me what I said, and I don't think I ever told Jimmy.

In Barcelona it was worse. If he and his managers had agreed to any filming of his shows Chuck would always turn up early to check things out; again, this was a tour when Jimmy wasn't there. It was an open football stadium, and the gig was actually in the open air. Chuck, Cherie and I walked into the backstage area. A group of young student-like men and women greeted us warmly, one girl speaking excellent English. They took us to Chuck's dressing room, everything laid out, and we had coffee and cakes.

"We are so pleased that you are here, Chuck, it is a big festival in the city this week and you are the highlight."

"That's nice," said Chuck.

"As agreed, we have the money you asked for in cash for the filming."

"Thank you," said Chuck, looking at the money in a package and handing it to me. I went into a small anteroom and counted it, $10,000. I nodded to Chuck, who seemed to brighten up all of a sudden.

"That's great," he said. "Now what four songs do you want me to play for the recording and I can play those first."

The room went quiet. The girl said, "No, no, Mr Berry. The money is for us to record the whole show for one hour. The programme is going live on the television tonight."

Quiet again, then Chuck said, "You've made a mistake. If you wanted the whole show for a television network live you would have to pay me $100,000! No, you'll get four songs."

They left the room in silence.

"Now what?" I asked Chuck.

"Whatever you do, don't give the money back," said Chuck. "You can't keep it here, take it and hide it somewhere, not at the hotel."

This was Chuck at his worst, and it wasn't going to get any better tonight. I took the package, got in a cab, and went to the main railway station. There I found a left luggage locker, put the package in it and slammed the door, straight back to the gig. I had my story planned if I was asked to return the payment. Chuck was pacing and now wanted to talk to his managers in the US. I met the band, our bass player, keyboard and drummer. He was in no mood to smile with musicians, so I kept them away from Chuck. Did they know his music? They said they did, thank God for that and the young interpreter guy they had given me as my helper. About an hour before showtime the girl from earlier walked into Chuck's room with two suited men, obviously television executives. They apologised for the mix-up and said the network had decided that they would not be filming any of the show so could they have their money back.

"Don't look at me," said Chuck, "ask him," pointing to me.

"I'm very sorry, gentlemen," I said. "I had orders to pay any cash that you gave me straight into the account of DIBA International Concerts, the Dutch company handling Chuck's tour. I've already deposited the money. I don't have any authority or knowledge on how to withdraw any money."

They both looked at me, smiling but not happy. They said to me they would return to take details. I left the building and quickly called Dick and explained what I had done, all I needed for him to say was that I'd done right if they called him.

Showtime. I walked out onto the stage with the three guys who still had not yet met Chuck. I looked out onto a sea of about 12,000 faces and shouted the introduction. On came Chuck, high fives each musician and smiling, I took up my place in the wings with my interpreter mate. Two songs in Chuck looked across and called me onto the stage.

"Change the bass player," he said. I had one ready; Jimmy said if he wasn't playing bass to have a couple of bass guitarists handy cos if Chuck didn't like the guy, he would change him there and then. Two more songs in Chuck beckoned to me again.

"Change the drummer, I can't work with this guy."

I tried to make light of it. "I'm all out of drummers, Chuck," I said.

"Well, I'm gonna play this slow blues for a few minutes. If you haven't changed him by then, I'm walking."

He went back to his microphone, reading a poem to the crowd. I quickly told the interpreter guy to come with me, we jumped over the barrier and into the crowd.

"Now shout 'any drummers, any drummers want to play with Chuck tonight'."

Chuck had started the slow blues song; I didn't have long. Out of nowhere came a gang of five guys shouting excitedly at me. They were saying that they had their friend, he played drums, he was very good (I learned later).

I quickly said to the interpreter to ask the question, "Can he drum properly? Does he know Chuck's music?" Yes, he could drum, he was sixteen years old, didn't know much about Chuck at all but liked rock 'n' roll. I got him away from his mates into the stage wings. Again, questions hurriedly into Spanish questions.

"Can he keep straight time?"

"Yeah."

"That will do." I explained there will be a lot of breaks so he would have to watch me sitting behind the bass amplifier and when my hand went across my throat that was for the break and I would bring him back in again with my hand waving. Oh Christ, Chuck looked across at me as I nodded.

"Time for a new man!" he called out to the crowd.

I beckoned the original drummer to leave his kit and walk off, he wasn't happy either. Our new young drummer got up on the drum riser and looked out at the thousands looking at him. He nervously adjusted the cymbal stand and shifted on his drum stool, he looked at me behind the bass stack, terrified. I smiled at him and gave him the thumbs up.

"'Up in the morning and out to school," two, three, four, stop.

"'The teacher is teaching the golden rule," two, three, four, stop.

His eyes were glued on me, and it was working. By the end of the show this great little drummer was having the time of his life. When Chuck backed off the stage giving me his guitar, with a sign for me to finish the number, he did as good a job as any professional would have done. To cheers he came off the stage and stood next to me. Hold on there, I motioned.

Chuck called me in, "Who's that kid you got, he was OK, can you get him in here?"

Christ, I thought, Chuck's going to pay him. I called the boy. Chuck shook his hand and said something the lad couldn't understand, then instead of paying him he gave him a signed picture of himself. I took the lad back to his friends who lifted him up onto their shoulders, cheering him and shaking my hand. I expect he will remember that night for the rest of his life, I know I will. I walked backstage again straight into the two TV executives and the police.

"Mister, we want our money back and we think you still have it."

Chuck came over and I said I would sort this out and he should leave without me.

The police wanted to take me downtown, so I went with them. I explained to anybody who understood English, but nobody was listening. They took me to a cell, and I didn't protest. Sooner or later, someone would come – they didn't! I'd given the TV men DIBA's telephone number earlier; surely, they'd have checked my story with Dick. Nothing. They let me go without saying much at dawn, so I walked back to the hotel enjoying the early sunshine. I found Chuck sitting in the reception asking what time we were leaving. I hadn't even thought about it.

"Oh, by the way, we'll have to make a quick stop," I said. I hadn't mentioned the station locker, not even to him.

Often, I called the promoter a day or two before our show. I would check that amongst the important things he had the musicians in place: "Yes, yes," they would say.

When I arrived at the gig I would often be confronted by a whole band, thinking that they had the gig. I quickly explained I only needed one drummer, one piano player and a bassist; if the guitarist of the band played bass, chances were he would get to be first reserve if Chuck wanted a change.

The normal reaction to my words was, "Well, if we can't all be involved, none of us want to play with Chuck."

"OK," I would say. "Bye." Now it was the promoter's problem – no band, no Chuck, no money back. He would talk 'em round, perhaps promising a photo with all of them standing next to Chuck or more money, their grandchildren would never know the truth.

Twenty-nine

MORE CHUCK, MORE PROBLEMS AND GOODBYE TO MY MUM

I had a call from Mark Howes, a promoter whose office was in Sussex. Arthur Howes was his dad and a name famous for promoting the Beatles on their early tours of the sixties, now retired. Mark had taken over and was doing a real good job like DIBA had. He had joined forces with a promoter from Glasgow, Robert Pratt, for this UK tour for Chuck. Robert later took over managing Chuck; he already had Don Williams, the country singer. I'm not sure how long he managed Chuck for but I'm sure it couldn't have been easy. Don, on the other hand, must have been a real pleasure. The tour had gone well with no dramas. Mark and Robert had taken care of everything well and there were no fines. However, we were camped for a few days at the London Hilton hotel opposite Hyde Park when Chuck called me to his room. He was livid, his wallet was missing from the bed stand where he said it had always been kept. I called the room service manager, together with the hotel manager, and they both came to the room. He was adamant that the wallet had been stolen, he wanted the doors locked and everybody searched immediately. The manager, in a somewhat cooler frame of mind, called the porters to the room to move all the furniture so that the room could be searched thoroughly. Of course, the wallet was eventually found; it had fallen over the back of the nightstand, not landing on the floor but resting on a wooden ledge at the base of the piece of furniture – everybody happy again, at least for a while.

One morning I had a call from reception, saying there were two men to see me. At first, I thought it was the police, having had a call from Chuck over the wallet episode they had just got around to sending someone over, but no, it was two young men from Hamburg. They apologised and said that they knew this wasn't the normal way of booking Chuck for a concert, but they already knew his tour dates were about to finish, so could they book Chuck for the day after in Hamburg – for cash, of course. I had coffee with them, promising I would speak to Chuck as soon as possible. They would return in a few hours. I caught Chuck lounging in his room having some tea with Cherie; I told him of the meeting.

"$18,000 in cash before I leave this hotel." I'd take care of the flights; they'd take care of two rooms that we need for the hotel. Again, no Jimmy.

"Steve, you take care of the stage equipment and tell them what I want and how it works, OK?"

"Right," I said.

At the next meeting I sat the two Germans down and laid it all out. The money they had, but Chuck would have to sign for it; hotels no problem; musicians no problem. A couple of these guys had worked with Chuck in Germany before and the piano player had studied Chuck's records and was very excited to be playing with him. Next, I went through the $2000 fines with them, saying it was imperative that they take in what I said; they were furiously making notes. We shook hands and they said they would return with the cash. I reported to Chuck, who seemed satisfied. He wanted to be there when they came so I suggested I take them to my room where they could pass the money over in some sort of privacy. When they arrived, I called Chuck and he came to my room. He was friendly and smiling and took the money and signed their receipt. He left saying he would arrange the flights and tell me so I could tell them of our arrival time. On the morning of the Hamburg show we returned the Mercedes to the hire company at Heathrow and went straight for the Hamburg flight; Chuck said he wanted to see the gig early. He had arranged the flights with some of the many thousands of air miles he had accumulated and arranged his return flight to the USA from Germany and not the UK. Everything for the rest of that day went like a dream. The show was great and afterwards he sent Cherie back to the hotel and asked me to go with him to the Reeperbahn just for a look round, he said. We arrived back at the hotel around 1am and just before he got out of the car, he gave me a wad of dollars.

"Thanks for your work on that, Steve. We did good, didn't we!"

I didn't count it until I was in my room: Chuck had given me $1,100 for that day's work.

The next Chuck European tour was with DIBA but no Jimmy again. It didn't get off to a good start at all. Chuck was in trouble at home; he owned a thirty-acre estate in Wentzville, Missouri. He'd built five houses and a restaurant on the site and called it Berry Park. Something had happened at the restaurant, and it was now national news in the States. Chuck, protesting his innocence, left hurriedly for Europe to tour and now the European press were keen to get the story. So, at Oslo International Airport I met Chuck and Cherie, and as they came out of the luggage department with his trolley, he was already swinging his briefcase at photographers and reporters who were getting too close. We arrived at the hotel and the promoter was in conversation with Cherie.

"Don't talk to her, I'm Chuck Berry, I'm the legend. If you're gonna talk, talk to me!"

Oh no, not that chestnut again – this was going to be a miserable two weeks for me. Wherever I could I got Chuck and Cherie out of the different airports out the back way, with the help of the airport staff. During that time, we had a couple of fines imposed on four promoters who hadn't read the rider but signed it. The last two shows were in Sicily at Palermo and Syracuse; we had them in that order on the itinerary. We arrived in Palermo, the capital, and there was a suited and booted delegation to meet us. Chuck wasn't having a good day. The Mercedes car was waiting for us and as we opened the boot to load our luggage Chuck noticed a bit of domestic carpet lining the trunk space.

"This ain't no hire car," he said to me.

He got into the driver's seat and saw a crucifix hanging from the mirror, opened the passenger glove box and found a taxi meter that had been removed from its permanent position and put away, ready to do its day job again when we were finished with it. Chuck got out of the car, took out his guitar and luggage, and went back into the terminal. The reception gang wondered what was going on. Luckily a couple of the guys could speak English, so I explained the rules and they looked bewildered, not having a copy of the rider with them. I agreed with them that we would drive the Merc to the hotel where they could see what they had signed. If the money was not paid to Chuck in cash immediately after that there would not be a show. Chuck drove the car, cursing everything. At the hotel he sat in the lobby with his luggage, not moving until the money arrived – it did. The suited English-speaking gent started to say it would take us about an hour to get to the other side of the Island for tonight's show.

"Hold on," I said, "in the itinerary we are playing Palermo tonight, not Syracuse."

They had them the other way round, everything was ready in Syracuse for tonight's show, my Mafia friend said. Chuck was in no mood to get the news but went to his room, cursing again. I couldn't see the problem with the two venues. The show went well in Syracuse and Chuck, as normal, went to his dressing room to cool off. Before the drive back to the capital, he called me in.

"I'm not doing tomorrow's show," he said. "Tell them that they should not have messed up. I shall be going home a day early tomorrow morning."

Oh fuck! I knew that this wasn't going to go down well with the Sicilians, Chuck was fucking them over. The more I thought about it the more I was convinced he was doing this because he thought that if he arrived a day early there would not be the posse of newspaper men with cameras to meet him. The police were also waiting for him to return home and they had the day after on their calendars.

I went to tell the Sicilians and said I would answer their questions in the morning, the big one being "We would like our money back for the cancelled show, not our fault!" The next morning, I was on the phone to

Dick and Bauke's receptionist. She was a very friendly girl who knew just about everything when we were touring.

"Hi Steve, oh Dick is in Aruba in the Caribbean and Bauke has gone sailing with his family round the Dutch and German rivers. No, they haven't taken their phones."

Now I was in trouble! I explained everything to the men in suits; a few moments later they found me again.

"OK, Mr. Steve, Chuck will leave this afternoon for America. You will stay here in this hotel until we get our money back." No smiles this time. "If you want to leave the hotel, one of us will go with you. Please use the pool and the restaurant."

"OK," I said, having no plan B.

Chuck said goodbye to me and drove himself and Cherie to the airport, leaving me with the men. I called the receptionist again to see what could be done about contacting Dick and Bauke.

"Dick is away for another three weeks and Bauke as well," she said.

"Oh shit!" I said.

I was soon bored by the pool; I felt I needed to be doing something. I took a large notepaper block from my tour case and started to put into poem form every dirty joke I could think of. The title of this literary masterpiece was going to be How Your Bottom Works and Other Rude Stories. The next day I called the receptionist to see if she had come up with anything.

"Oh, hi Steve, are you still in chains? Have they given you the water torture yet?"

"Yeah, yeah."

She had had a brainwave, though. Bauke had done this sailing trip before and had mentioned a really nice restaurant that his wife had loved; perhaps he was going there again.

"I think I can remember the name of the place."

"Brilliant, anything would do, please make the call."

She did and the restaurant owner couldn't remember Bauke, he certainly hadn't booked anything ahead. He would leave a large note on the door that he couldn't miss should he arrive. Great, but I was still looking at another two and a half weeks.

The hotel was nice, right in the city of Palermo. One of my friendly guards was Nicky, and when I asked what the other hotel was like in Syracuse he told me it was on the beach, much better.

I asked if I could have a transfer after Nicky told me how much cheaper that hotel was than the one in the city centre. To my surprise and looking at my good behaviour record I was moved to the beach hotel in Syracuse. The suited men were always polite to me and I to them, and when I got settled in, I noticed that they weren't around so much anymore. I did get the English-speaking boss visiting me every day to see if there was any progress from DIBA; he knew about both men being on vacation. The weather was glorious, and I suddenly had a brainwave and asked him if I could invite my wife to come for a few days or until I was allowed to leave.

"Yes," they said. Next day Anne arrived, having taken the girls to her mum's where they were going to get spoiled to death by their grandma. Day after day we lay on the beach, ordering fresh fruit in a bowl covered with ice and drinking anything we wanted. Every time I finished another dirty joke poem on paper, I would read the poem out to Anne, and we would howl with laughter. It wasn't only jokes I was transcribing. I was also including funny things that had happened to us as a family.

A couple of years before we had been to Majorca, and while on the way to dinner one evening we had crossed the water garden bridge. In front of us was an old couple walking with their friends. Suddenly the old guy dropped a very loud fart, and his friends started to look at each other and laugh. He said to his wife, "Gor blimey, was that you, Doreen?" to escape the blame himself. My little girls thought it hilarious that someone would fart so loudly in public. When we got home, they would fart, and then blame me, always me. So the story, and others like that, were put into rhyme; now this was going to be a bestseller.

A few more days passed, and Anne and I were really enjoying the Sicilian sunshine when I got a call. It was Bauke. He had stopped at the restaurant and had seen the note. I explained the whole story and he immediately spoke to the Sicilian promoter and the town's council, and within a day the refund was on its way. Anne and I packed to go home. I had been here eight days. Bauke said he would pay me for my time, but the truth was I didn't want the extra. He had paid me well as he always did, and Anne and I had had a great time.

We'd been home about forty-eight hours when the phone rang. It was John, my brother-in-law, Janny's husband. They were back from South American duties and had bought a large house in West Monkton in Somerset. Now they were closer to my mum and they could see a lot more of each other. Mum was there and had gone to bed with a headache. During the early hours Jan had heard a loud banging noise and went to investigate. She didn't have to go far. My mum had got out of bed, either to use the toilet or to tell Jan she was feeling worse. She had collapsed and toppled down the stairs, banging her head badly. Jan found her in a heap with a lot of blood coming from somewhere. The ambulance was called, and paramedics thought she was having a brain haemorrhage.

"That was last night," John said, "you'd better come now as they are not sure that your mum is going to survive this, Steve."

We packed a change of clothes, and the girls went again to Granny's, and by the early afternoon we were there. I went to Mum's bedside. They had taken her teeth out and tied a cord around her cheek to hold in a breathing tube; she was on a life support machine and not expected to live. Jan had asked if she could stay that way until my brother Mike could get back from Beijing in China. He was well settled there now, doing a great job as the naval attaché to the British Embassy. He had jumped onto the next plane when he'd heard the news and he would be there the next day. Merry, my younger sister, was already there. As luck would have it, Mum had been taken to the hospital in Taunton where her sister lived, my Aunt Rosemary, and her daughter Rosalind was the ward sister at the hospital, and she saw that my mum had the best possible care. Mike walked in and after greetings and hugs we all spoke to the doctor. It wasn't good. If she woke up out of the coma it would mean she would be more or less a vegetable, not able to move or speak. The only way to know if she had the strength to breathe on her own was to turn the machine off; if she didn't breathe on her own, she would die immediately. The blessing was she was in no pain. The decision was made by us to turn the life support machine off.

"Who would like to sit with your mum?" asked the doctor.

Rosalind was there, turning the machine off, and the doctor would have to be there to record the time of death. Merry was in tears, Jan was comforting her, and Mike said that he didn't want to see her die.

"It's me, then," I said and went to sit by my mum. Rosalind told me to talk to her, it would make me feel better. I started to joke around with Mum saying that with that cord around her face and no teeth she had looked like Popeye, but inside I was breaking up. Now all that had been taken away she looked like my lovely mum again, sleeping peacefully. Suddenly her face twitched, and her shoulders moved, together with her arms. I shot out of my seat and looked at the doctor. He came over and explained to me that this can happen when a body is winding down.

"Nevertheless," he continued, "she has a very strong heart. It will stop eventually, though."

Twenty minutes later it did, and the doctor recorded that Nanny Pat, Grandma Patsy and Mum had died, but she had broken free and most probably run straight into the arms of Harry, her husband and our dad, hopefully. Anne and I didn't hang around. Jan's large house was getting crowded with Merry and Mike and her own family soon to arrive, so we drove home, only to return within the week for the funeral. The service was at a small church in West Monkton and Mum was laid to rest in a beautiful graveyard under a large oak tree.

Thirty

MEETING JIM DAVIDSON, AND I THOUGHT I WAS FUNNY!

All of a sudden, I took a long look at the job I had. I loved meeting other bands and acts and having different problems every day to sort out, but I needed to be nearer to my family. I expect every tour person thinks like that after they have lost someone close. I decided to get a more permanent position and perhaps do a bit of tour managing now and again. Just by chance I ran into my old mate Dave South. He had been touring with all sorts of acts since leaving Curly; The Stranglers, Sex Pistols and one gig he fell into was with a young comedian who wanted the people to hear his jokes, so he hired a large PA system, large enough for a band. He had a band and they and the jokes were loud. Dave loved the gig and Jim Davidson loved him. I went to see him at Baileys in Watford and stood with Dave at the sound control desk, wetting myself with laughter. This was a comedian who didn't care what he said, it was so funny, the music was kicking too. I went backstage to meet Jim and told him I had as many jokes as him although I expected he had heard most of them. I continued to go along with Dave when I could, helping out where I could.

Dave had sold his share of the old Curly PA system back to the company that made it and they put it in their hire company stock. Jim had bought his own system now and Dave was more or less working for Jim full-time. Jim's manager, Laurie Mansfield, had played a large part in the production of a brand-new London musical, Buddy. Jim was asked to invest; he said he would so long as they used his PA system. Needing more equipment for the theatre and his own act, Jim and Dave went out to buy more. This gave Jim the idea to form his own PA sound hire company.

One night he said to me, "Right, I'm forming a new sound hire company. Dave, you will be on knobs. I'm the cheque book. Steve, will you be on the telephone?"

"Yes," I said, "I can do that, right up my street." I knew enough acts and bands – how hard could it be?

Dave had been working for Jim since 1980 and had met Jim's cousin, Julie; she moved into his house in Hemel Hempstead. It wasn't long before she was pregnant, and they were regular visitors to Anne and me who were less than a mile away in Boxmoor.

When the Falklands War was over there was a military township built called Mount Pleasant and it housed thousands of British troops stationed there so as not to give the Argentinians the idea that the islands were ready to invade again. Jim was very keen to give the boys his show and wanted to go. He was just about the first show to entertain there, and he was soon followed by a regular programme of shows from the UK.

Julie was getting close to giving birth when Dave had to leave with the Jim show party to the Falkland Islands. We promised Dave we would look after Julie, although he should be back in time. One night the phone rang. It was Julie, saying something wasn't right. We got in the car and went round. Anne decided that hospital was the best place for Julie and just as well, as a few hours later Julie gave birth to Ria, a three-pound premature daughter. I called her mum and dad who came from London; trying to find Dave was another problem. Eventually I got through and Dave was very surprised and pleased, and told me that he would wet the baby's head in Army fashion later that week. Soon after getting back, they decided to move to Lincolnshire, and bought a house in Chapel St Leonards, outside Skegness. He had also found a warehouse for the new company equipment in Boston. And so Alpha Audio was born. Jim had thought of the name; he had wanted AA in the sound directory for PA Systems, so that his company would be the first on the listings.

I was put in a very nice office in Regent Street in the centre of the West End of London. It was part of Laurie's suite of offices. He had staff looking after many acts, so the place was always bustling.

The Jim show and Dave were working very hard that summer. I had been at the office for a couple of weeks when Dave called me one morning.

"Steve, can you get in your car? Go to this address in Richmond," where a lady was making the costumes for the dancers in Jim's summer season show in Torquay. The show was opening tonight, and she had suddenly realised that they were three costumes short; the woman had them ready for me. I drove the car to Richmond and knocked on the door. The costume lady was enormous and waddled down the hallway, beckoning me to follow.

"Could I use your toilet?" I said. "I'm breaking my neck for a pee."

"Of course, duckie," she said, pointing to the toilet door downstairs. It was a lovely sunny day outside and she had left her red curtains closed so the room was in a dull red light. I quickly undid my trousers and, looking down, I thought I saw a butterfly sitting on the toilet seat, its wings closed. I flicked it off the seat. Wait a minute, I thought, that's no butterfly, that's the fat lady's poo! She had left a nugget on the seat and now I had it on the back of my fingertips. I'm glad I was right-handed. But putting my winkle away and doing up my trousers one-handed was a problem – I washed my hands for at least five minutes. She asked me if I was all right in there, but I said nothing. When I arrived at the theatre in Torquay I relayed the story to Jim and he was laughing, it really tickled him.

While I was there, I was asked to do another small job. During the show Jim dressed as Buttons and Hilary O'Neill, his female support artist that year, dressed as Cinderella. They would be doing the Kitchen Scene from Jim's winter pantomime. With lots of rude jokes he would enter the stage, seeing Cinders so miserable that she couldn't go to the ball. Trying to cheer her up he suggested they go to the small table at the centre of the stage and make a pie together. The table was covered to the floor on three sides by a cloth; the large pie was already bolted to the tabletop. It had a hole in the centre where they were going to put the ingredients. My job was to be under the table ready to grab the ingredients, the long string of sausages and the other stuff, and pull it hard and it would pull the sausages quickly so that it seemed the sausages were flying into the pie themselves. I had been under the table since the curtain went up for the Kitchen Scene and I felt a huge fart in the departure lounge. Seeing as they weren't going to be coming to the table for a few moments I gratefully let it go. God, it was awful, I knew that this wasn't going away anywhere quickly. Jim approached the pie.

"Come on, Cinders," said Buttons, "let's make a Jesus Christ!" Jim glanced down to see me, the tears rolling down my cheeks and my jumper in my mouth. He got the giggles too and it wasn't long before Hilary came to the table and got the good news. They both could hardly get their lines out, let alone the romantic song at the end of the scene – I wasn't given that job again.

Ever since my first meeting with Anne's dad, John King, down in his garden shed in 1970, he and I had been firm friends. We laughed about most things, I always tried to help him out with his cars and even bought an old Morris Oxford from him when he wanted a change. The girls, of course, loved him to bits. He would send them to the local shop to buy his tobacco and laugh when they returned with the tobacco and perhaps a children's sewing kit or colouring books that they had bought with the change. He was a Navy man through and through; after signing up for war duty he was sent to the Caribbean to cruise and protect our islands from possible invasion from the Japanese or the German fleet coming up from South America. As wars go, he had a good one, didn't see much of the enemy but did see a lot of American sailors, more or less doing the same job. John was a big man with fists like two hams and loved a scrap, so if he wasn't in the brig or on punishment duty, he would be getting brown and telling jokes. When he came home, he opened a greengrocery, met and married Anne's mum, Marge. He told me stories of the islands and said one of his dreams would be to go back to St. Kitts where he had had the time of his life.

It was a sorry day in 1990 when John went to the doctor with a bad cough and chest pains. Since boyhood he had been smoking, always rolling his own cigarettes, and when lung cancer was confirmed, he didn't stop, saying he could beat it. Anne and I came up with an idea that we could take him and Marge to the Caribbean to cruise round the islands, including St. Kitts. John and Marge jumped at the idea, insisting they pay for themselves. So, plans were made to go early in January 1991 on a Cunard Caribbean island cruise ship; there would be no children on this ship. As the months went by, we could talk of nothing else, and John regularly attended chemotherapy sessions.

Four weeks before the start date John's doctor advised him to leave it for a year so that he could improve. Getting sick on a cruise could be very costly, especially if they had to airlift him home. He smiled when he told us that he was going to wait, perhaps go next year, and after that he was completely clear. They insisted that we go; perhaps Cunard would make an exception and we could take Jo and Zoe, who were sixteen and eighteen. I went to the Cunard offices in Southampton to change the tickets personally; next it would be passports for the girls. It all came together at the last minute, and we all went to say goodbye to Nanny Marge and Grandad.

"Take plenty of pictures of the islands," he said, "then I can tell you and show you where I had my best punch-ups."

The next day we were off. Stu took us to Gatwick Airport, and we took the flight to Puerto Rico to meet the Cunard Princess. From the airport to the quayside buses were laid on, Caribbean steel bands played all around the ships – party time! John would have loved this. For the next two weeks we were cruising to a different island while we slept and woke up each morning ready to explore and sit on another dream beach.

We flew home through the night and arrived very early to be met by Diane, Stu's wife; her car was smaller. So Anne sat next to Di, and I sat next to the girls with suitcases on our laps. We were all trying to tell Di what a great holiday it had been, all at once, and when we were well on the way home Anne asked if Di had heard how her dad was. Stu and Di were family to us and knew about John's cancer.

"Oh Anne, has nobody told you? Your dad died four days ago."

Jo whispered to me behind a suitcase, "Did she just say Grandad has died?"

I nodded with tears in my eyes. He had been a great friend and I considered him as grandad to the girls, but a dad to me. How Anne held it together on that journey I will never know. After calling her mum on the phone on our arrival at the house, she sobbed for hours. Soon after our departure John had deteriorated, and it was as if he knew he was not going to make it on that trip of a lifetime; he pushed us to go with the girls instead, never mind the reimbursement from Cunard. He said it was so late to cancel he didn't think that Cunard would want to give much back, and he was right of course. When I was with Cunard in Southampton, I'd been told they were only going to allow the girls to go because they were family. No money would be given back, it was just too late.

John's funeral was a sombre affair. He was cremated, and the Royal Navy Association Members turned up with medals on and flags and he was given a colourful send-off. Next Marge had arranged that, according to John's wishes, he wanted to be buried at sea, or in this case his ashes scattered into the ocean. The Royal Navy Association helped, and it was arranged that we would report to HMS Nelson at the Portsmouth Dockyard for a small service. The six of us would be allowed to go on the Royal Naval barge out to the naval burial ground to scatter John's remains and say our final goodbye. Anne, me, Marge, John's son David, and daughter Irene (Anne's sister), and her husband Peter were the six who went to Portsmouth that early foggy morning. We were shown into a small chapel and met by the naval padre who read out John's service record and concluded with a small prayer. Just then a naval rating walked in and whispered into the padre's ear and left.

"Erm, unfortunately the weather is against us this morning and the launch is not able to take you out to the burial site. Then that now concludes the service."

The other families fled out of the chapel, but we wanted to speak to the padre.

"What happens now then? Will we be asked when the weather clears?" we said.

"We don't normally inform families again to join us."

I looked at Marge, whose lower lip was trembling. I suddenly blurted out, "Padre, what if you notified us of the day and time and we came alongside the launch in our own launch to witness the scattering of the ashes, would that be possible?"

"Yes, I would say so," said the padre.

At that moment I'd had a flash of us standing on Jim's £700,000 Princess Afghan Plains and blurted out my request; now I had to ask Jim.

I went to work the next day and told him the story. Jim's answer, "Get the date and time, I'll arrange the boat. We'll need catering and drinks."

"I can do that," I said, grateful that we had at least got the boat.

A week went by, and I was calling every couple of days. Marge and the family were getting quite used to the idea and looking forward to going on this luxury motor yacht. At the end of that week, I was told it had already been done. The padre had not mentioned that we had our own boat to come alongside, permission would have to have been given for Afghan Plains to enter the burial site anyhow and he was doubtful that we would have got it in time. Marge shed a tear at the news. Jim was a little disappointed as he would have loved to show off his skippering and his seamanship skills to the Navy, but there was nothing more to be done. God bless and rest in peace, John, dear friend.

Thirty-one

FUN, FUN AND MORE FUN

Dave had taken on more sound guys to help get the sound system ready for Buddy. His mate Lance Lovell joined the team. This was going to be a lot more intricate than a band with a comedian front man. When they needed me, I went to Plymouth to help fit up the theatre. Buddy would be there for one week then move on to the West End. When it opened the press loved it, the people loved it and Alpha Audio loved it, the money was coming in thick and fast. Soon musical theatrical entrepreneurs were looking at the same sound design and we soon had enquiries from other planned shows. We needed bigger and better warehousing, perhaps with an office above, nearer to London. Jim and I found a suitable place in Sunbury to the west of London and just to the side of the M3 motorway. It was thirty minutes from there to London's theatreland, perfect for us.

Working for Jim was a delight. He was as funny in his day job and real life as he was on stage and had us in fits of laughter nearly all day. I tried to compete with my jokes but only one in fifty got through the heard it barrier. We hadn't long been in the new premises. It had a small kitchen, toilet downstairs, with a warehousing space, stairs as you came through the glass doors entrance up to a large open office, with a private office for the boss at the far end. We had bought desks and cabinets and computers and Jim had bought some leather sofas from home; one we put in his office and the other was for guests. We looked at the kitchen, ordered a fridge/

freezer and microwave together with plates and cups and knives and forks. Next was food.

"Come on, Stevie boy, we're going shopping."

Jim was a household name and on television every week, so supermarket shopping with a trolley wasn't going to be normal. We ended up at Tesco and as we entered heads turned and people said, "That's Jim Davidson," or "Hi, Jim." We filled the trolley quickly with frozen meals for the boys, fizzy drinks, beers, and a couple of good Scotches and vodka, wine for the girl visitors and receptionist. Whilst we went round, he was making people burst out laughing, especially old ladies as they walked round with him.

We arrived at the checkout and there was a queue of about eight people. The woman in front of us was really well-built and was wearing a well-worn shell-type tracksuit. She had her trolley and her eldest son, about six years old, was ready to push it forward. She was pushing her younger boy, about three years, in his pushchair and constantly yelling at them to do this and don't do that. We stood behind her for a moment and then Jim said, "Having trouble with the twins today, are you, love?"

"They ain't bleedin' twins!" she ranted. "This little sod is eight years old and the little bastard in the pushchair there is three. What makes you think they're twins?" She had raised her voice and now had the full attention of our queue and the queue next door.

"Well," answered Jim, "I can't think of anybody who would want to shag you twice."

It's a strange sound when twenty or thirty people are desperately trying to stifle their laughter.

Jim loved to work, to tour and do the summer seasons; this was six to eight weeks at a seaside resort, where he could move his boat into a marina, if possible, otherwise it was the Grand Hotel of this town, and I loved to take time from the office and go and spend some time with the group. It was fun meeting Jim for breakfast, closely followed by lager and lime. We would be drinking at lunch until around 4pm and there would be plenty of drinks in Jim's dressing room for the show. At the end of the day we would all be slightly drunk but happy. Dave had noticed that Jim was drinking a little too often, so we abstained from the breakfast drinks and kept an eye on him, as when he had had a skinful he would often sack everybody and not remember anything the next day, so we didn't even mention it.

At a major music and lighting exhibition in Frankfurt, Jim had given each of us some money to spend and we had gone out into the night for a drink. Laurie, Jim's manager, had come along as well. In the morning Jim was still a little drunk and I had a job getting him out of bed ready for the trip back to the airport. He kept telling me he needed a drink and asked me to find something. At nine o'clock in the morning? All I could think of was to empty his and my minibar miniatures into my pockets. Every ten minutes he'd say, "What ya got?" I'd put my hand in a pocket, and pull out small bottles of vodka and grapefruit, Scotch and advocaat. We arrived at the airport and had to run to the gate; everybody else was ahead of us. I prayed. The German police stopped us to be frisked with their electric table tennis bats, Jim was being funny as usual. As the guard doing the frisking on Jim came up his inside leg, he accidentally collided with Jim's three-piece inside his trousers.

"Steady on!" cried Jim. "Whatever happened to tits first?"

We all had the same ticket, but Jim was put in the Club Class row next to Economy. From there he stood and had the plane in stitches. Getting off the flight an old man, seeing that I was with him, quietly said he had pissed himself literally and had to find a toilet, bit late I thought.

His drinking was getting worse, very much worse, but he could still do the show to thousands of adoring fans. It came to a head the day we had the Alpha Audio Christmas dinner. A good local restaurant was chosen, and the sound crews were invited, together with Laurie Mansfield and Kevin, now Jim's driver. Jim had been drinking in the morning so by the time we all sat down to our food he was gone. Earlier in the week he had told me to make a quick speech after we'd eaten, letting everybody know of the great year we'd had financially and to outline the programme for next year. Jim was so drunk he wouldn't have even heard a word of it. It wasn't great at Jim's house either. At his lovely old forge house in the country near Ewhurst his wife and small children had had to put up with Jim's behaviour. As a last straw, Tracy, his wife, had taken out an injunction order against him coming to the house. After the dinner it was starting to get dark, and Kevin had taken Jim to the local pub not far from his house. He knew about the order; as he got more drunk, he said he was determined to go home. Kevin called Dave and me for help and we immediately turned the car round and made it to the pub. Kevin's plan was to get Jim in the car again and drive around until he was asleep. Kevin had made a reservation in a small local motel, so we followed the Bentley until it pulled into the motel. With the room door open, we carefully got Jim out of the car and into the room, when he suddenly woke up and ran out into the night.

"He might sleep it off in some ditch," said Kev. "I'll drive round and look for him, you guys needn't hang around."

We drove away only to get another call from Kevin. "He's got a lift from some girls that know him, they've taken him home. Come back before the shit really hits the fan."

We got to the house, there was a ruckus going on and Jim was beating on the door. Tracy came to the door asking him to leave before the police came. Bengy, his little dog, a King Charles Spaniel, got out while she was talking to him, and he picked it up and said he wouldn't give it back if he couldn't come in. I took the dog from Jim as he shouted at his wife. She slammed the door and while Jim was still swearing and shouting, I quickly ran round the back of the house and tapped on the kitchen window. Tracy and her mother were sitting at the table looking petrified. I held up the dog so she could see it. She quickly opened the window, and I passed the dog back.

"Please get him away from here, Steve."

"I'll try," I said.

When I returned to the front of the house there was a man confronting Jim. Dave was standing by Jim at his side. The man was trying to give Jim a copy of the injunction order but Jim didn't want to accept it.

As I walked up, he said, "'Ere, hand it to my lawyer then." The man passed me the paper. Just then a policeman showed up. A large police sergeant got out of his car, he couldn't have been too long from his retirement, and he stood quietly by both men. The guy from the court explained who he was and what had just happened, then he left. The sergeant took me to one side and asked if I was really Jim's lawyer.

"No," I said, "I'm not."

"OK," said the sergeant and spoke calmly to Jim and after a while he and Jim left for Guildford police station. Jim spent the night there and on the promise of good behaviour, spent the next few days at home. He and Tracy talked a lot and immediately after Christmas Jim booked himself into The Priory, a rehabilitation clinic, where he stayed for the next six weeks.

The time flew by for us, we were all busy at Alpha getting another show system together. Jim wasn't allowed phone calls, although he did occasionally give his wife a call to see if she and the kids were OK. His boat had been moored at the marina in Torquay since the summer had finished, so he had brought it around the coast to London Bridge marina for a while. It was a beautiful 55-foot Princess motor yacht with three cabins, lounge, kitchen area and a flybridge. He had named it Afghan Plains, and now he was back with us again, not drinking or hardly at all – thank God he hadn't lost his sense of humour. I liked to be in his company and considered him a real friend. One day he invited me to go with him to a cinema in Leicester Square to watch the world premiere of the new Star Wars movie. I wasn't as big a fan of Star Wars as Jim was, and I looked forward to a great night out. The plan was to park the car in Berkeley Square, where Morton's, the club, was and go by cab to the theatre. We would end up on the boat and spend the night there before collecting the car in the morning. The red carpet was out for the cast and other celebrities and people were pointing and shouting at Jim as we made our approach. A glass of wine for me, Jim, I'm not sure about. After the film another glass of wine was at the hosting party and then back to Morton's in Berkeley Square for a few more drinks for me. Just then Jim told me that he was going to stay with Laurie and tossed the keys at me.

"Take the Bentley home, I'll see you at work in the morning."

"OK" I said.

I had driven the Bentley once before. This will turn a few heads in my cul-de-sac, I thought. This was going to be fun. I left Morton's about 1am and the traffic was light as I made my way to the M1 at Hendon. I hadn't been on the motorway more than a couple of minutes when a car came screaming past me with no lights on at all. That guy's going to get nicked, I thought, so I raced up behind him, flashing my lights. He kept on not taking any notice of me, I kept on behind him, flashing. Then I noticed lights flashing behind me, blue ones. I pulled over and he stopped behind me. The policeman asked what I was doing, I explained, and asked if they had noticed the guy in front of me had no lights on at all.

"You were going over 100 mph, sir." It certainly didn't seem like it in this luxury car.

"Have you had a drink tonight?" he asked.

"Yes, some," I said.

He produced a bag, and I blew into it. He returned from his police car a few minutes later with a second policeman who was travelling with him.

"Sir, you are over the limit so I'm arresting you for drink driving. You will now get into the police car and this officer will bring your car to the car compound at Hendon police station."

I was stunned. I felt OK, not drunk at all. At the police station I was led to a cell and the door was slammed shut – what now? I had heard that exercise helped dispatch the alcohol level from the body, so I ran up and down for ages on the spot, doing twenty press-ups every few minutes. After forty-five minutes the door was opened, and I was led upstairs to the duty police sergeant.

"Right, sir," he started. "You were found to be over the limit when you blew into the small roadside bag, now you must blow into the bigger machine, more accurate. You get two attempts. If either of these attempts show you are under the limit you are free to go."

I prayed, dear God, get me out of this. God knows what Jim's going to say when I tell him his Bentley is in Hendon nick. And then there was Anne, what would she say? And how was I going to get to work? I blew in the big machine and the result was instantaneous.

"Well, sir, on the machine you are under the limit, so you're free to go."

Oh, sweet Jesus, I thought, I must go to church to thank him properly. I grabbed my jacket, and the keys were given back to me.

"Oh, there is, however, the case of you doing 102 mph, you'll be hearing from us."

"OK," I said thankfully.

After a week I was summoned to appear at Watford Magistrates Court. I smiled at the judge, who was a coloured woman, as I explained why I was speeding. It was my boss's car, and it was so easy to go so fast in such a luxury car that just purred. She smiled back.

"I understand about the Bentley," she said, "we have one at home, and as you were trying to notify someone that he was breaking the law, you broke the law yourself. You will lose your licence for two weeks and pay a £200 fine. I will not put any points on your licence."

I could have kissed her, but politely said, "Thank you, Your Honour," and left. I went home on the train. I quickly looked at the bus timetable and there was a bus from Hemel Hempstead to Terminal 4 at Heathrow every morning, so the night before I was going to work, Stuart took me and my bike to Heathrow where I chained it to the fence near the bus stop. The next morning, I took the early bus, unchained the bike and then it was a half an hour ride to Sunbury. For two weeks it worked like a dream; I was getting fit losing a few pounds during my sentence.

The call came through to Alpha Audio from somewhere high up. Could we please supply a small PA system with microphones and stands to St. James' Palace where Queen Elizabeth the Queen Mother was wanting to put on a small party for her friends one afternoon. Dave and I had to go down there in normal working clothes but change into black dinner suits for the performance. The Queen Mother had loved Vera Lynn and her wartime songs and now Dame Vera and her pianist were singing them again to a small group of invited guests sitting around our Royal lady in comfortable chairs. The Palace gave us every help and included Dave and me in the after-show snacks and drinks. We stood in line afterwards, saying hello and shaking hands with the Queen Mother. She told Dave how much she had enjoyed the show and thanked him for his hard work. Then another smartly dressed lady, who I recognised as Princess Michael of Kent, came and started to talk to Dave and me. I was amazed that the Princess was able to ask questions about the sound equipment and sound itself; the Royal Family must be taught to talk about all sorts of stuff as next week she might be in a conversation about pig breeding to some farmer lucky enough to meet her. She had put us at ease and was happy to have her picture taken with Dave and me. That picture still sits on my wall today.

Burns Night.

Thirty-two

GREAT YARMOUTH

Then Jim announced that Great Yarmouth Council had given him the Wellington Pier Theatre to do up. He loved that old theatre, as his parents had taken him on many holidays to Great Yarmouth during the summers and to him it was like coming home. So, I stayed there with Kevin and our mate, Stukie, and we started to knock down the bits we wanted gone. Jim had also donated time and money to the Caister Lifeboat (they had named an inshore rescue boat after him) and all the men there were keen to help. John Cannell, Mickey Knut and Sid Fosdick were there every day with us. Enter Edward Moore and his new company ELM Contracts and they were going to do the complete refurbishment. I even did a bit of plumbing there to keep my hand in. The plan was to do a great job and then ask the National Lottery to help fund it; they came several times to see the work, but I think Jim paid the six-figure bill himself in the end.

Dave and the boys from Alpha turned up to fit the sound system in and I, together with Kevin and Stukie, mounted the lights. New stage curtains were bought and when we'd finished the paint job the beautiful little theatre really did look the business. Jim planned a stunning opening show. First, a ballerina would float across the stage that had to have a thin coating of dry ice.

"Stevie, we need a load of dry ice for this number. Make it so."

"OK," I said.

My first plan was to put a 3-inch plastic drainage pipe across the front of the stage and the two small dry ice machines would pump the helium air smoke from each end of the pipe; with holes drilled along the drainpipe the dry ice would float over the stage evenly.

"Brilliant," smiled Jim, "now let's test it."

We warmed up the machines and dropped the block ice into the hot water. The dry ice started to flow out of the holes but at the same time the pipe became a twenty-five-foot whistle.

"Stop, stop, stop," from Jim, "we can't have that."

"OK," I said, "we need more holes in the pipe."

Out came the electric drill again, lots more holes.

"Try again," shouted Jim.

It was silent now and started to work. Just then a suited figure walked in and after watching for a few minutes asked, "Is that dry ice?"

"It most certainly is," said Jim, before asking, "and who are you, mate?"

"Health and safety. You cannot have dry ice flowing off the front of the stage if you have musicians in the pit."

"Who says?" says Jim.

"Health and safety, that's who," said Mr Suited and Booted. "If they get sick, they can sue you!"

"Sod them then," said Jim, "the dancer will dance to recorded music, and while she's dancing, they can have a cup of tea backstage. OK now?"

"Better," said the man, laughing.

That wasn't the end of the dry ice saga. Besides the two small machines Jim had bought a monster machine ready to give out dry ice up to three feet thick right across the stage. Not knowing exactly how dry ice would perform from this giant machine, Mickey Knut and I set up this monstrosity in a small room to the side but lower than the stage. We had to wear thick gloves to load the carbon dioxide blocks from the freezer, where they lived, into the hot machine. We only had so many blocks so it was decided we would use it for the dress rehearsal and the show itself. Jim was directing the show.

"Stevie, is that dry ice machine hot yet?"

"Yes, Jim, we're ready to go."

The music started; the dancers were ready. "Cue the dry ice," he called.

Mickey and I worked furiously, chopping up the carbon dioxide blocks into the machine, this new machine was the business.

"Cue the dry ice!" shouted Jim. "Where's my dry ice?"

There was so much heavy dry ice smoke being produced that the pump wasn't strong enough to pump the smoke up high enough onto the stage. The little basement room was filling up quickly, the level of smoke now up to our chins. Mickey ran out as if he was going to be drowned by it. I stood still, and I couldn't see a thing in front of my face. I heard someone come running down the stairs.

"Where's my bloody dry... Oh, Jesus, what's this? Steve, where are you?"

"I'm here," I shouted.

"Christ!" he said.

I had shouted in Jim's ear when it was only three inches away from my loud voice. We burst into laughter. We brought the machine up to the back of the stage for the show and everything was fine. A great opening show, Jim had directed it really well.

I'm not sure who thought about it first. Sound crews and lighting crews fitting up touring musicals doubled in number when the show had to come down in that particular town, it was then a race to get the equipment packed away and the miles of cables recoiled and put into their flight cases. The work would start as soon as the curtain came down after the last performance and take to around two or three o'clock in the morning to finish. Then what? Not worth going to a hotel; they had to be more or less at the next theatre at the same time as the trucks were arriving. What if there was a van or small coach with beds in it so the crews could get some sleep before the next load in, somebody said. The idea grew on us. I had built a small tour bus out of an old Markus Deutsch van and that had worked well. Alpha had two identical Mercedes vans and Jim decided that one could be put over to be converted.

"Stevie, make it so." It took a couple of months to do, and we had professionals put in a coach headlining and windows. I built the six bunks and Lance covered the wood with this grey carpet and strong glue. Proper coach seats were bought instead of second-hand airline seats, and a coffee area with water heater and TV and video machine were installed. We were all thrilled at the finished job. Lance let the companies know it was now available, the only one of its kind, and the bookings came rolling in. Either Lance or I would drive while the crews slept: God, they needed it. It was Jim who came up with its name, 'The Kipper'; couldn't have been called anything else really.

When Jim came back to us back from the clinic we expected him to be into God or some religion, as many of the reformed celebrities were when they were released. Not Jim; he had taken a very keen interest in Masonry and had been invited to join the showbiz Lodge at Chelsea. Our company accountant, Robert Simons, was also on the square, so they had great conversations about this charitable society. Then one day I was called in to see them both and I was invited to join them. I accepted the invitation and went to speak to an older gentleman high up in the Lodge rankings. His first question to me was, "Do you believe in a God?"

"Yes," I answered, and from there on the conversation was very straightforward. I would have to learn long formal answers to the questions I was asked by the officers and when I had done that, I would be installed into the Masonry brotherhood. Each visit to the Chelsea Lodge, (which was actually in Queen Street, nowhere near Chelsea) would end with us all sitting down to dinner and laughing and joking a lot. As the Chelsea Lodge was the recognised show business Lodge, there would be a short cabaret of elder retired musicians and comedians who would get up and do a turn for old times' sake. They were all retired but brilliant entertainers, and they were loudly appreciated. There were some secrets in the society to be observed and the initiation of the young Masons was one. Very few people outside Masonry actually know what happens. I had heard though, through the grapevine, that all newcomers had to kiss a goat's arse, and one said, "You get stripped to the waist and they spank your arse." Oh no!

On the day I was initiated all the members filed past me to go into the Temple and I was blindfolded. I was going to be led in when everybody was seated. One of the initiating officers was a little late in going in and raced past me, his chain of office with something metal attached to it jangled as he sped by me; it sounded just like a small cow bell. Oh shit, I thought unable to see anything, there is going to be a goat after all – there wasn't. Jim had been led in like that some time before and was now moving swiftly up the Masonry ladder.

Thirty-three

PLAYING AGAIN, TROUBLE AT HOME

For a while now I had been playing again. I thought I might try something tried and tested, a wedding orchestra. I formed a twelve-piece band easily from past playing mates and local musicians. I bought pink jackets and dance band-type music stands with the initials 'SSO', the Sovereign Sixties Orchestra, also in pink. The piano keyboard was placed in a pink grand piano frame that I made from light plywood so it would fold down. The presentation was first class, the music kicking and the girl singers doing a really great job. We'd been doing that for a year when I was asked to put together a Blues Brothers tribute band. I asked Nicky Payne, Stuart, and Tony from Adam, to join. Nick found the other musicians from his playing circle in London, and I asked Dave Williams, a very old pal of mine from Watford, to play guitar. I couldn't believe how good this band was going to be at the first rehearsal, the singers Paul Cox and Al McClean were the reincarnation of Jake and Elwood Blues. It wasn't hard for me to find two black suits, ties, and trilby hats. The first gig that came in was from Amway, a pyramid selling company that spent thousands on their conventions in great venues. I'd hired Lance to take the equipment to Cardiff's Motorpoint Arena, I hired a coach, and we sped down to South Wales. It couldn't have gone better. They loved it and we were booked for several more shows. The money was good, especially when we played two venues a night (the NEC and the Birmingham Symphony Hall), even better when we played the Sunday morning worship sessions. Everybody in the band either had other music commitments or jobs, so playing every week wasn't imperative. I loved that band.

Back at the Alpha warehouse Jim was keen to expand his office space and Lance was called in to build new offices at the back of the building. He and his brother-in-law worked well, and Jim offered him a full-time job with us. He had a Class 1 driving licence, knew about sound mixing – he was perfect for us. Stuart, my old playing pal, also got a job working for the production team of Buddy and he mixed the sound for the show at Victoria Theatre in London for several years before moving to Spain when his marriage folded.

Things at home were, I thought, going along OK. Over the next few days, I tried to figure out how I could have been so wrong. Anne had risen through the ranks of management with the Abbey National Building Society and now had taken a job as a company lecturer. Her boss was a woman of her own age and the two seemed very close. It was Anne's job to lecture managers about the different aspects of the Building Society; she would spend time with her boss friend and then travel to lectures, sometimes staying in hotels for a couple of nights. I was at home almost every night now with the girls and between us we could knock up some fabulous, interesting meals. We had just had a great weekend and she was off the next morning, but at breakfast she was snapping at me and the girls and I, for one, was snapping back; in the end she stormed out of the house. The more I thought about it the more I thought the argument was futile and decided to send flowers with an apology note to her hotel. I called her boss, and she gave me the name of the place Anne was going to be staying. I sent the flowers, then called a couple of hours later to see if they had arrived. The hotel didn't have Mrs Farr registered or booked for those days. I felt uneasy, so I called her boss back, asking why she had given me a bum steer. I must have caught her off guard as I stumbled round the explanation that Anne had asked for some time off and she hadn't gone to that hotel, she didn't know where she was. Now I was worried, had she been seeing that guy from before? I sat down with Jim and Dave and told them what was going on.

"You need to sort this out today," said Jim. "Find out where she is and go sort it, don't come back until you have done that."

I had been calling her mobile continuously and she eventually answered; she hadn't liked that particular hotel so she hadn't gone there.

"But you weren't booked in there, you never were, where are you now?"

"I'm on the M3."

"Right,' I said, "go to Fleet Services. I'll meet you there and you can explain all this."

"OK," she said.

As I drove down the motorway all sorts of things were crashing through my brain. How was I going to handle it if she wanted to part? I had been sitting in the car by the entrance to the restaurant at Fleet Services for two hours now; she wasn't coming, and I called her again. This time she answered quite quickly.

"Where are you?" I shouted, starting to get annoyed.

"I've had some trouble with the car. I'll go home, and I'll see you there."

When I got back to the house it was about 6pm and the girls were in but no sign of Anne. I told them of the day that I'd just had. Just then I heard her key in the door, she came into the kitchen and blurted it all out. She had met this guy from one of the courses and they had been seeing each other for about six months. He lived in Kent and that's where she was going when I called her. I thought I was taking this pretty well. I hadn't got angry or upset, not like the girls though, they went for her, saying they didn't want anything more to do with her. Now Anne was getting upset.

I told her to go over to her mother for a couple of days and then come back when we were all a bit calmer; she did that. A few days later she returned, saying that she was in love with this guy, and they eventually wanted to be together, he was single and eighteen years younger than her. Joanna, my eldest, was just starting to buy her first house by herself, saying she was glad she was getting out of it. Zoe, on the other hand, was close to her mother and didn't want the family to break up. As for me, I didn't quite know what to think. Why wasn't I getting upset? Perhaps deep down I saw our relationship going stale and I'm sure, when the dust settled, we would like each other again. Now, though, perhaps I could start rethinking my life, perhaps out on the road again. Anne didn't want to go anywhere for the time being so I said I would convert the study downstairs to a bedroom for her; it had a bathroom next door. I would stay upstairs, and we would eat together at least three times a week. We agreed we would bring nobody into the house to sleep the night while the girls were there.

A few weeks later I was busy helping Jo move only two miles up the road to a small, terraced house which she was very proud of.

Another year on and with Jo gone and Zoe out with her friends the house seemed strangely empty to me, so I stayed at the office at Alpha often with Dave when he was always working to get sound equipment ready and out in time. For some time he had been separated from Julie, and had met a pretty blonde singer, called Karen. They had met as she often used to support Jim on his shows. One evening they were talking on the phone, and she suggested that I meet a friend of hers who was in a similar situation to me. Mary was living with her two children and her husband was long gone. The following evening, I was talking to Mary on the phone. She seemed really friendly, and we got on right away. We spoke every evening after that and were soon talking about our sex lives or the lack of them. She told me that an old lady had told her to use a sex toy when there was no man about, but not wanting her kids to find vibrators in the bathroom, she had elected for something else. I was intrigued and I asked what; rather than tell me she offered to come over to the office one evening when everybody had gone home, and I was all for it. I was delighted when she walked in a few weeks later. She was pretty, with a great smile and we talked and laughed as though the conversation would never stop. I had bought wine and the office lights were dimmed and with the leather sofas it looked like a fitting place for our first meeting. I'd been thinking about tonight all day. So it wasn't long before we were in each other's arms and the clothes were coming off. Now we were both naked and she reached for the carrier bag she had brought in. She smiled and said, "Do you want to see what I have brought?"

"Of course," I said.

From a box she lifted out an Oral B electric toothbrush. Again she explained that the old lady had said it's a great sexual toy, and looked very innocent on the shelf of the bathroom. As she spoke, she put the toothbrush together as expertly as if she was preparing a sniper's rifle. Once together she tested the battery with a few short stabs, reminding me I did the same thing with my strimmer in the garden before I went to war on the weeds. She lay back and started to work on herself not saying much but grinning from ear to ear. I sat by her staring intently; after a few moments she stopped.

"What can I do?" I asked eagerly.

"Nothing right now," she said. "I know, go and make a cup of tea."

The kitchen was down the cold stairs by the warehouse, and I flew down there. I didn't want to miss much. Of course, the kettle took forever and just as I had made two hot mugs of tea, there was a cry, "Stevie, come quickly!"

Jumping the steps two at a time completely nude with two steaming mugs of tea was a risky business with hot tea jumping and splashing everywhere; I didn't care if any of it splashed onto my three-piece, quite frankly it could have done with the warmth, it was that cold a night. I burst into the office to a different Mary from the one I'd left, she was now yelling, staring at the ceiling, her body gyrating. I put the tea down, not too close to her because things might be getting worse. I had to be involved somehow. I dropped to my knees and tried to get my head between her legs. It was as if the electric toothbrush had a mind of its own and attacked me on a few occasions in my mouth, in my eyes and even up my nose! I started to laugh and so did she. She threw the toothbrush away, still buzzing, and we passionately finished the evening off, twice. We were still laughing and joking as we dressed and then realised that the tea had gone cold. Shame.

Mary came over to Alpha several more times and I went to hers, in Essex where she lived. She went into a London hospital to have a serious operation and I visited her there with flowers, but we didn't see much of each other after that. Later Karen told me that she had met a really nice guy and they planned to marry. I was very pleased for her – marriage certainly wasn't on my schedule. Some weeks later I retold the story to Dave and Jim and forever after Mary was named Oral B. Jim even turned it into a story for his stage show and he finished it off by saying, "Stevie has never had a filling since!"

Thirty-four

P45 TIME, THEN YARMOUTH AGAIN!

The lighting side of the company had been growing steadily alongside Alpha Audio. Jim wanted to call the company Cellulight Limited and it wasn't long before he had his cheque book out again to buy a host of moving lights and controls. He wanted an American system called Synchrolights and it wasn't long before we had to find our first lighting designer to understand them and put complicated instructions into its computer. He used them on his summer season shows and pantomimes to great effect. Enter Billy Potts, a well-known moving lighting engineer who worked mostly for The Stranglers. His first job was to create something special for Jim's show in Torquay. He cleverly devised a lighting show that started automatically when the music began, therefore no operator was needed; the sound engineer just had to hit the play button on the recorded music. He was then asked to build a lighting rig and design a moving light system ready to go to Poland. Jim had put together a large event for the troops in Poland, starring himself, of course, and the whole company was looking forward to taking the show there. Jim was taking his band and Karen plus dancers, so it was imperative that the lighting designer was there to erect the show and run it alongside the sound crew.

I had been working with Billy Potts on the lighting rig and as we finished it, he told me he would not be going to Poland to run it. I was dumbfounded as it was only a few days before we left. I had to tell Jim, and when I did, he went nuts, blaming Dave and me for hiring such an unreliable guy, and we didn't have time to replace him. Then, out of the blue, he sacked Dave and me. We thought nothing of it and went to the pub for an early lunch. After the break we called in and were told to go home. Dave was furious, and the next morning came round to my house, saying it had been nothing to do with him and he considered he had been unfairly dismissed. We started to make plans about seeing a solicitor to see if we had a case, but it didn't come to that. Robert Simons, the company accountant, stepped in and worked out a final payment to suit us both.

I was happy to be at home and did some odd jobs. When I had left Dick and Bauke in Holland to work for Jim, I had found a great guy and experienced tour manager in Chris Markland; he had slotted right in at DIBA International. He called me to see if I still had my large Mercedes.

"I need you to drive Gerry Marsden (of Gerry and the Pacemakers) around for a day or two."

"OK," I said, "I'll enjoy that."

Some months later I had Jim on the phone.

"I've been given the Winter Gardens next to the Pier from Yarmouth Council. I'm going to make it into a nightclub. Will you help me, Steve?"

"Yes," I said straightaway.

The Winter Gardens was a large hall made completely of glass in steel frames. It was huge, bigger than a tennis court. There was a lot to be done. Me, Kevin, Stukie, John Cannell, Mickey Knutt, Sid and Edward and his ELM company were all called to arms. It was to take about six months, so I rented a cottage in Caister, just outside Great Yarmouth. The work was fun, and it was great to see this old building that had been a dance floor, then a roller skate arena, turn into a modern nightclub with lasers bouncing around and then out to sea. The Alpha boys came in and put the sound in and we had new guys on the lights, Wayne and Neil, to build the lighting and laser rigs. The club was on one floor with a food section and four bars.

"Find some young staff, Steve," ordered Jim. Now I was hiring. Loads of young people turned up for the short interview I had devised. Basically, they had to tell me about themselves, then I would say yes or no. An older guy, about forty or fifty years old, sat down in front of me. He lived in a squat and was wearing pyjama trousers and an old-fashioned dinner jacket. He'd been homeless and was desperately looking for work, perhaps getting his own flat again. He promised me he would work hard and never let me down. I had a job for Norman.

"You will be in charge of the glass-washing machines, Norman. I will show you what to do and you'll be so busy you won't have time to come out into the club for a wander or a drink. Do you think you can do that?"

His face lit up as the tears ran down his face.

"Oh, yes, sir," he said.

"I'm just Stevie, Norman. Your boss is Jim Davidson, and he would want you just to call him Jim. OK?"

All the staff were bought black trousers and Hawaiian shirts, and the girls had black skirts. An hour before we opened Jim met the staff at his new club. The hype around the town had been fantastic and we expected hundreds of people on that opening night. He looked round his staff and stopped at Norman and looked at me. I smiled and said I'd explain later. When I did get to talk to Jim he said, "Well, why not? Let's keep an eye on him though."

The gents' toilets were large enough to cope but the women's toilets or cubicles weren't, so we had brought in some very posh mobile toilet units and opened a side door so that they could be reached. They had to be fenced in, though, to stop gate-crashers. The place was buzzing when I was told the women's toilets were backing up. I was in my suit and went to investigate; I immediately knew what was wrong. The manhole cover by the mobile toilets had to be raised to get to the blockage. There was no time to call a plumber or sewage clearing company, it was ten o'clock on a Saturday night. Mickey Knutt and I found some tools and managed to get the manhole cover off. The shite was right to the top.

"I need an old broom handle and a towel and some string," I said. These were found and I made a large wad out of the towel and tightened it to the broom handle with string. Next, I lowered it into the manhole and pumped it up and down, trying to push some force against the blockage. At one point I was going like a steam train, pumping furiously, when the glasses, that I had put in my top jacket pocket for safety, jumped out straight into the poo and sank. Just then there was a gurgling noise and the level of the sewage dropped drastically. There was no way I was going to look for my glasses – manhole cover back on quick! John Cannell and Jim thought it was hilarious. John knew the Yarmouth councillors, having been one himself, and said he was going to speak to the health and safety officer to ask his men to keep an eye out if they came through the sewage works.

Still laughing, Jim said, "Forget that, buy some new ones on the company tomorrow."

On the second night I was told by the staff to go to Norman's glass kitchen quickly. He was pissed. "I told him he wasn't to go to the bars," I said, "he'll have to go." When I got there, he wasn't completely drunk; he was on the way, but he was still doing his job. I watched him from the door before he saw me. As the staff were bringing in the empty trays of collected glasses, if there was a drop of beer in the bottom of the glass Norman would drink it. I went in, laughing.

"Norman, don't do that. You can't be drunk and do this job, you promised me."

"OK," he said, "I still promise."

He never did that again. Through the summer Jim bought him clothes and shoes and at the end of the summer Jim made him Employee of the Season and gave him an extra £100. Norman wept for joy and hugged Jim – good old Norman.

One weekend my girls came to see what I'd been up to and were very impressed with the Winter Gardens. To my surprise, Anne came with them, and we had an early dinner together. Later, walking to the club, Anne said she had come to ask me if we could sell the house. She needed her own place; she had been nearly two years living downstairs. I agreed and told her to put it on the market. We had paid £14,000 for that council house some twenty-four years before, I had put on an extension kitchen, and we had many improvements done through the years. It was sold in less than a week. Two families, or fathers, wanted it for their daughters when they were getting married at about the same time. One would offer, the other would increase that offer, and then one of the fathers came to see Anne one evening (I was still in Yarmouth at the club) and offered £15,000 more than the asking price if she said OK and took the house off the market immediately. She called me and I said yes.

With the club up and running well I really didn't want to be the manager. I think Jim saw this and said that this coming Saturday night would be my last. It was; his daughter had wanted the job and I wished her every success.

Thirty-five

THE FAMILY BREAKS UP, SO I'M OFF TO THE FALKLANDS!

At home we had to decide what was going to happen next. We only had a few weeks to find somewhere, or two somewheres, for us to live. It was decided that Anne would go to her sister Irene so she could take the dogs with her; Jo had her own place now; Zoe was going to her grandma's (Anne's mum not too far away from Irene); I was going to stay with Stuart in Berkhamsted and we would look for a place for me to buy. As the vacancy date came close, I went to a removal company to arrange for all our furniture, tools, garden stuff to be stored. When the day came when we were splitting up, never to be living together again, the teary goodbye was cancelled when Zoe came racing downstairs saying that one of the old removal men had used the toilet upstairs and stunk the whole upstairs out. We were laughing as we walked out of that house.

I moved into Stuart's, with Lance's help. He had left Alpha Audio, wanting to start his own business with his first artic truck. He said to me, "Sell your Mercedes and buy a van. A man and a van will never be out of work." I did exactly that and the first week I was trading I made three times the wages that Alpha had paid me. Another Alpha mate's wife, (a sound man, Andy May) helped run a rock 'n' roll catering company called 'Eat to the Beat' and she gave me lots of work, moving catering equipment around London and the UK. We became very good friends. Meanwhile, Stuart and I were looking at houses for me, although nothing the size of the Boxmoor house; I fancied a small old-fashioned cottage and we viewed a few over the first months. Then his relatives asked for accommodation. They were coming from America and planned to stay for some time, so I vacated Stu's and went immediately to Tony's, very near to Whipsnade Zoo in Bedfordshire. Since finishing with Adam, Tony and his father had expanded the business and he was now living in a grand house with his wife Cathy and two children, Maddie and Jackson. Jackson was about eight years old and when I moved in, he would jump out on me, with his hand making the shape of a gun, and would make bullet noises, sometimes machine gun fire. I would retaliate with my imaginary gun with noises included, and he would get shot and writhe all over the floor. He did it to everyone who visited, including Stu, so he was now not called Jackson but Exploding Boy. We still talk about Exploding Boy now, twenty odd years later.

I was sitting in Tony's kitchen when I got the telephone call from the removal firm that had taken all our possessions into the store. There had been a fire, and everything was gone; would I go to the office in Hemel Hempstead to fill in insurance claim forms.

"Surely, not everything?" I asked.

The fire heat had been so intense that my stone statues from the garden had cracked and split, and my aluminium ladders had buckled; everything was gone. The girls, when I told them, were upset, but looked forward to buying new. I collected the claim forms from the office and a few days later met with Anne and the girls so they could list their clothes and bedroom stuff. It would be a while before I would hear from the insurance company. At last, a company rep asked to see us. Anne and I arranged for the two men to come to Tony's house one afternoon. We sat down and went through the forms I had submitted, and they asked some strange questions. Somehow, they didn't seem to be ordinary claim agents and I let them know that they were acting more like the police; the two men looked at each other and then explained that's more or less who they were, the insurance police. There had been so many claims regarding this fire that the company was suspicious of those claiming.

Anne and I started to shout back, that this fire had left us with nothing, and we would fight them in court if necessary. All the claims had come down through the removal company and it was for a staggering amount of money, so they had to be sure. For weeks it went quiet and then I was told to get a solicitor to handle my claim against the insurance company. Later I went to court with only a few others to make our claims bona fide. My solicitor called me a few weeks later to say that the removal company had been found guilty of fraudulent claims and the insurance company would now not be paying anybody. Anne and I were furious, and I went immediately back to my brief; he suggested we now sue the owner of the company and claim against his business, and his house if need be.

Weeks passed again; when I heard from the solicitor, the owner of the removal company and his son had been convicted of moving illegal immigrants into the country in their trucks, and they had been given seven-year jail sentences. It was now not possible to sue through his house. We still had nothing, and I'd just bought a brand-new Barratt's home in Leighton Buzzard. I'd got fed up with trying to find a cottage with character, so I opted for a new three-bedroom detached house with garage and garden. It was going to be Christmas in a few months. Zoe and Jo bought me a Christmas present early in the form of a huge television. I had chosen the house option that had given me a gas fire, gas hob, oven and cooker, cooker hood, dishwasher and fridge, then had ordered the house to be carpeted by a large department store in Watford; I also bought chairs and settees and beds and it came with a very large account that I could pay off every month (perfect for me).

Since our sacking at Alpha, Dave had found a job working with CSE, the company that arranges and sends the different musicians and acts to the Armed Forces wherever they were stationed around the world. He had his warehouse at the CSE site in Chalfont St Giles in Buckinghamshire. He had been to Belize, Cyprus, Malta and other hot places, having a great time doing the job that he loved doing. I asked if there was any opening for a tour manager/lighting engineer: he said he would keep his eye out for me.

Now I was settled in Leighton Buzzard, I went to a very large parcel delivery company to see if there was any work for my van and me. They tried me out and I passed with flying colours but offered only filling-in work, when the drivers didn't turn in. I told them of my other catering and music work, and they seemed satisfied with that. I would get a phone call around seven thirty in the morning if I was needed and I was usually loaded, paperwork collected and away by 9am. The money was good, especially as they were paying for a man and his van.

Because the profit on the Boxmoor house had been very good, I'd paid most of it down on my new house, not leaving much on my mortgage, so the payments were quite easy. The van work was flooding in, moving theatre lights or sound equipment, catering kitchens or parcels, I loved being that busy. Even Andy's wife, Bonnie, the catering queen of Eat to the Beat, put her secretary my way when she wanted a room to rent.

One evening Dave called me from CSE. Would I be interested in going to the Falkland Islands to run the lighting rig for Shakatak, a charting band from the eighties? He would be doing the sound. "Great," I said, "yes please." This was all new to me, working for the Forces. I prepared the lighting equipment with Dave at the CSE warehouse and then we drove it down to the military air base at Brize Norton. There we loaded it all onto special trolleys that an air ground crew (all RAF guys) would load onto the aircraft just before we left; nothing could be forgotten. Mount Pleasant was a huge military camp but there were no trees on the islands, let alone music shops. On past trips Dave had left all his big speakers and mixing decks there and I was going to leave most of my lighting equipment. On the travel day we were securely checked onto the air base and then went to the restaurant for a meal before we left. The flight was going to be full of squaddies going to do their six months' stint on the island. The flight itself was going to take nearly 24 hours, with a stop on another military island on the equator called Ascension. When the flight was up and away the stewards, all RAF personnel, handed out Sony video boxes, battery run, about the size of a box of chocolates. There were many movies to choose from and there was no limit to the number you could watch. At around the halfway stage we would land on Ascension and be taken off the plane into a secure compound. There were toilets and a shop and a café, all with a high wire fence. The military obviously didn't want anybody wandering around their air base. We would be here for up to two hours while the plane, a Lockheed Tristar, was refuelled and restocked with more movies and food. It was off and another eight hours to the Falkland Islands. As we came in to land the Falkland Islands were made up of hundreds of uninhabited islands, all very bare and again with no trees. Camp Mount Pleasant was about six miles from the Islands' capital, Stanley. I later learned that huge cruise liners always made a stop at Stanley, God knows why! It was only a thousand miles from Antarctica and the South Pole. The capital was one street, the water and the beaches were always freezing cold, and any bather would last up to about four minutes before losing muscle control and drowning.

The runway was on the military base so once we were on the ground soldiers were marched off to their accommodation, and we civilians were driven in Land Rovers to our block. Each of us had our own room, basic but comfortable. The concert party was Dave, me, the band and supporting acts, normally a comedian or a magic act and, of course, dancers. The next day we set up the equipment for the first show that evening. We were instructed before we left to pack a decent jacket, trousers, shirt, and tie, as we would be hosted in the Officers' Mess after the first performance. The young officers would move in on the pretty dancers, giving them the edge on the enlisted men. From day two the cast and crew would be hosted by a different regiment each night; our favourite was an evening with the Gurkha Regiment, as their food was Nepalese/Indian and very tasty.

Shakatak were received warmly and their time on the Falkland Islands was soon over. I had a great time horse riding and doing other activities that I didn't normally do during the day. On the morning of our leaving the weather was rainy and very foggy. We were delayed for a few hours, until the powers that be decided it was clear enough for us to go. The plane was full again, with servicemen who had done their six months' duty and were now more than ready to get off the Falklands. My seat was next to the girl sax player from the band and we soon got talking about saxophones and different bands. I had the window seat and only minutes after take-off looked out and saw that the engine was on fire. I called somebody immediately, but I expect they already knew in the cockpit. The fire was dealt with quickly and the captain announced to the passengers, "I'm afraid we have had a small fire in two of the engines. Don't worry, we have three. Anyway, I must turn around and go back to Mount Pleasant to have them checked out and I'm going round in a large arc so as to dump the fuel. We can't land with the tank so full."

I watched as the fuel came flooding out of my wing. Onboard there was a deep drone of moaning from the squaddies who just wanted to get home. We came into the land and at the last moment lifted away from the runway; the captain repeated the landing process again and at the last moment aborted putting the plane down. He spoke again to the passengers and crew, "Ladies and gentlemen, with the weather so bad and now trouble with our instrumentation I cannot safely land," (cheers from the squaddies), "with most of the fuel gone I'm going to limp to Montevideo in Uruguay."

Argentina was closer but there was no way that they would allow us to land and if they had they would have jailed all of us. If we kept our speed down, we could reach Montevideo. My saxophone girl held my hand, getting upset; she had a young baby son at home, would she see him again? The only thing that worried me was that if we had to crash land into the sea the bloody water would be so cold, I hated cold water. The joking and laughing stopped, as if every passenger was contemplating 'what if'. Those hours passed very slowly, and the lights were dimmed. At last, we heard the captain's voice again. "Well, ladies and gentlemen, we've made it and we will be able to land in Montevideo."

Up went the lights to cheers from us. We landed in Uruguay, being chased by ambulances and fire trucks. Wow! I'd seen this in the movies. We parked well away from the terminal building and before we were transported out, we were put into small groups. I was with Dave and the dancers; we were taken to a five-star hotel in the city. We were going to be there for four days, as the RAF were flying out replacement engines and they were giving the plane that extra careful once-over. All meals would be taken at the hotel. The food was great, we didn't mind that, and spent most of our time on the city streets of Montevideo, taking it all in. We were even invited to a wedding party in the hotel; we were famous now, we'd been on the news, and we were the survivors – free drinks all round! Fabulous. We eventually arrived home to a surprise. We had been given an extra four days' pay. That was the first of five trips to the Falklands for me. We still used those old Tristar airliners, apparently, they were bought from Freddy Laker so they would have been well into their forties, let's hope they are all in retirement now.

Next up was a tour managing job for CSE, this time for a very successful Abba tribute band Bjorn Again. They were first put together from the ideas of two Australian guys, Rod Stephen and John Tyrrell. Rod played bass guitar and John was a drummer. The band they formed took off like a rocket. Everybody knew the Abba songs and Bjorn Again looked and dressed exactly like the Swedish originals. The show was slick and professional, and the Army and the Navy and Air Force loved them, everybody loved them. They soon played for celebrity occasions and even Royalty. Rod and John soon stopped playing in the band and managed them. The offers came streaming in thick and fast, so thick and fast that a second Bjorn Again was carefully formed and the front two singing girls were carefully chosen for their voices and their looks. It was the Bjorn Again 2 that I had the pleasure of working with. We went on tour to Croatia and Bosnia. There was still a large constituency of British Army in the region, helping settle the country down after the war there. As we moved between camps, village after village was still completely burned out and if we stopped for any reason and got out of the vehicles, we were forbidden to go off the road as there were thousands of mines still to be cleared. We still heard horrific stories of children running to play and being blown to smithereens or losing limbs. I would be meeting Bjorn Again a few times in safer surroundings.

Old Reunion.

Thirty-six

EUROPE, THE BALKANS, AND THE MIDDLE EAST

1999 was going to be a very busy year for me. CSE had taken me under their wing, knowing that I could cover tours either as a lighting technician or a tour manager, sometimes both. I had been in my house in Leighton Buzzard now for two years. Because of the fire everything in the place had been bought from new and now two years later it still looked like a show house because I was hardly ever there. It was lucky I was at home when my brother Mike called. He and Pat would be passing and could they call in and see me one evening at the house. I was delighted and planned a sumptuous menu of food I was confident of cooking. It was great to see them, and I was very keen to hear all about my nieces and nephews. Then the conversation turned serious. He explained that he had prostate cancer and now it had gone through into his spine. He didn't know how much time he had left, but urged me to get checked out, as it could be hereditary. I was devastated. They stayed that night on my drive, sleeping in their motorhome, and I had to leave early in the morning for a parcels job, so I left them sleeping.

He called a couple of days later to see if I had booked an appointment with the surgery to have my prostate test. My doctor, a great little man from India called Dr Shaffi, said he could do it right away when I explained the story to him. "I want you bare from the waist down, you can keep your socks on and you can put your clothes over there where I'm going to put mine," he laughed. Putting on his rubber gloves he gunged his fingers into lots of slippery stuff and I could feel him put his fingers up my bum.

"Not too unpleasant?" he asked.

"No, no," I said. "I hope you are going to buy me some chocolates after this."

"Maybe," he said, "now this next bit will be a bit unpleasant.'

He produced a large glass tube about the size of a mastic gun and greased it up with the gungy stuff and put it inside me. He explained he needed to see where the prostate lived. He was bloody right; this was very unpleasant. This was the first time anything had gone up my bum that way, up to now it had always been a one-way pipe! As I dressed, he laughed and joked with me, but the good news was that I was completely clear of any prostate trouble, and he would be able to test me with blood samples taken every six months. I called Mike and he was pleased. I later told Jim of the mastic gun test and we laughed for ages.

At home the parcel company would still phone to see if I could cover somebody who hadn't turned in, and a band I'd formed a year earlier had the occasional gig. When I formed the Blues Brothers Tribute Band it was Jim who had suggested that I call the band The Blues Brothers' Other Brothers and we had a good laugh about it. The name stuck; great band, great musicians and singers.

The year started with a week in Northern Ireland lighting a children's show that played for the servicemen's children in the country's military camps. The show was a bit like a pantomime and the kids loved it, especially the main character, a young man called Stephen Mulhern, great with the audience and doing magic tricks both on stage and after the performance too. Then it was home for a couple of days then to the airport to meet Mark Walker, an up-and-coming comedian, son of TV personality Roy Walker. We were going to Abu Dhabi, to entertain the troops stationed there. He was a great impersonator and did a brilliant Billy Connolly. We made friends and got on very well. We had four dancers and a juggler to make the show into an evening's entertainment. On the way home to the airport Mark asked me to stay with him as he had a plan to get bumped from Economy to Club Class at the last minute of boarding. I was intrigued to see what was going to happen. The others boarded the plane. Mark kept well back until the last call then finally rushed to the gate. We entered the plane as the hostesses were closing the doors; he asked where his seat was and was told to sit anywhere and get the seat belts on. Of course, he sat in the Club Class section, smiling, and I sat down next to him. Surely it wasn't going to be that easy? It had worked before, Mark said, smiling. Alas, not on this trip. Once in the air the same hostess who had ordered us to sit down quickly came and looked at our boarding passes and took us back to our seats in Economy – nice try, Mark.

In a couple of weeks, I was to meet and do a short Northern Ireland tour with an old adversary of mine, Jimmy James. I had met him once before when I was doing a TV show with Johnny Wakelin; he was fine and didn't mention the old dispute over wages and us selling his equipment to compensate. We shook hands warmly and the tour was a success. The band were young and enthusiastic, they reminded me of me and the Curly boys when we joined him. He even had a girl in the new band, and she sang well, and they were good together. I was to meet them again next year.

I had a great time with Bjorn Again and got on well with managers, Rod and John. I had a week off, so I took the offer to take the band to do a short corporate visit and show in Seville in Spain. This was followed by another in Tenerife. On these short trips across Europe the band had to take their own equipment, so when we presented ourselves at the check-in, we had several trolleys of luggage. In London, British Airways took it all in their stride and the trolleys were whisked off to the plane; at the other end I organised the equipment not to be put on the luggage belts but trolleyed to the waiting transport. In Seville coming home we had a problem. The airport authorities said we must pay to have the equipment flown back to the UK. I demanded to see somebody in authority and waved a paper at him. The two pages I had in my hand were headed with the British Airways logo and it was a copy of our out and return flight times. Somebody in authority got the gist of what I was going on about. I said it was confirmation from BA that we would not be charged for the equipment. I was amazed that it worked, and the gear was loaded onto the plane. Rod and John were grateful that I had saved them several hundred pounds. In Tenerife I managed to put three full sets of golf clubs on the trolleys and I and the two band members had a wonderful early morning round of golf in the warm sunshine.

Abu Dhabi again, this time with Bobby Davro. This trip was going to be slightly different. Having done the show on the base we were to go to meet HMS Birmingham for a grip and grin session and Bobby would do a few funny bits. A great lunch followed. Having been to the Royal Hospital School run by the Admiralty and my brother having been skipper of a nuclear submarine, I'd never been on a British warship – for me it was a great afternoon. I even met a couple of officers who knew Commander Mike 'Chinese' Farr OBE RN.

Home, then straight out to Abu Dhabi again, this time with Bucks Fizz. At the airport I recognised only one of the original band members, Bobby Gee. They were very popular with the servicemen and expats and went down like a storm. The next morning, I was out shopping with Bobby, to pick up a few gifts for home, when there was a terrible rumbling in the ground. We both stood still and looked anxiously at each other, then nothing. Later that day we heard there had been a massive earthquake which was named "Chamoli" in Northern India, several thousand miles away. It was big and had killed several hundred people.

The next week it was back to Heathrow, this time to meet Bjorn Again, the mark 3 version, as Bjorn Agains 1 and 2 were already booked elsewhere. We were off to Glasgow then on another, smaller British Airways plane that covered all the west coast Scottish islands. We had a show to do in Saxa Vord, that took three days, and then it was home again and out again, the same journey but this time another island, Benbecula. These small camps were manned by the Navy and the Royal Air Force as British submarines rehearsed in that region; they played cat and mouse with the Air Force, everybody getting some great battle rehearsal time, and then coming in and learning to meet the enemy in the bar. These bases were going to be closed down soon so these beautiful houses were available to the servicemen for £1000 each. The beaches were miles of sand but freezing nearly all year round, even in summer. There wasn't much else on these islands at all, and the bus shelters had shelves of books and easy chairs, which didn't say much about the punctuality of the buses.

The Falklands was looming again, this time with Tony Hadley of Spandau Ballet fame. After the break-up he had teamed up with Spandau drummer John Keeble and they had formed a very polished band. They loved football so we formed a five-a-side team to take the Army on. I don't remember who won, but I do remember that John Keeble was a great goalkeeper. Tony was very popular with the squaddies, able to converse with the infantry, in the sergeants' mess and the officers' mess. He did mention that his mum had always wanted Tony to join the Army years before, so for the journey home they dressed him up in a captain's uniform and John talked his mother into meeting him at Brize Norton when we landed – surprises all round.

The year was getting along. I was busy almost every day with either van deliveries for the parcel company or Eat to the Beat catering company, when Renata Foster, head of entertainments CSE, called and asked to see me. They had booked Jim Davidson to do a grip and grin tour for the troops in Macedonia, a volatile hotspot at that time. Jim had been the first entertainer to do a Falklands show after the war there; he was an old and experienced hand. He, at the same time, had just formed the British Forces Foundation, a charity taking entertainment to the Forces in the Middle East. He reckoned that his charity did it better than CSE and would be quite critical of this tour if things weren't quite right.

"You know him well, Steve. Can you and Dave South make it go as smoothly as possible?"

Dave was going to be doing the sound on the tour, and he brought his mate, Billy Connolly's man, Malcolm Kingsnorth, to do the lighting. The show had another comic, Dave Lee, and, of course, dancing girls. The tour didn't get off to a great start. The party flew into Thessaloniki in northern Greece by British Airways, and we arrived around eight o'clock in the evening. Neither Jim, Dave nor I had been to Macedonia before, and we had no idea how long our road trip in Army Land Rovers was going to take. When we were told it would be about 8 hours Jim said that hotels should have been booked so we could leave early the next day. I phoned CSE, only to find they had gone home, and Renata wasn't answering her mobile. I quickly booked the whole party into an airport hotel. There were fourteen of us, God knows how I was going to pay for that. I would be trying to contact Renata at CSE during the evening. Jim was getting annoyed that we couldn't contact anybody. "What if there had been a real emergency?" he said. "Don't worry, Steve," he would pay the bill if I couldn't reach anybody in the morning. Of course, when we arrived at the first camp and got into show mode the mood lifted. British troops love Jim Davidson, he understood everything military from rifles to ranks and he would have the whole audience in stitches throughout the show. The fact that he had brought sexy girl dancers for them to ogle as well was a great bonus.

Our last show was out almost on the frontline in the countryside. He was going to do a grip and grin (more handshakes and smiles) to a tank regiment who had been tucked in the trees and the tank crews were living under their tanks. He also wanted to do a small show for them, and a stage was made up out of a huge tank transporter vehicle. It was just about mid-morning and Jim was laughing in conversation with the crews when suddenly the alarm went off. Action Stations were called and the crews moved so fast, they ripped down lines of clothes and got into the huge guns and got on the move. Jim and I could only stand out of the way and watch. A few moments later we heard some very loud firing – was it a practice or was it real? Just then my mobile phone rang, and I answered it.

"Hi, Steve, it's Parceline in Dunstable. Can you come in today? Only one of the lads is a bit sick. Gor blimey, what's that banging noise?" I laughed. He wouldn't have believed me if I had told him the truth.

"Sorry, not today. I'm in a war zone."

"Oh. Trouble with the wife, eh. OK, see you soon. Bye."

Later that afternoon when the tank crews returned, Jim went to the makeshift stage, and the crews and the rest of the company were seated on the grass bank; it wasn't long before he was in full flow. Just then a lady member of the company got up and as Jim could see that she went to one of the portaloos by the side of the show area, he started to give a portaloo commentary. Then he had the idea of wouldn't it be funny if some squaddies lifted it up and moved it whilst she was still in there. To great encouragement from the audience, it was done. The lady emerged smiling but clearly not happy. Apparently, the fluid that kills poos went everywhere and she did end up making a complaint to CSE, not that Jim cared; he was going to be very busy with his own charity, which he ran for a short while, and before he left it for another charity for servicemen, called Care After Combat, he had introduced (at a mighty gamble) Katherine Jenkins, the well-known opera singer, to the Army. Katherine was keen to do it, would the squaddies like it? Katherine loved it and they loved her, and she went back time and time again.

It was this year that I started to think about being with someone again. There were a few dates I had been on, mostly with women that I'd known before, and there was, of course, Oral B! So I joined a dating agency and put down a little about me. "My job takes me everywhere, I own my own house, I love to play music in bands, and I really like skiing." When Anne and I had parted, the first thing I did was to tell the girls to book a short holiday so we could regroup and discuss how we were going to continue without Mum. To my surprise they booked a week's skiing in Andorra, something none of us had ever done before. I had written about it as an up-and-coming school activity in the sixties at Teacher Training College but I'd never put a pair of skis on myself. So after a few lessons on a local dry slope, we went to find the snow. For those who have never tried skiing as a winter holiday, it's a must. Anybody who tells you that they have never fallen over while learning is a liar. During the day we were together in our beginners class, making friends instantly, laughing and joking whilst picking each other up.

Back at the hotel in the bar before and after dinner the laughing at the day's skiing disaster stories continued and then it was out in the clear cold night air to a jumping bar with dancing. I loved it, so did Jo and Zoe. The next year we took friends, the next year their friends, and the next year a group of about twenty strong. Always a different skiing resort. We had a meeting a few weeks before we were going to Alpe d'Huez. I, as the organiser, had planned something different. We would meet at two places early on the departure day and be taken by luxury coach to Waterloo station to catch the Eurotunnel Express to Paris. The dinner was booked in a restaurant near the station and then it was on the disco night train to travel through the night to Grenoble. Each person had a couchette (bunkbed) booked that they could use when they had had enough of the bar and the throbbing music. I didn't last long as the disco coach was jam-packed and ankle deep in swilling beer as the train rocked through France at speed. We arrived in Grenoble around 6am and it was another couple of hours on the French coach to the ski resort. Most people went to get their hired skis and boots and get started as the lessons began that morning. Another great week.

I was surprised just how many women wanted to meet me. I started to talk to a few on the phone; meeting them would come later, the agency said. Millennium New Year was looming. I had already been asked by Rod and John to take Bjorn Again to a massive outdoor event in Belfast. The show had been organised well and Belfast went nuts when it was New Year. Perhaps this year was going to be the year I would meet someone special and start a new part of my life; I hoped so.

Me giving Frank Bruno the eye.

Thirty-seven

HELLO SUE, GOODBYE DEAR BROTHER

One of the first tasks of the New Year for me was that I was going to be best man at my friends' wedding. I was dating a pretty blonde bombshell called Marion, and had met her next-door neighbour, a young very up-for-it guy, called Michael; I had become very interested in his games project. He had invented a couple of very complex puzzles and I was keen to put in some money so that he could expand and make some samples up. We formed a company called The Alternative Board Games Company. Marion's friend was an accountant, Peter Hall, our new partner, and he took care of all the paperwork. One of Michael's puzzles, a colour-matching task, has never been done to this day. Michael had met Amera and they were married on January 22nd 2000. Two days later we were all off to Gressoney, including his new wife, to ski.

A couple of weeks later Jim Davidson called me and asked me if I would go back on tour with him. We would be using the theatre's sound and lighting systems, instead of our own but I would be carrying his own onstage monitoring system and the merchandising in a small van. He would be travelling with Flo, his new minder. The tour dates weren't as intensive as in previous years and I got on very well with Flo. Kevin also had come back periodically as Jim's driver.

I was able to do other work. Eat to the Beat hired me to do an insurance tour. I was to meet two girl chefs, another girl would be going to work front of house, together with a guy who would be driving a very posh brand-new Chrysler Grand Voyager; he would be ferrying the clients from their offices to the double-decker bus parked in the country. Tony, the boss of Eat to the Beat, had hired the use of a double-decker bus and inside, the whole downstairs section had been beautifully converted into a large lounge area with comfortable seating. Upstairs had two jobs. There was a very large table, seating twelve people, with a screen at the front where the windows had been. This was the lecture area during the day and in the evening, whilst drinks and canapés were being served downstairs, the long table was dressed for dinner or lunch. The insurance company was recruiting smaller agents to push their expensive policies, This was no ordinary policy, this company insured your private jet or your luxurious yacht and, of course, your mansion. Each day the bus would be parked in the grounds of a country park or stately home, and it was my job to move the mobile kitchen, again expertly converted from a standard truck. Once parked up next to the bus, I would find and connect a water supply and a drain for the waste water, then I would check the gas bottles for the cookers, and light the pilot lights on the industrial stoves. When dinner was over and people were saying their goodbyes, me and the girls were busy cleaning up ready to get away to the next venue.

During the day I liked to keep busy too, so I helped Suzie, the chef, peel potatoes and do the veg. She was very young, had a wonderful smile, great sense of humour and I was always keen to be in her company, joking and laughing, doing anything she needed doing. Her dream, she told me, was to have her own restaurant some day and I hope she got it. On the last evening the big insurance bosses came and invited us, all of us, to have a drink with them at the hotel. We gathered in the bar, and it seemed that we were the only ones there. The bosses stood around, not much conversation going on, then the main boss came over to us and did a really loud fart.

"There," he said, smiling, "that should break the ice."

I looked over at Suzie who was open-mouthed, horrified. I was crying inside with laughter.

I loved these different sorts of jobs, meeting different sorts of people, and whenever I could I drove the kitchen truck around for Eat to the Beat.

Now it was back to the Falklands, this time only for one week, with Liverpool football legends Emlyn Hughes and Duncan McKenzie. They didn't have an act planned, they introduced themselves to the crowded room full of servicemen of all ages. Emlyn was a household name and many remembered Duncan in his playing days. Once the club rivalry started the conversation between the two men was funny and interesting. Next, they invited questions from the floor, and this would take a good hour and a half. Of course, everybody wanted to know about Emlyn's relationship with Princess Anne and, of course, A Question of Sport on the television. In the afternoon, after lunch it was another mess with a whole new bunch listening and thoroughly enjoying the sports entertainment. During that week Emlyn played in a couple of five-a-side games with the enlisted men. He was middle-aged but still held his own with great soccer skills, competitiveness and he was still very fit. It was a very good week for CSE, who were now going to introduce more sports personalities into the military entertainment programme.

Back a few days later I had Frank Bruno and BBC sports commentator Gary Richardson on another one-week tour, this time Bosnia and Macedonia. Frank still looked good in a T-shirt, he liked to train or run each morning and then we would go to work. Gary and Frank had worked out a script with questions and answers that made the huge crowd that had come to see them listen carefully and laugh when Frank sent himself up.

Gary: "Is that right, Frank, that you now have a detached retina?"

Frank: "Yeah, Gary, before we used to live in a council house."

Another great week, Frank did everything they asked of him.

Then it was back to the UK to Jim and summer gigs. These venues were nearly always seaside theatres, and we would do the rounds, a few days in Torquay, one in Bournemouth, Skegness and, of course, his beloved Great Yarmouth. Jim had fallen in love with the town. His mum and dad had taken him there as a young boy, he liked the people with their funny accents, and they loved him. They loved him because he was battling to keep the venues and entertainments open. Jim, the indoor circus owner,

Peter Jay, and the fairground owner, Albert Brown, together with the owners of the arcades and the seafront shops, even introduced a passport whereby, if you used these facilities, holidaymakers would get some sort of a discount. For years he had been a great supporter of the Caister Lifeboat and bought them their first inshore rescue rib; they had named it the Jim Davidson. Bernard Matthews, the Norfolk Turkey giant, had bought the large seagoing vessel for them. On his show Jim would say that Bernard had paid for this large boat because he was richer. "He's got more turkeys than me, but I've had more gobbles than him!" he would say. So it was, every Saturday night that Jim's show went into the Wellington Pier. I knew John Cannell, now the bar manager, Mickey, Sid, all the bar staff; after all, I'd hired most of them. On this particular Saturday night in July, I noticed the very attractive, middle-aged lady sitting at the end of the bar and asked John who she was. He explained it was the mother of one of our very pretty barmaids, Natalie, and she would walk down to the theatre most nights so she could walk back with Natalie to the house. Her name was Sue and she had lost her husband two years previously. Jim had finished his show and the audience were leaving, so I took my chance and went to talk to her before the bar became packed. She had a lovely speaking voice, no sign of a Norfolk accent, a beautiful smile and I thought my conversation was going quite well. Just then Jim burst through the bar with Flo, Kevin and some of the show cast in tow.

"We're off to Avenida's, Steve," he said. "You coming? Bring your friend if you want to."

I hadn't eaten for hours, I was starving.

"Would you like to join us?" I asked Sue.

She declined, still giving me that wonderful smile, but I secretly thought she was terrified. Besides, she'd come for Natalie.

"I'm here next week, perhaps you would like to go then."

"Perhaps," she said.

During that week I spoke to John on the phone to get more background on Sue. She had two very pretty daughters; Nicci, the elder, and Natalie who had just finished college and had put out feelers for joining the police force forensic team. Unbeknown to me, Natalie was also grilling John about me. Jim's reputation with other women was a bit wild, so why shouldn't I be? John calmed her fears, letting her know of my family and my broken marriage. The next Saturday I was able to talk to Sue for much longer before the Jim machine burst through the theatre on the way to eat at his favourite Greek restaurant. Sue was invited again by Jim; this time, to my delight, she accepted. I hoped the conversation and language wouldn't be too bad, as she seemed so nice. Her father had been a squadron leader in the RAF and she had been educated in Germany, Ceylon, and the UK. Her brother had been sent to boarding school, a bit like me, so we had lots to talk about. At the end of the meal Jim would always be the one to pay the bill; he did it every week, no matter how many people were around the table.

At the end of the season Jim asked me to stay an extra week to help close the theatre down for the winter with John. That being done, I saw Sue most evenings and we would go to see any remaining shows in Yarmouth or dine out in the country in a restaurant, mostly recommended by John. I bought her to see my house in Leighton Buzzard and she liked it very much. We were getting along like a house on fire. Jo and Zoe met her and liked her very much. Stu, my best friend and playing partner, now settled in Spain, was inviting us to visit so we went, and he was suitably impressed. For some time now Stu had been on to me to relocate to Spain to be nearer to him and I had been seriously thinking about it. Sue and I were very close now, and when we had the conversation, I asked her if she would come too, if I went. To my amazement she said she would like to give it a try. I said we would make more visits to Spain to look around at the property market.

Sue asked me if I would accompany her to a family wedding. Her only uncle's daughter was getting married just outside Northampton and I jumped at it, eager to meet as many of her family as I could. Her mother was still living but couldn't make the journey, and her father had married again since his divorce and was now retired and stayed in Devon, where he lived. It was the morning of the wedding. Sue and I were in the hotel room when my mobile phone rang. It was Janet, my sister, telling me through tears that Mike had lost his battle with cancer and had died the previous day. The funeral would be in Inverness, where he and his family lived. Would I be going? Would I be bringing Sue? I told Sue what had happened, and we spoke about the funeral the next day. It wasn't going to be the right time for Sue to meet the rest of my family so we decided I should go alone. I didn't, as Jo, my daughter, came with me. We flew into Inverness to be met by friends of Mike and Pat, as there were a lot of people coming. Pat had organised the villagers who put up as many as they could. Jo and I would not be together. Each of us went to a different family for the night.

The funeral was a sombre affair. At the cremation the coffin was brought in and there was a line of Sea Cadets accompanying it. The naval ensign was draped over the casket, his naval hat with its gold braid and his naval sword were laid alongside. The worst moment at a cremation service is when the curtains slowly surround the coffin, and it disappears on its way to the furnaces. Janny, Mary and I held hands tightly as the silent tears rolled down our cheeks. Goodbye, dear brother.

Back at the house Pat was determined for it not to be a solemn wake. The music was on and loud and the drinking and the laughter started.

"This is how Mike would have liked it," she said. We certainly gave Mike a great send-off.

I didn't stay too late. I went home with the young couple who were putting me up for the night. They refused any payment, saying Mike had served the community so well, running the health service since he had retired from the Navy. I woke in the morning to find a little girl sitting at my feet at the end of the bed, holding her teddy. She looked at me.

"My mummy is cooking you breakfast."

"Ooh, thank God," I said. Too much drink last night, not enough food, I was starving.

I had arranged to meet Jo at Pat's house so that we could say our goodbyes. Wendy, Mike's youngest daughter, asked to show me the garden. His land went down to the edge of the loch and there were mountains beyond. She took me to a very large smooth rock and said this was the place she and Mike had sat and read many stories together. When we returned Pat said that Mike had asked for his ashes to be scattered in this area. I feel I haven't given enough space in this book, so I enclose his obituary from The Times to show he had a wonderful, colourful life as I did, but different colours entirely.

Thirty-eight

THINGS DON'T GO RIGHT IN THE DESERT

Jim had seen The Blues Brothers' Other Brothers and liked them a lot, what's not to like? Two great front men in Paul Cox and Al McClean and really, really, good players playing great soul music. He offered me one night a week during the summer season that year at the Wellington Theatre; I took it, of course. It was going to be a bit of a gamble. Would we make enough money to pay the wages for the boys? The band thought we would. Wouldn't it be great if we added something extra, an Aretha Franklin or a Tina Turner? I put it to the band. First half of the show The Blues Brothers, second half Aretha or Tina, some different stage shirts, same band, of course. One of the band had seen a girl, working in London; her name was Marcia Raven, and she came highly recommended. She wouldn't be hard to find, and I managed to meet her in a north London pub. She had brought a few pictures of herself on stage. With this great band Marcia was going to be absolutely fantastic, just as long as the voice was fairly similar, as she really did look the part. As a finale both The Blues Brothers, Jake and Elwood, would join her on stage, fabulous! I told Jim and he offered his recording studio floor at Pinkhurst for us to rehearse and for him to check out our new Tina; she was very smiley to Jim. I would have to keep an eye on her.

I had posters made and, nearer the time, radio advertisements and announcements beamed across east Norfolk. Sue was involved in keeping the stage shirts clean and pressed so every week the band looked great. The stage set was simple with a central drum riser and a set of stairs going down into the audience where Paul and Al would get the audience to join in. We didn't sell out the Wellington Theatre by any means but made enough money to pay the wages and expenses for those who used their cars to bring the boys and Marcia up to Norfolk every week.

On one occasion we were using musicians we hadn't met before. There was a sax player and a trumpet player who came from Jools Holland's band; they fell right into it, loving every moment. The season was over too soon. I didn't know when I would see them again as there was nothing in the book and everybody was so busy.

Renata, the boss lady at CSE, asked me over for a chat. She explained that with the build-up of military hardware and men in Oman, everybody in the military was expecting it to kick off in the Gulf States pretty soon. The government and the powers in CSE wanted to show their appreciation to the thousands of servicemen who were going to be in Oman, stationed in Camp South in Thamarit, and Camp Fairburn in A'dam; the two camps were 400 miles apart. My job was to fly to Muscat, find myself at the Hotel Intercontinental, a five-star hotel, and wait for the Army to pick me up. I was told that two other men would meet me at Heathrow: Matt Glover, son of John Glover, artist and tour coordinator, and also the production manager. I'd met him before with Tony Hadley, who'd done a bit with the troops in the Falklands, and Dave Gibbon was going to be the lighting designer and operator. At the last minute I was told that neither of those were going to go with me, no reasons given. I was met by a RAF officer who had been asked to accompany me on this little visit. I was to meet the Royal Engineers and the military staff to discuss how they would put on an open-air concert for five thousand men. We arrived at the hotel in Muscat and messages were left saying that the Army would pick us up at 8.30 in the morning to drive to the concert site. That evening I met Dave Emery, who had an enormous sound and light company in Dubai, called Gear House. Dave had worked with Take That when he lived near Manchester, so his input was going to be greatly appreciated. CSE had given me the title of CSE Production Manager. It was down to me to bring all the factions together for show 1 and show 2.

The next day we drove for hours into the desert and when we arrived it was just desert, nothing else. There were a few earth movers and a road-making machine and no one had arrived yet and when they did, they would be under canvas. Dave's main concern was that this show was going to happen in two months' time; would the roads be made strong enough for the artics full of concert equipment, artics full of staging and enormous heavy generators for the power that was needed. The Royal Engineers major drew with a stick in the sand. His men and his equipment could make a thirty-foot high amphitheatre so that the squaddies could see the stage, and the area in front of the stage and the stage area would be levelled flat. By the end of the day, we all had a plan which was printed out with rough measurements. Another major was providing stage crew and truck unloaders; we would need plenty of them, especially if the trucks had difficulty getting to the concert site from the main road. Dave was providing security barriers across the front of the stage and the portaloos that were to be used and expected to be used by all, including the acts; good luck with that one, I thought.

Something else we learned at that meeting was that CSE was sending a huge satellite dish and another man from Sky to erect it. Above the stage they had asked Dave to provide an enormous cinema screen. This was for the World Cup football qualifying game between England and Greece, happening on the afternoon of the first show. As it was up anyway, Dave offered to bring some cameramen to film the gig, which would also come up on the screens. This was going to be some concert. So late in the afternoon, with everything agreed we got under way to do that boring journey back. We were in three 4 x 4s and there were a couple of Jeeps with armed personnel as our escort. On the way home we were able to stop for a drink somewhere. After dinner at the hotel Dave and I went to the bar for some well-earned alcohol. We sat and watched an eight-piece Filipino band, incredible. They covered tunes and sounded exactly like the original bands; their Queen's 'Bohemian Rhapsody' was a masterpiece.

I shook hands with Dave the next morning. He was confident that his sound and lighting crews could do the job, but he was asking, could the Army? Let's hope so.

"See you in a couple of months," I said.

During those weeks Renata kept in close touch with the Army in Oman and brought me up to speed when I called in. Two months passed and I was back in Muscat at the Hotel Intercontinental. I met with Dave Emery the next morning and we were off in convoy to Camp South, a completely different scene now. A huge amphitheatre had been made and the canvas tents were going to be our accommodation for the next four nights. These tents were also going to be dressing rooms for Geri Halliwell, Steps and Bobby Davro. The main camp was a quarter of a mile away, but there was always something or somebody being ferried in so getting to meals was never a problem. As the trucks were running late, as Dave had predicted, it was a great relief to see them back up to the stage and the Army getting in to get them unloaded. We worked well into the night.

Somebody had had the great idea of setting up a shower but had not been able to finish it. Step up Steve Farr, ex-plumber to the stars and now the Army. The water heated itself in the sunshine and the best time to shower was either dusk or soon after sunrise. There were a few complaints from Dave's crew about having to sleep in the tents. I'm not sure what they were expecting. One guy refused and climbed into the back of an empty lorry container, something about camel spiders. After an early breakfast the crews got back to work, and the Army had to put the stage together, the full-sized concert stage. When the trussing was lifted into the air it was loaded with static and moving lights; the cinema screen was then put on top. Thankfully no wind was forecast. Behind the great mound of sand and rock that had been made into the amphitheatre was another line of tents with no sides and trestle tables lined up so that the audience could be served with beer, plenty of beer. The soldiers had arrived a week or so before and this was the first time they had been allowed to let their hair down.

On the show day we were ready. There was music being played and all the lads who had helped were milling around, waiting for the celebrities to arrive. Bobby Davro was first, mucking around and joking with the men, then Steps walked over from their helicopter with lots of filming and short interviews as CSE planned to make a video of the whole event.

By the time Geri Halliwell arrived with her entourage of dancers the place was buzzing. The CSE bigwigs had arrived too; Renata Golding, my boss, and the managing director of the company, David Cryws Williams, lots of high-ranking officers acting as the military liaison, I even saw Matt Glover, who was supposed to be with us from day one of the production. Apparently, he caught the flu and stayed with the main party and his dad.

The beer started flowing about 4pm and the thousands of troops sat on the sand banks and waited for the England v Greece World Cup qualifying game to start. It was still hot; it was going to be a hot night tonight. It was a good game of football and ended with England needing a goal from a free kick to win: David Beckham took the kick and the ball sailed into the net. The place erupted, England had won and moved to the next round of the World Cup. The soundman on the main PA system turned up the music. Very shortly Bobby Davro would be kicking things off. He was dressed in Army fatigue trousers and an England shirt; the large audience were chanting England football songs. Bobby Davro went on stage shouting at the crowd who were shouting back; he had a can of beer in his hand and foolishly he shook it up, so it exploded over those standing behind the barrier and immediately he was pelted with a hundred beer cans and had to run off the stage out of the way. He was supposed to be on for fifteen minutes; he stood his ground, hoping to calm things down, but the cans kept coming over. An officer came onto the stage and ordered the men to behave; fat chance! Up next, Steps took the stage. Cans kept coming and the crowd were pushing forward and the younger squaddies who were, perhaps, real Steps fans and had got early places at the front, were now being pushed and crushed against the barriers. Again, the show was stopped, the officer ordering the crowd to stop pushing; fat chance again. The Military Police arrived and helped get the crushed and injured over the barrier and led them to waiting first aiders and ambulances in a few cases. Water was sprayed into the crowd. Things now were getting serious, the Military Police were telling the front section to push back, and they went into the crowd to get this done, then all hell broke loose. Drunken squaddies, scorched by the sun, started to attack the MPs and everybody else who wanted a fight, it wasn't just young servicemen and women who were being crushed by the pushing. There were plenty now coming over the security barrier with cuts and bruises. I was standing in front of the stage, helping get bodies to relative safety and taking them backstage to the tents that were now like a scene from M*A*S*H. Just at that moment David Cryws Williams stopped me.

"Steve, can you help me? The sole of my shoe has come loose, do you have a piece of that sticky tape or anything that you can put round my shoe?"

"Not now, David," I barked, without swearing.

He had no idea how serious the situation had been. Again, the officer came onto the stage and threatened to close the show if they didn't quieten down. The beer tents had been closed. Geri Halliwell and her sexy dancers drew the Army's attention and for a performer who was just starting off on her solo career, her show went down really well. She danced her socks off with her troop and, of course, the Army loved it. It was all over, the Army walked back to Camp South and the entertainers got in their helicopters and were taken back to the hotels. The next day they were whisked off to visit some Royal Navy ship and do a grip and grin visit with plenty of smiles and photographs.

It was now our job, again without Matt Glover, to dismantle the whole concert area and pack it into trucks. We worked until about 2am; the stage and the lighting gantries would be dismantled in the morning. We walked over to the camp to get some breakfast and to my horror there was nothing. No one had said anything about giving us breakfast; the Army had had theirs, hours ago. I explained to the person who was in charge of the kitchens that some of us had been up all night doing our job so that we could get the trucks packed away to travel the hundreds of miles to the next show. I was hungry and mad that Renata had not thought of telling anybody that Dave Emery and his crew and I had to be fed in the morning. At last, we got eggs and toast with tea.

By mid-morning we were ready to leave. The old civilian bus turned up that was to take us to the next show site, Camp Fairburn. That bus lasted about half a mile before it went bang. Thank God it didn't get out of the camp; what would have happened if we had been stuck in the middle of the Oman desert? Another bus was found, and we arrived very late and very tired. This was the Royal Marines base in Oman, and we were shown tents for the night. The journey had been long, we had taken plenty of bottled water and had to find our own food at a café in some village along the way. I was going to have a lot to say to David Crwys Williams and Renata when I got home. In the morning it started all over again, but we only had a day to put the second show up, as the show was tomorrow evening. Over breakfast our Royal Marine stage crews told us they were really pissed off that because of the fighting and bad behaviour of the Army in Camp South, no beer was going to be given during the concert.

"Will they turn up?" I asked.

"Doubt it," was the answer.

Pissed off or not, the Royal Marines got stuck into the job and were ready to go. Come show day, a different show altogether. Bobby Davro was now able to do his act without dodging cans. Tonight, Steps would be headlining after Geri Halliwell – wrong move, I thought. Just as Steps were doing their show Renata told me to be ready to leave; the whole concert party were making an immediate exit by helicopter to Muscat to get the British Airways midnight flight back to London. We had been given a tour itinerary booklet from the start and my name was not on any leaving list for that night. I assumed I was going back to Muscat with Dave Emery and then getting my flight to London in a day or so. Apparently, President Bush had kicked the action off in the Gulf and now everybody was on war standby. Dave Emery was not best pleased with me or CSE when I told him we were ducking out before the load out. First it was Matt Glover, the production manager didn't show and now I was leaving too before the end. He walked off, cursing CSE. I just hoped they paid him and his team well, they deserved it and more.

On the flight back all I wanted to do was to eat something hot and sleep. I did notice one thing, that I was the only one sitting in Economy; the concert party was over thirty people. Can they get that many in the First and Club Class sections? I thought.

A few days later I went into CSE and had a meeting with Renata and David Crwys Williams. I told them about the lack of food, the right hand not knowing what the left hand was doing; the fighting and the crushing was something no one would have predicted, but all in all CSE hadn't come out of this smelling of roses. Just as we were finishing David told me he had something for me, and I had done a great job. He passed me a brown envelope. I opened it and pulled out a large, signed picture of Geri Halliwell. At that moment David Cryws Williams reminded me of Chuck Berry. Later Jim Davidson told me that the government had questioned CSE about the staggering expenses bill for this concert; Geri Halliwell had charged over £90,000! It couldn't have been cheap with all those expensive air tickets on the BA flights. Jim was licking his lips as he wanted his charity to take over CSE entertainments.

I thought that after my damning speech to Dave Cryws Williams and Renata at CSE, my days of working for them were more or less over. Renata called me one evening.

"Steve, they tell me you have a very good Blues Brothers tribute band, is that right?"

"Yes," I said, "and if we are doing a full night's entertainment, we carry an amazing Tina Turner." I threw that in quickly in case she might want us for a gig sometime.

"Oh, that's fabulous," she said. "Our next Falklands band have pulled out, the singer tried to top himself. Can you get it together to be ready to go for a ten-day stint in three weeks' time?"

"If the money's right, Renata, we could go."

The money was better than all right. I could pay the band and Tina a very good wage and there was enough to pay myself back for the money I put in for the wages for the Wellington Pier when there wasn't enough in the kitty. I said I would call her back the next day. I had to find everyone and get them to come to this lonely cold little place with no trees at all. Within 24 hours I had the full band with no substitutes, with Nicky Paine and Larry Winch and me on the brass; even Marcia was excited to go. Stevie Dickson, our drummer, said he would take his cine camera to make the whole trip into a CD. Nick asked if there was a good telephone line from the Falkland Islands as his mum wasn't well, and he wanted to be in touch with her whenever he could.

The sound engineer and the lighting tech I knew well, and I put myself in as the CSE tour manager; that meant I was getting two wages and that would pay for the sleepless nights in the desert the month before. We didn't need to rehearse much, and I loaded the backline onto my van and took it the day before we left to Brize Norton RAF base, where the flight handlers took it and put it on the plane. Just before we left, CSE gave us another week in Northern Ireland, great, money right up to Christmas. Also, the complete fee for the Falklands shows was paid into my bank account and I paid everybody into their accounts online from there. The itinerary for bands visiting the Falklands, or Mount Pleasant, was always the same no matter who they were. On our arrival it was the officers' mess that invited us for dinner. Everybody had been told to bring a decent shirt, tie and jacket, no trainers, and after the meal the young officers would love to talk to the acts, especially if there were women in there. Second night after the first show the sergeants' mess would host the entertainers with food, pots of beer, a quiz perhaps or a movie. After that every evening a different regiment would take the entertainers for food, games, karaoke, anything to brighten up their lives a bit. They were here for six months at a time; we were there for just ten days. Our first night in the officers' mess went off with a bang. After a wonderful dinner with wine and a toast to the Queen, our keyboard player had arranged that the electric piano be brought in. He played for the mess and often an officer would get the chance to sing a song, good or bad, it didn't matter. The officers thought it was wonderful and gave the singer tremendous encouragement and applause. No one before us had thought of bringing in the piano; we were off to a flying start. Our first show had gone really well. The concert venue wasn't a large room, holding around two to three hundred men and women, but it did look crowded when they all got up to dance, so we had fair to good houses every night. On the second night during a boozy session in the sergeants' mess I got a chance to talk to the young woman officer who was going to be handling our itinerary.

"What itinerary?" she asked.

I was a little lost for words and I explained that I had been there five or six times before with different acts and knew the drill, as I worked for CSE besides playing in the band. She apologised, saying that CSE hadn't given her any directives that the act, that's us, should be hosted by the different regiments at all. I was starting to get angry; why had CSE changed the goal posts? We had stepped in at really short notice. Just then I had a brainwave.

"OK," I said. "Can I see the head man of the sergeants' mess?"

The young lady officer stood by while I had a chat with the chief of the mess. I explained what normally happened to the entertainers after the show and that I thought we had been badly let down.

"If that's the case," I said, "I will host my own band after every show with your permission in your mess. If we require food, I will gladly pay for it as I will the drinks, if that's OK?"

Thankfully it was OK. What a shame; I'd told the band about after dinner show hostings and the different foods we would be tasting, neeps and tatties and maybe haggis from the Scottish regiments, and perhaps a fabulous curry from the Gurkha Regiment stationed there. As the tour manager I was carrying about £2000 kitty money as a working float, that should cover it. It certainly wasn't the lady officer's fault. She arranged for us to fly to see the seals island, to see seals and penguins, thousands of them, and visit remote outposts, normally radio hacking stations that had only a few men, for a grip and grin session and a bit of a laugh. On the last night the officers and mess sergeants surprised us with a group of Gurkha chefs who brought in one of the speciality curries; the food was absolutely fabulous.

The last show done, we packed everything into our flight cases, and in the morning they were taken up to the flight and loaded. The equipment was flying back on the same flight as us which suited me fine. Nick was still worried about his mum, so we took the transport to the departure building, only to be told that the weather was getting bad, and the flight had been cancelled. "Try tomorrow," the flight sergeant said. We did and again we were turned away; the third day we got away, to arrive back in Brize Norton 48 hours later. The next time I spoke to Nick, he told me his mum had died before he arrived at her bedside. The delays weren't our fault, but it still made me feel awful. I suppose because it was my tour and my responsibility, perhaps I should have left him at home. No, he wouldn't have liked that.

It was only just over a week before we were off again, including Nick, to Northern Ireland. The Army barracks there were much smaller than they had been in the Falklands; the audiences were as good, though, and they were hosting with great beer and food after the show. Still, the week flew by, and our equipment was being moved by the CSE sound and lighting engineers by truck, so we travelled on that short tour back and forth on Aer Lingus and not by an RAF flight.

It was great to be home for Christmas with the girls and Sue. Her two daughters, Nicci and Natalie, were roughly the same age as my Jo and Zoe. All of them had boyfriends so they were out most of the time. Still, Sue and I were happy to be together whatever we did. With New Year over, I was off to the Middle East again, this time to Incirlik in Turkey. NATO had a huge airbase being constructed there and it was my job to see if CSE could put on decent-size concerts. I had to check out the concert room and was there enough power for sound and lighting, and where would the backstage area be, what about the dressing rooms. I was only there for three days, and in that time, and with the help of an RAF corporal who was with me over the period at the camp, I had a three-piece suit made by a little tailor who had a shop just outside the camp gates – great suit for not much money, that tailor must have been very busy. My corporal told me he did a great line in blazers and dark Crombie coats.

Thirty-nine

WILLY NELSON, THE ALBERT HALL, AND THEN CHUCK BERRY!

Phone ringing again, this time Robert Pratt from Scotland; would I tour manage Willy Nelson's UK tour for him? Oh, sure, he was one of my favourites and he didn't disappoint. He travelled in his own bus with his manager and his sister, who played the piano on stage with him. In bus 2 was the band, bus 3, me with eight Texan technicians. I was told to watch out for the crew boss, Purdy Young; not a young man but as cunning as a fox. He tried to get me running around for him, wanting extra this and extra that. I liked him a lot and laughed at his requests, I even took him shopping in Glasgow; he couldn't understand anybody, and we bought his mother an English teapot and had it sent directly to her. When he called her to see if it had arrived for her birthday, he made me talk to her. She liked a London accent. She said a few words but now it was me who couldn't understand what this elderly Texan lady was saying.

At every show I would be standing in the wings, waiting for Willy to take to the stage. As he approached, he would always say, "Howdy, Steve, my bunch been behaving today?"

"Perfectly, thank you, Willy."

"Oh, that's grand," he said, "thank you, Steve. Have a great show."

During the day and right up to the time Willy was to go on to do his show nobody saw him; he stayed in his bus, smoking, Bodie said. On the last night we were in Belfast and that's as far as I went; the Willy tour was moving on to Eire (and the promoter was changed, of course he had his own tour manager). I went to say goodbye to Willy's manager before the show and he told me that Willy would like to see me for a chat. I felt honoured to be invited onto his bus. We sat and chatted about my music career and, somehow, the conversation got to Masonry; I told him that I was on the square. Willy's father had been a high-ranking officer in Texas and when Willy's name was put forward to join, the application was dismissed because of his drug convictions and prison sentence. I thought it would have been just the same here too. I really enjoyed talking to him, he was like the Royal family, able to talk to anybody about anything when he met them. Everybody loved Willy Nelson.

Jim was after me again, wanting me to go to Germany to suss out the gig possibilities as his charity had booked Status Quo for the show and Jim would start the show off. I was used to checking out empty fields now with the Army; I was back the next day. Within a month we were there again. It was great to see the band again, the show went really well in great weather. Jim was pleased that his charity staff had handled it professionally.

At a show in the Bournemouth International Centre, I ran into Derek Block. I hadn't seen him for at least fifteen years, and he didn't look any different from the day that he gave me the first Gary Glitter job in 1985. I met him by the merchandising stand after Jim's performance and introduced him to Sue. He looked at us, smiled and said, "I've got a job for you two."

Cleo Laine and Johnny Dankworth, the famous jazz couple, were having a celebration show and night at the Royal Albert Hall, where anybody who was anybody in jazz was going to be there.

"Would you and Sue run the backstage for me? I'll need security, too; can you take care of that?"

"Of course I can, Derek," I said.

As the date grew nearer, I went to the Albert Hall for a meeting; good meeting until I said, "I'll be providing backstage security for Mr Block."

'I don't think you will,' said the suited voice, "the security backstage must be very well qualified to work at the Royal Albert Hall."

I called Flo, and his partner at that time, Goose, an ex-sergeant major in the SAS and told him about the job. I also said about them being qualified; they laughed at me. They had a security company that held courses for close protection government work and these two guys had security passes to work in and around Royalty. They still said they would enjoy a night out at the Royal Albert Hall. I went back to the staff at the Albert Hall; they were very impressed and said Flo and Goose would be welcome. They were expensive but Derek Block didn't mind that. On the day, backstage was bustling, loads of jazzers were there speaking and laughing with each other, catching up. I found Sue in deep conversation with Bruce Forsyth, and later with Julian Webber. Sue would bring the artists to my side at the side of the stage. There was a strict running order, so we made sure next up was in the wings five minutes before they were introduced. That's when I was standing next to George Martin, then I reminded him that he'd been in a band with me and Paul McCartney. He was still laughing as he went out on stage to join Cleo and Johnny and five thousand people.

Just by chance another old face loomed up to meet me that weekend. The next day, Chris Markland, the tour manager I had given all my European DIBA work to, called to see if I could take care of Chuck Berry doing a private show in London. This was going to be very easy for me. No hotels to check, no band members to change, no cars to check, no money to hold, he had taken care of that himself weeks before.

There was excitement backstage when we were told Chuck's car had arrived. I waited just inside the door. I didn't know if he'd been told I was taking care of him for that day or not, and when he saw me, he ran to me and hugged me like a long lost relative – it was good to see the old bugger. Cherie was with him, and I was glad that I'd taken Sue as now she could have lots of girly chats. Chuck, as always, sat himself in his dressing room, not wanting to go backstage and meet fans or support acts. He did, however, get to meet the guy who had paid him to do this private show. No little amount, he came and went, and Chuck and I talked, and I unloaded all my newest jokes on him. But there's always something, though; the support act was a blues band and the harmonica player was a guy called Chris Jagger, brother to Mick. He had plenty to say, telling his mates that he was going to go out on stage and play harmonica with Chuck. I put him straight very early on, oh no he wasn't – Chuck doesn't like other musicians especially ones he doesn't know getting on stage during his show.

"He'll know my name," Jagger said.

"Chris, I doubt if he even knows your brother," I said. "It's still no, and if you make a dash for the stage, I will pull you off and run you out and security will throw you out of the building."

Chuck always used the same guys when he was touring in the UK; they could have handled Chris Jagger jumping unannounced onto Chuck's stage, but I'm sure Chuck would have been smiling but not happy. Thankfully the show went without any hitches. After a hectic but happy weekend, Sue and I travelled back to Yarmouth.

It was back to work, doing lots of Jim gigs and odd things with Eat to the Beat. The parcel delivery people, seeing how busy I was, didn't call so much anymore. Then the Falklands came up again. It was Jimmy James and the Vagabonds again, but this time I took my best mate, Stu, he was coming with me. By now he was a great sound man, having his own studio at his house in Berkhamsted and, of course, working at the Victoria Palace doing the Buddy show. Jimmy was very pleased to see us both and during that tour I was able to explain why we had taken the drastic step to sell all his sound equipment.

It was great to have Stu on this tour. He jumped at the chance to go to the Falklands; he was one of those guys who wanted to see as many different countries and cultures as he could. He spoke fluent Spanish now and had bought a couple of houses there. He was going to see a lot more of me and Sue as we always stayed with him whilst looking for a place of our own. The weather was wonderful, a little too hot sometimes, and as we drove round the countryside, I noticed how dry everything had become. I needed to see more green, and Sue agreed. Along the coast there was always a forest of tall cranes building taller, grand apartment blocks and massive resorts, and I remember saying to Stu one day that the coast was going to run out of water with all those extra people moving in. Sure enough, it happened, and even now with small villages the water was cut off for a few hours during the day during the hot periods. We drove up north to look at properties around Barcelona and coastal properties near Blanes and Torremolinos; still dry, still brown.

We had driven to Stu's from the UK on one occasion, driving down through Madrid from the ferry port of Bilbao, and now we decided to drive up through France to catch the ferry at Caen. Over the border we saw what we were looking for, green fields, mountains and forests, lots of rivers, lakes and water. We talked, saying that perhaps France was a better proposition.

Once we were home, I looked up French Property News, a property advertising magazine, on the internet. The houses were old, rustic and cheaper, much cheaper than Spain. The country was full of old houses that needed some restoration and a lot of love. Each house seemed to have enormous gardens and even enough for a smallholding. We spent many hours glued to the computer screen. We didn't want northern France; the weather there would have been too similar to England, so we concentrated on properties about an hour from the Mediterranean. Then one hit me. It was a semi remote property, had a river with a waterfall, fifteen acres of ground, needed attention; £65,000. I couldn't believe it. If we bought a property like that, we would have lots of money spare to do the place up with perhaps a swimming pool as well. I made a call, a lady answered. I was the first to call after the ad was placed. Within days, Sue and I were on a plane to Rodez in the Aveyron and picked up a hire car with careful instructions from Barbara, the lady of the house, to come over and we found it. She had made lunch for us which we were very grateful for. Sue was eager to walk round the house and the river and the waterfall, Barbara provided the wellingtons. The house was of medium size with plenty of outbuildings; there had been a small mill, and the steel wheel and frames were still there but they had been dismantled. The house inside was a bit scruffy. Barbara had four children, three boys in their teens and a younger daughter. Her husband had gone, and lived in London, but he was helping her with the move. We were still excited and talking about it when we returned to the local auberge where we were staying. We had booked in there for a couple of days. Sue and I decided to go for it and went back the next morning. Barbara was excited, she was going to move quite close by because her children were settled in school. They all spoke fluent French and perfect English when we were there. The phone rang a couple of days later; it was Barbara's ex-husband from London. He knew I had offered the asking price for the house.

"It's gonna take a while for Barbara to move out," he said. "You were the first to see the house, she hasn't even started to look for somewhere yet."

"That's OK," I said. "I'm in no rush."

I didn't tell him that I had put my house up for sale, something I did that week, it was sold within a couple of weeks.

A couple of months went by and then it was Peter, her husband, on the phone again.

"Do you still want to buy Barbara's house?" he asked.

"Of course," I said. "I've waited for you to tell me that Barbara has found somewhere else to live, we had a deal."

"Well. Barbara has found somewhere local. There is someone else at the house now wanting it; if you still want it, can you put £10,000 into my account today?"

I started to get angry. You didn't buy a house like this in France, I'd have to get advice quickly.

"I could do it, but it won't be today," I said.

"Oh well, this guy's got his cheque book out, so I'm going to sell it to him."

That's when I called him every swear word that I knew; not much chance of me getting it now, then. I threw the phone down and picked it up again and told Sue. Although disappointed, we both knew there were a lot more houses out there at good prices so we would carry on looking. I explained to my house buyer that there would be a short delay and they said there was no hurry, thank God.

Another month passed, then one sunny morning the phone rang. It was Barbara from France. She sheepishly apologised for her husband. He had a share in the house, and he had sold it for slightly more money (he obviously got his £10,000). I said I was no longer interested and would punch Peter if ever I got the chance. She then explained that if I had liked that one, which we did, one of her jobs was to help English people find properties and she would do that for us if we liked. Sue and I had liked the area very much so it was decided that I would go for five days. Barbara would have two days, another agent two days, showing me as many properties as I could see. I told Barbara that I was coming back to stay in the same auberge that Sue and I had stayed in so that she could show me around.

Forty

SPAIN WAS TOO DRY, FRANCE WAS JUST RIGHT!

When I arrived at the auberge she was waiting. She was with one of her sons, who apparently didn't go to school much. At the time I saw three houses, all at around 100,000 Euros, none of which floated my boat. I made a call to Sue every night, she had to work. On day three I presented myself to an estate agent in Albi, the nearest city, and the agent, about my age, chain smoked and offered me a portfolio of properties to look through while he was on a phone call. He said he would be there for a while.

"OK, let's go," he picked up his keys and, of course, his cigarettes. We walked to his car, a large Audi that needed a really good wash. Inside was no better, just a stink of Gauloise cigarettes. We were soon at the first house; too small and too steep a piece of ground at the back. No. On to the second, again at speed, another no from me.

"OK," he said, "we must go back now."

"Where to?" I asked.

"To my office, I have another meeting after lunch."

Lunch for him was going to be two hours, standard practice in France.

"When I called, I asked you for a day," I said.

"Not possible," he said, no apology, again, standard French practice.

"What about the house I had picked out of the portfolio?"

"Oh no," he said, "that's too remote for you."

"Here, how would you know? Well, I want to see it."

"Then you must go alone."

The conversation ended there.

At twelve he was at the office, and he gave me the sales sheet for the remote house. It had rough details on it. I took it from him and told him I was going to go by myself. It took me nearly an hour for me to find the village of Laval-Roqueceziere, and then I would never have found the house without the aid of an old man; he couldn't speak a word of English and my French was almost non-existent. Down the hill, alongside the village, you come to a crossroads with a religious cross in the middle, turn left and follow it down to Vareilles (the house). At the end of a pretty tree-lined lane I first saw the property. It was fabulous, this was a bit more like it. I stopped at the iron gates, which had a lock on. I could see the stone steps and pathway leading to the front door. Just then the door opened wildly as two dogs came racing towards me; they couldn't get through the gates though, so I stood my ground.

"Get away from here! What do you want? I will set the dogs on you. I have a gun!" Thank goodness, she spoke English.

"Pardon, madame," I called. "I've come to see your maison." I was waving the paper.

"Where's Monsieur?" The fag man. "Why isn't he with you?"

"He wouldn't come, madame. He said it was too remote."

She was cursing him under her breath. That's why, he didn't want to face this dragon, he told me she was living alone.

"You can walk around the house, but you are not entering," she said to me.

"OK, madame."

She opened the gate and made no move to show me around the grounds.

The next day, as I didn't want to see Monsieur Fag Man again, I went to the next town to look in another estate agent's windows to see if I could see anything else. I kept thinking about the house Vareilles so I thought I would sneak another look. The plan was I would park up down the lane short of the house and take some photos. As I stopped the car another car pulled up behind me. It was the lady of the house, this time without the dogs; she wasn't shouting so much today.

"I've spoken to the agent, I said he must be here. He said no, so you can look inside now if you like."

Today might be just a waste of time, there again, it might not.

Madame Lemaitre was a widow, her husband having fallen ill and died a year before. They had bought it as a wreck, and in that time, he had managed to do an awful lot of work. He had been a tiler by trade and the floor tiles had been expertly laid through the ground floor, together with the small bathroom and shower, all fully tiled. There was a tiny kitchen, and the biggest room of the house had a timbered floor, a beautifully beamed room with a toilet at one end. In the middle of the room was a huge stone fireplace. She didn't live in this room at all. Next to the kitchen was another open fireplace; there were even radiators in this part of the house. The boiler didn't look too old, and it was all fired by butane gas, which was held in a large tank outside. She lived in this room of the house; she even had her bed there. The upstairs rooms I counted were three and there was nothing in them except one; she had made a shrine to her husband in this room. The bed was there, not made up, and on the pillow was his trilby hat and around it there was a circle of soft rabbit toys. They had bought this small farm to raise rabbits in cages, not for their meat but for their wool. She told me later that every day she had taken each rabbit out and combed it for the wool and then collected it and spun it into Angora wool balls. The rabbits had gone, although there were still several barns full of rabbit cages, about 700 in all. I could see through this; I was already thinking of holiday gites we could build. Another walk round the large garden and that's where the pool was going to be. I said to Madame that I was very interested and could get back with Sue next week.

That evening I told Sue I thought I'd found the one. As I left the house, I took a few more pictures of the pretty lane and one of the woodlands that came with the house. I was full of it when I got to Sue's house. We arranged to return the next week as promised. Sue immediately liked it and we walked over and around the property, saying that we could do this, and we could do that, to make it our home. In the house I pulled out my camera but she immediately made me stop.

"No pictures!" she screamed.

That evening at the auberge we met Philippe, a Dutchman, who was living close by, in a wood somewhere, doing up a wreck, and he took his meals each evening at the auberge and stayed drinking into the night. He and the auberge owner were friends now and Sue and I later relied on them for some help. I told him what we had just bought. I showed him some of the photographs and he said he was an artist and would go over and make some sketches. I told him not to run into Madame Lemaitre but to sit on the hill opposite and to sketch the house for us sometime soon.

The next morning, we returned to Vareilles to say I wanted the house.

"How much will you pay?" she demanded.

"What you asked for on the flyer," I said, which was 137,000 Euros, in English money £79,000.

"When will you give me the money?" she said.

"I don't think it works that way. I'm going to the notaire's office this afternoon."

"I've already seen him," she said.

So, the wheels were set in motion, my offer to purchase her house now on record. I dare any man to sit in her kitchen and say, "I'll get my cheque book out, love."

During the next few weeks, I heard nothing, and then had a demand from the notaire's office to pay the deposit and attend the first meeting with the sellers. Sue stayed at home, and I had already agreed with Philippe, who spoke perfect Dutch, French and English, to attend as my translator; he agreed, and we agreed a daily fee. If a married French couple sells a house and one of them, as in this case, was deceased, his half automatically goes to the descendant. So it was that Madame's long-lost daughter suddenly appeared with a fat husband and an eight-year-old daughter that Granny had never seen, lots of tears of joy.

We discussed the property. There was a stone barn, that was big enough for two-storey, one-bedroom gites (holiday cottages). The daughter said she wanted it as she used to play there as a child. I sat glumly and listened until the notaire asked me for my thoughts. Through Philippe I said that the building was part of the property for sale and if she still wanted it the sale stopped now, I would walk away. Silence in the meeting room. I looked at the notaire. He was nodding his head at me; the daughter had quiet words with her mother and agreed that the outbuilding was included; that was my second victory of the morning. Earlier Madame had shouted at the notaire to throw Philippe out of the meeting.

"If he goes, I go," I said, and that was that.

Now the notaire turned to me and asked if I had any questions. I had just agreed to give Madame Lemaitre extra time, about six weeks, to find a home. The dates were set; in French law, if she was still in the house on that day the police could come and throw her and all her belongings onto the street. I asked if I could start depositing my goods and furniture in one of the huge empty dry barns as I had a lot to bring and she agreed. Later that month, loads of screaming at the notaire's office; I had put a fresh padlock on the barn doors, he said it was my right, and she had thrown a book at him. As we were leaving that first meeting the fat husband of the daughter asked to speak to me.

"If you want her out early, I can take care of it," he said, in fairly good English.

"The old man (her husband) cut a lot of firewood for his wife before he died and it's all in the barn." I'd seen it, there was certainly a mountain of it.

"If you give me 500 Euros, I will leave it for you when I get her out," he said.

I knew his game; she would never see that money if I agreed.

"No," I said, "you take it with you," knowing he wouldn't.

So now it was a waiting game while the French authorities did their work. The notaire's office (there is one in every region) handles the house sale for buyer and seller to keep the waiting time to a minimum, but it was still going to take a few months, especially as I had given Madame Lemaitre extra time to find somewhere new to live. She was going to be near her daughter and, of course, her new granddaughter. Ten years before she and her husband had thrown the daughter out, saying that if she married the fat guy she would be disowned. She hadn't seen her or her granddaughter till that first meeting at the notaire's. I'm not sure what she thought of the fat man; not much, I hope.

In those few months Sue and I were going to be really busy. Firstly, we had to pack up the contents of the Leighton Buzzard house and arrange for a trucking company to take them to France, to be stored in one of the large barns as agreed. I wasn't going to use a removal company; much too expensive in my eyes. The particular company I had hired did it this way. One driver arrived with a forty-foot container; I then had three hours to get it loaded, after that it was golden time for the driver and lots more money. Flo, Jim's minder, and his son Sean arrived. Now I had two big men and me, the driver also helped a little bit. We were done in time and the truck went immediately to Purfleet on the Thames estuary, where the container was loaded onto a ship to cross the Channel. A European driver and his truck would pick up the container and drive it to Laval-Roqueceziere and I had drawn a map by hand from the main road 10km away from the house. Barbara, my friend (with the very dodgy husband Peter), had offered her sons to help unload, same rules, three hours to clear the trailer.

I was waiting for the truck at the house four days later; Madame Lemaitre was being nosey whilst keeping out of the way. She took an instant dislike to the three boys, all in their teens, because they had arrived on their motorbikes. The huge load arrived, and the driver called me from the top of the drive. He then walked down the leafy lane to the house. He was a Dutchman and decided the best thing he could do was to reverse down the hill all the way. Twenty minutes later he had expertly manoeuvred this enormous truck and container to the side of the house. These three lads weren't going to be as fast or as strong as Flo and Sean; the Dutchman said he would help and suggested we load everything onto the grass, thus getting the container empty well within the three hours and avoiding extra charges. The boys and I could get the stuff into the barn when he'd gone. It worked out well and whilst he was working hard for us the driver told me that his son was a very young musician, as he had seen the instruments being unloaded. I gratefully gave him an acoustic guitar for his boy and he said that was better than any tip.

There was to be a second load to go down to France. Sue and I had decided to store the rest of the furniture until we knew definitely that we would be moving in. I moved into Sue's house in Great Yarmouth until we had a moving day. Sue had also given her notice at work; they were pleased she was starting a new phase of her life. She would be keeping her house as we needed somewhere to stay when we came back. Natalie was taking it on. Nicci already had her house just a couple of miles away.

Jim was planning his next tour. He called it 'Jim's Silver Jubilee' and it was to be his biggest and finest to date. He asked Sue if she would sell the tour merchandising, no small feat on this tour. I put together two large chrome shelving stands either side of a large TV screen, six or seven feet from the ground. Sue played his past TV shows and videos continuously as soon as the theatres opened – to date he had at least eight videos which were now in VHS and DVD form – selling T-shirts, books, programmes, mugs and keyrings. Two large tables ran the length of the stall, covered in a dark blue cloth. The whole thing, when lit, looked most impressive – Jim loved it. After the show I would have to help Sue with the selling as we were so busy and then get the stock away and the shelving down to be loaded into the waiting trucks.

Of course, I knew all the musicians; Jim used the same guys on the summer seasons. Andy May was the sound engineer and the very talented Nigel Catmur designed and lit the stage set expertly. Neil and Wayne were there to help him with the lasers. Sue hadn't done anything like this before. She loved it but was totally exhausted by the end of the night. I loved having her with me as we were now inseparable. She had stepped into my life, straightened me out and her daughters Nicci and Natalie had welcomed me into their family. I certainly wouldn't be straying anymore – I'd found my perfect life partner. Marriage hadn't been talked about. I was quite happy with that, had she wanted it I would have said a big "Yes"!

So now Jim wanted me and Sue on the smaller tours with him. Great for me, I didn't have to worry about poor Sue being left in France after we had moved in.

By now Madame Lemaitre should have found her house and been out of mine, but we heard nothing. Some weeks before I had paid the balance of the new house in full, together with the legal costs. The buyer in France pays for everything, including the notaire's fees. I called to see if he had heard. He hadn't and told me she had been so awkward he hoped she was still there so he could throw her out. Sue and I decided to go to France and find out for ourselves. We arrived back at Vareilles, the name of the farm, and I immediately noticed that grass was growing along the bottom of the gate. She'd been gone for weeks and told nobody. Where were the keys that were supposed to have been dropped off at the notaire's office? When

I spoke to him, he immediately phoned the number she had given and after a very heated conversation told me that the keys would arrive in the next day or two. We were here now, and I wanted to get in today. There was a small single window in an upstairs storeroom, so I decided to break into my own house. An elderly gentleman appeared from nowhere, asking me who we were; he spoke no English at all, and my French wasn't much better. I tried to explain that it was my house now and I had no keys. He got it and went off to find me a ladder. The breaking in bit was easy with the aid of a small rock and once I had found a door with a key in it inside, I was able to let Sue and my new friend, Fermin, in. He owned a small derelict house at the end of the lane and the fields that surrounded our houses. He actually lived on the other side of a small mountain in front of our houses, but still grew his vegetables here.

We must really have upset Madame Lemaitre's fat son-in-law. He had strewn rubbish around every room and had cut every ceiling light so close to the ceiling that there were no wires for me to reconnect my lights to them. He had loosened every waste trap in every sink, so that when the water was turned on, any waste water would have flooded over the floors. When we did get the keys a couple of days later, when we opened the garage there was an oil storage tank with 'Death to the British' written in French in large chalk letters.

Next day Barbara and her boys showed up to help move stuff from the barn. She became quite angry that a British couple should be treated this way, so she called the police. Two young police officers came and listened to Barbara, and on seeing the message asked me if I wanted to take it any further. I said no, and then they said it might be good if he had a visit from their local police station to hear their displeasure. That's enough, I thought.

We were now back in the UK, working regularly with Jim and we took advantage of any breaks in Jim's touring schedules to arrange another container truck load to France, same company, same rules. To load it in Great Yarmouth there were Natalie, her boyfriend at the time, Neil, and his brother, Sue and me. Not quite as much as the previous load, so we did it easily in time. Then quickly down to Vareilles again to meet it. All I had this time was one of Barbara's sons and Sue. Again, I got the call to say that the truck was at the end of the drive, this time from a short Frenchman, almost as wide as he was tall. I told him it would be almost impossible for him to turn round down at the house, and it would be best if he reversed down the half a kilometre.

"Impossible," said the Frenchman.

"You are the second load to arrive," I said. "The Dutch driver of load one did it OK."

"Oh, did he?" said the Frenchman, laughing. "If he can, I can. Vive la France!"

Safely down, he jumped out of the truck and waved the boy away, saying he could do it with me a lot faster. He passed the broom to Barbara's son and said his job was to sweep the container when we had finished. We went well after the three hours of unloading time. The Frenchman said not to worry. Sue went off to prepare a good dinner for us three men. With that and a good tip, the driver was full and happy. Apparently, the French are not good at tipping, so today had been his lucky day.

So far Madame Lemaitre and her fat son-in-law had been the only awkward French people we had come across; everybody else seemed very nice. Our postman turned up one day with some housewarming cards from family. He came to the door and asked if I was Monsieur Farr. I said I was, and I introduced Sue Sales as my partner.

"'Has Madame Lemaitre gone for good?" he asked.

"Sure," I said; with that, Sue and I laughed as he did a dance across the lawn, waving his arms in the air.

From now on it was going to be hard work. There was stacks to do and I wanted to do most of the building work myself. The new bathroom we immediately planned was no problem at all. I would have to learn about bricklaying and plastering as I went along, but with the Stevie Farr attitude, how hard could it be? We didn't mind when our efforts were interrupted when we had to return to the UK and carry on with Jim's work. Life was great, Jim was great, and he was always pleased to see us, often calling us The Clampetts from the American TV show The Beverly Hillbillies when we loaded the van with ladders, carpets, bedding and even the kitchen sink.

A few years before Jim had bought a really beautiful country house called Pinkhurst, near Cranleigh. He had sold the lovely cottage in Ewhurst when his marriage to Tracey had ended. After a couple of girlfriends, he met the love of his life, Michelle, and they worked hard to make Pinkhurst their dream home. I always hoped that one day he and Michelle would visit us in southern France. They did. Travelling up from the Mediterranean coast in their Range Rover, they made great time until they had to cross the world's highest, tallest bridge at Millau. Jim wasn't great with heights. To get across he needed to fix his eyes directly on the road ahead while Michelle asked general knowledge questions, from a quiz book they had in the car, to stop him thinking about the drop. They made it and loved our little farmhouse and were grateful the bridge wasn't on the route home to Britain.

It wasn't long before Jim, Sue and I were on the road again.

Commander Michael Farr.

Forty-one

A BIT OF A BANG ON THE HEAD!

We had arrived in Bradford and the hotel was right behind the stage door of the theatre. It was one of those grand old buildings from when the main railway stations had their own hotels. Jim, Flo, Sue and I were staying there. The day was pretty normal. Sue and I would go to the gig to load in the merchandising boxes and the flight case of radio mics and monitoring system. The sound and light crews knew us and were very experienced, so the sound check, which I did without Jim, went without any hitches. Sue would set up the merchandising shop, and if there were no more problems, we would go off early to get something to eat. I had to lay out Jim's shirt, trousers and shoes, making sure all were clean, and he would arrive in his dressing rooms around 6pm. I'd go in to check he was OK.

"Everything OK, Jim?" I asked.

"Great," he answered. "Stevie, I'm going to read for a while, can you turn the piped music off?"

There's always a speaker in every dressing room to call acts to the stage and if it was a pantomime or big cast show it saved the stage manager a lot of time finding the acts and telling them it was soon time for them to be on stage. We never needed calls as I was always on the case and brought Jim into the wings of the stage in good time. I reached up on a chair to the speaker and turned it off. The music was still coming from somewhere. I thought perhaps they had a small box speaker on the floor somewhere and started to look around at the room. Jim got up to help, perhaps there was a speaker in the bathroom. No, nothing. I was on my hands and knees, loudspeaker hunting, when I crawled past Jim. Hold on, the music got a little louder. I stopped. The music was coming out of Jim's arse.

"The music's coming out of your bum," I said, smiling.

"What?" he said. "Impossible!"

It was then that he pulled out his mobile phone out of his back trouser pocket; he hadn't turned it off and now it was playing soft rock music. We burst into laughter.

"I'll be dining out on that story, Stevie," he said.

Jim now wanted to tour three or four times a year, working almost every night. That suited Sue and me, as we could get back to our farmhouse in France as often as we could between tours. We had met two new friends, a retired insurance director, John Kemp, and his lovely Finnish wife, Stella, an ex-ballerina. John had worked for Lloyds in London and was responsible for designing special policies for entertainers and bands. He had prepared insurance for the Beatles' first tour of America, the cats in Cleopatra and the stuntmen in the early Bond films, so he had great stories to tell and I listened to them for ages.

I was the younger man and looked forward to working in their house when they needed me. They were back in the UK the next winter, at their house in Amberley, and I had been asked to plaster a beamed ceiling on their landing. I had the house to myself, so I rigged up a long, raised platform so I could be close to the work. Once everything was in place and ready, I moved quickly to spread the plaster onto the ceiling. I didn't see that one of the heavy oak beams had a nasty pointed end to it and turned my head straight into it, two inches above my eye. The pain was excruciating. I was dizzy but not knocked out. I swore like a trooper and finished that part of the job and went home.

The house was empty and cold. Sue had flown home a couple of days earlier as she had a hospital appointment and she wanted it out of the way before this next tour started. I was ready to follow in the tour van the next day. That evening the headache I had from the beam was getting worse and didn't subside the next day on the journey 800 kilometres to the ferry. When I reached Sue in Great Yarmouth, I explained what had happened.

Loaded up with tour equipment, merchandising and shelving we made our way to the first tour theatre in Bromley. The pain was still in my head and didn't seem to want to go away. Jim looked at me strangely and at one point asked if I was pissed. I never drank on show days and asked him why he thought that.

"Oh nothing, you're walking a bit pissed."

Next day was Basildon. I set the stage equipment up and went to help Sue with her merchandising stand. My head was pounding. I walked into the gents' toilet in the theatre foyer for a pee. God, I felt awful. Trying to pull up my jeans was impossible; my arms and hands had stopped working. I had no control. I stumbled out of the gents', calling for Sue to help me. At first, she was annoyed that I was in the theatre foyer with my jeans at my knees. If this was a joke it wasn't funny. I tried to explain through slurred speech that something wasn't right. Sue shouted to the theatre staff to call an ambulance quickly.

Basildon hospital was just up the road and the paramedics were at my side in minutes. Sue had just enough time to call Jim. I was taken to have a brain scan and was diagnosed as having a brain haemorrhage. It was then decided to move me to Romford hospital, as they were better equipped to handle this type of procedure.

Jim arrived at the theatre and the stage crew ran up his microphone monitoring system. Everybody at the theatre being so helpful. The ladies working as ushers offered to sell his merchandise. Sue had left the van keys with the manager, who said the van could stay where it was until we needed it again.

By the next day I had had the operation to repair the blood vessels that were leaking into my brain, and I woke to feel an enormous bandage around my head. A nurse said they had shaved half my head and now I had two holes in my skull joined up by a large knife cut that was now stapled up. I noticed immediately that my headache had gone and cheered up. Apparently, before the operation I had been an arsehole to everyone, or so my daughters said.

Jim was often on the phone. At the show in Basildon, he had met the town's Lady Mayoress and explained what had happened that day.

Cheekily he had asked her to keep an eye on me. She did better than that, she turned up to see me. My first visitor! Stu phoned from Spain. Tony Hughes and Baz the drummer came to see me and when Jim made his entrance the doctors and nurses rocked as he had them in stitches, the laughing kind. Before he left me, he told me that he was paying me for the whole tour whether I came back or not.

Within a few days I was de-bandaged and wanted to go home. The hospital staff tested me to see if I could walk unaided up and down stairs and asked me general knowledge questions while I had to make a cup of tea for them. Passing with flying colours, I was back to being the full shilling. Jo laughed at my weird hairstyle and promptly shaved all the rest of my hair off. The two holes in my head were now two dents, only I wish they had put a little more cardboard in as filler as they are still two dents today.

Days after, I collected the van and returned the tour equipment to Jim's office. It was then that Jim told me he was retiring me, and as a retirement present, he was giving me the tour van.

If I was to retire this was a good time to do it. Sue and I had started a new life in France. Jim and I would always be the greatest of friends, a more generous and thoughtful man I've yet to meet.

The bang on the head didn't put me off working to improve the properties, but Sue was always on my case if I wasn't wearing my hard hat.

Then a couple of years later out of the blue I took a call from my Scottish promoter friend, Robert Pratt. Would I be interested in tour managing a nine-week tour of sixties music artists, nine of them on one show? I thought this might be a challenge so I said "Yes!" He sent me a list of the artists and the venue dates. Two months later he called again, this time to say that everything was cancelled as the Covid-19 virus was ripping through Britain. Everything was to be locked down.

Would the tour be resumed some day? He doubted it.

Just then I thought my funny odd career was finishing. I thought of Kenneth Wolstenholme's words as he wound up his TV commentary of the 1966 World Cup final.

"They think it's all over… it is now."

COMMANDER MICHAEL FARR, RN. OBE. OBITUARY FROM *THE TIMES*

Commander Michael Farr. Attaché whose relations with the Chinese survived Tiananmen Square.

Like Gordon of Khartoum, Mike "Chinese" Farr earned his sobriquet by a devotion to Chinese affairs and, in his case, comparatively long service in China as the naval attaché to the British Embassy in Beijing. He was, unusually, appointed for two tours, the first under Sir Percy Cradock from 1981 to 1983, and the second under Sir Alan Donald from August 1986 to August 1990, which encompassed Deng Xiaoping's ruthless suppression of the student uprising in Tiananmen Square in June 1989.

Farr was the first naval attaché to be appointed since the withdrawal of diplomatic presence coincident with the celebrated escape down the Yangtze River of the badly damaged frigate Amethyst in 1949, her replacement captain, Lieutenant Commander Kerans, having been the assistant naval attaché at Nanking.

Farr's first tour was marked by less easy diplomatic relations than his second, but his remarkable personality and excellent grasp of Mandarin Chinese enabled him to build unusually warm and fruitful relationships with officers of the Chinese Navy, who knew him as a friend and valued his advice as a professional submariner of distinction. He was permitted to attend seminars and deliver lectures on submarine operations at the submarine school at Qingdao.

His influence was never more evident than during the fraught days after the slaughter in Tiananmen Square. Infringements of diplomatic immunity, including armed threats to the international diplomatic enclave, proved excessively alarming for the inmates and their wives and children. As the senior British military representative present at the time, Farr produced an evacuation plan for dependents which was widely used by other embassies. Landing clearance for a British Airways aircraft proved impossible to obtain. A telephone call from a Chinese Air Force contact was taken at the Farr flat by his wife, Pat, herself an excellent Mandarin speaker. She recalls that when she heard that clearance had been arranged, she thanked the caller for his help and received the reply, "We are friends and always will be." Later it emerged that special forces from the People's Liberation Army had kept a particular watch on the Farr flat to see they came to no harm.

Sir Alan Donald remembers Farr as "a shining example of compassion and common sense". As well as having two children of their own, the Farrs adopted a four-year-old boy from a home in Hong Kong, and a handicapped girl from an orphanage in Beijing, when she was still in a cot. Because of his friendships, Farr was able to reduce months of adoption bureaucracy to 24 hours. He was the first Westerner to be allowed such an adoption. The Farr 14th floor flat was also home to cats, rabbits, ducks, cage birds, terrapins and a white mouse.

International relations were strained after the shootings in Tiananmen Square, but it was a mark of mutual respect between Farr and the Chinese Navy that they were talking together within a few weeks. He was appointed OBE for his services to China.

Educated initially at Watford Grammar School, Michael Farr was awarded a bursary to Eton in 1952 and went to Dartmouth in 1957. In 1961 he trained as a submariner and served in several submarines on the Home and Far East stations, notably during the confrontation with Indonesia between 1963 and 1965.

His Chinese language course in Hong Kong lasted from 1967 to 1970, but Farr's career as an able and active submariner dictated that this was not to be used for ten years. He qualified as a submarine captain in 1971 and commanded Finwhale and Porpoise out of Singapore before serving in the personnel division of the Admiralty.

A belief that one had to be married to get a place at the United States Naval War College at Newport, Rhode Island, had the happy effect of accelerating his wedding to Pat in 1975.

On returning to Britain, he qualified for service in nuclear submarines. After duty in Scotland with the Third Submarine Squadron, he commanded the Polaris ballistic missile submarine Revenge for two years, ensuring the continuing integrity of Britain's nuclear deterrent throughout a series of ten-week patrols.

His final tour before retirement was to superintend the secret Underwater Test and Evaluation Centre in the Inner Sound of Raasay in the Hebrides, where naval underwater weapons and sonars are developed.

Michael was well known as a lively raconteur and wit, with "a heart as big as all outdoors" as a contemporary described him. When in Hong Kong he ran the Duke of Edinburgh Award scheme for street kids and in Beijing was deputy chairman on the board of the International School. In Scotland he chaired the local Sea Cadets unit, was a governor of Fortrose Academy and secretary of the Kyle Playing Fields Association. He is survived by his wife and their four children.

Commander Michael Farr, OBE, British Naval Attaché, Beijing 1981–1983 and 1986–1990, was born on October 16th, 1939. He died of prostate cancer on September 22nd, 2000, aged sixty.